UNCANNY X-MEN: SUPERIOR VOL. 4 — IVX. Contains material originally published in magazine form as UNCANNY X-MEN #16-19 and ANNUAL #1. First printing 2017. ISBN# 978-1-302-90525-5. Published by MARVEL WORLDWIDE, INC., a subsidiary of MARVEL ENTERTAINMENT, LLC. OFFICE OF PUBLICATION: 135 West 50th Street, New York, NY 10020. Copyright © 2017 MARVEL No similarity between any of the names, characters, persons, and/or institutions in this magazine with those of any living or dead person or institution is intended, and any such similarity which may exist is purely coincidental. **Printed in the U.S.A.** DAN BUCKLEY, President, Marvel Entertainment; JOE QUESADA, Chief Creative Officer; TOM BREVOORT, SVP of Publishing; DAVID BOGART, SVP of Business Affairs & Operations, Publishing & Partnership; C.B. CEBULSKI, VP of Brand Management & Development, Asia; DAVID GABRIEL, SVP of Sales & Marketing, Publishing; JEFF YOUNGQUIST, VP of Production & Special Projects; DAN CARR, Executive Director of Publishing Technology; ALEX MORALES, Director of Publishing Operations; SUSAN CRESPI, Production Manager; STAN LEE, Chairman Emeritus. For information regarding advertising in Marvel Comics or on Marvel.com, please contact Vit DeBellis, Integrated Sales Manager, at vdebellis@marvel.com. For Marvel subscription inquiries, please call 888-511-5480. **Manufactured between 6/2/2017 and 7/3/2017 by QUAD/GRAPHICS WASECA, WASECA, MN, USA.**

10 9 8 7 6 5 4 3 2 1

PREVIOUSLY

DISCOVERING THAT THE TERRIGEN CLOUD CIRCLING THE EARTH WAS ON THE VERGE OF DISSIPATING INTO THE ATMOSPHERE, RENDERING EARTH UNINHABITABLE FOR MUTANTS, THE X-MEN DECIDED TO TAKE ACTION AGAINST THE INHUMANS. LED BY EMMA FROST, THE X-MEN STRATEGICALLY NEUTRALIZED INHUMAN THREATS, PREVENTING THEM FROM INTERFERING IN THEIR PLAN TO DESTROY THE CLOUD. FOR JEAN GREY, THIS MEANT PSYCHICALLY IMPRISONING PERHAPS THE MOST DANGEROUS INHUMAN OF ALL: KARNAK!

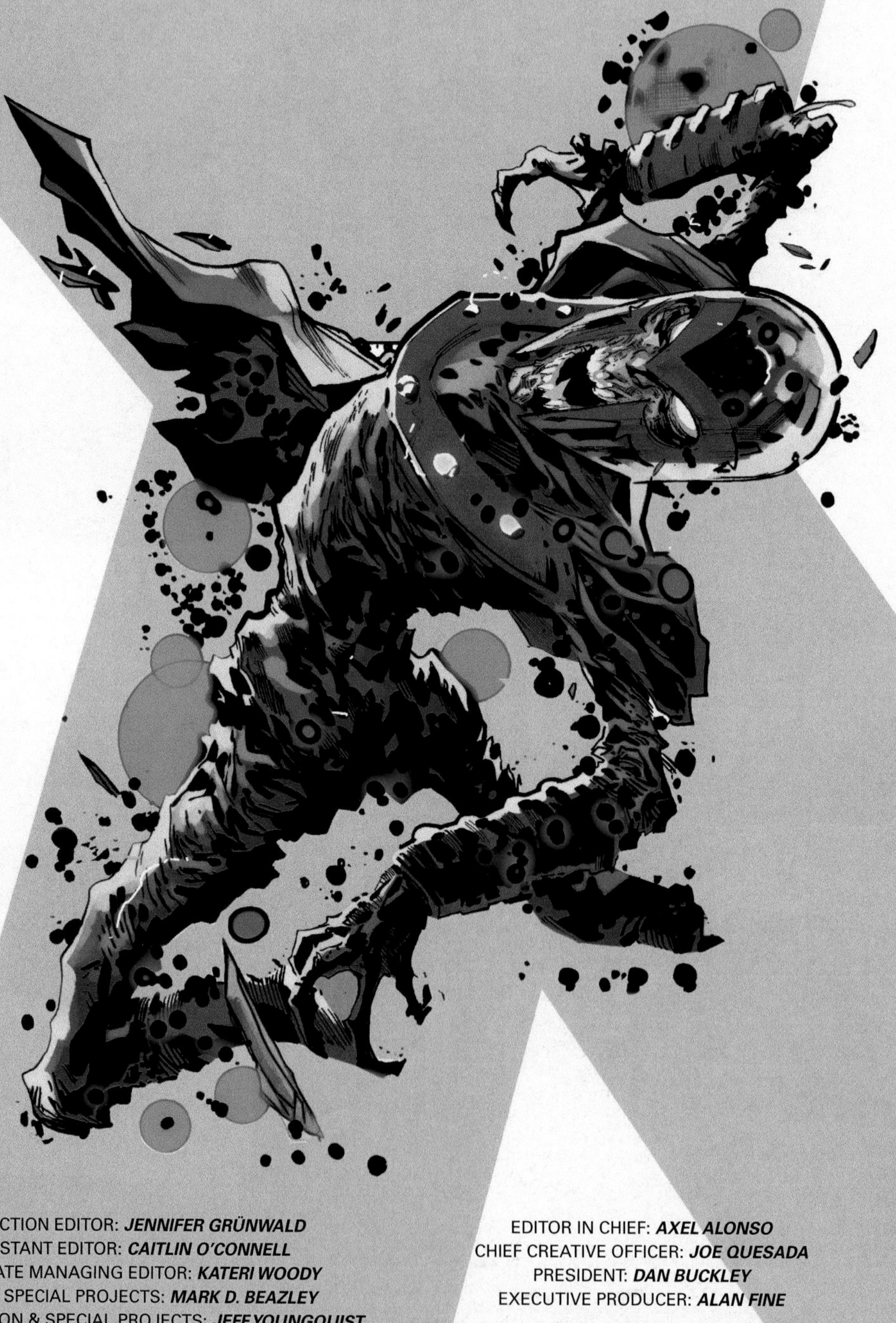

COLLECTION EDITOR: ***JENNIFER GRÜNWALD***
ASSISTANT EDITOR: ***CAITLIN O'CONNELL***
ASSOCIATE MANAGING EDITOR: ***KATERI WOODY***
EDITOR, SPECIAL PROJECTS: ***MARK D. BEAZLEY***
VP PRODUCTION & SPECIAL PROJECTS: ***JEFF YOUNGQUIST***
SVP PRINT, SALES & MARKETING: ***DAVID GABRIEL***
BOOK DESIGNER: ***JAY BOWEN***

EDITOR IN CHIEF: ***AXEL ALONSO***
CHIEF CREATIVE OFFICER: ***JOE QUESADA***
PRESIDENT: ***DAN BUCKLEY***
EXECUTIVE PRODUCER: ***ALAN FINE***

TERRIGEN MISTS CIRCLE THE GLOBE, WHITTLING DOWN MUTANTKIND'S NUMBERS AND SUPPRESSING ANY NEW MUTANT MANIFESTATIONS. BELIEVING BIGGER THREATS REQUIRE MORE THREATENING X-MEN, MAGNETO IS JOINED BY A TEAM OF THE MOST RUTHLESS MUTANTS ALIVE TO STEM THE THREAT OF EXTINCTION...

UNCANNY X-MEN

IVX

#16 & #18-19

CULLEN BUNN
WRITER

EDGAR SALAZAR
PENCILER

ED TADEO
WITH *EDGAR SALAZAR* (#18)
INKERS

NOLAN WOODARD (#16),
RAIN BEREDO (#18) &
ULISES ARREOLA (#19)
COLOR ARTISTS

#17

KEN LASHLEY
ARTIST

NOLAN WOODARD
COLOR ARTIST

VC's JOE CARAMAGNA
LETTERER

**KEN LASHLEY &
NOLAN WOODARD**
COVER ART

CHRIS ROBINSON
ASSISTANT EDITOR

DANIEL KETCHUM
EDITOR

MARK PANICCIA
X-MEN GROUP EDITOR

UNCANNY X-MEN ANNUAL #1

"BALANCING THE SCALES"

CULLEN BUNN
WRITER

KEN LASHLEY
ARTIST

NOLAN WOODARD
COLOR ARTIST

VC'S JOE CARAMAGNA
LETTERER

**DANIEL KETCHUM &
CHRISTINA HARRINGTON**
EDITORS

"LADY LUCK"

ANTHONY PIPER
WRITER/ARTIST/COLORIST

VC'S JOE CARAMAGNA
LETTERER

CHRIS ROBINSON
EDITOR

**ACO &
ROMULO FAJARDO JR.**
COVER ART

X-MEN CREATED BY *STAN LEE* & *JACK KIRBY*

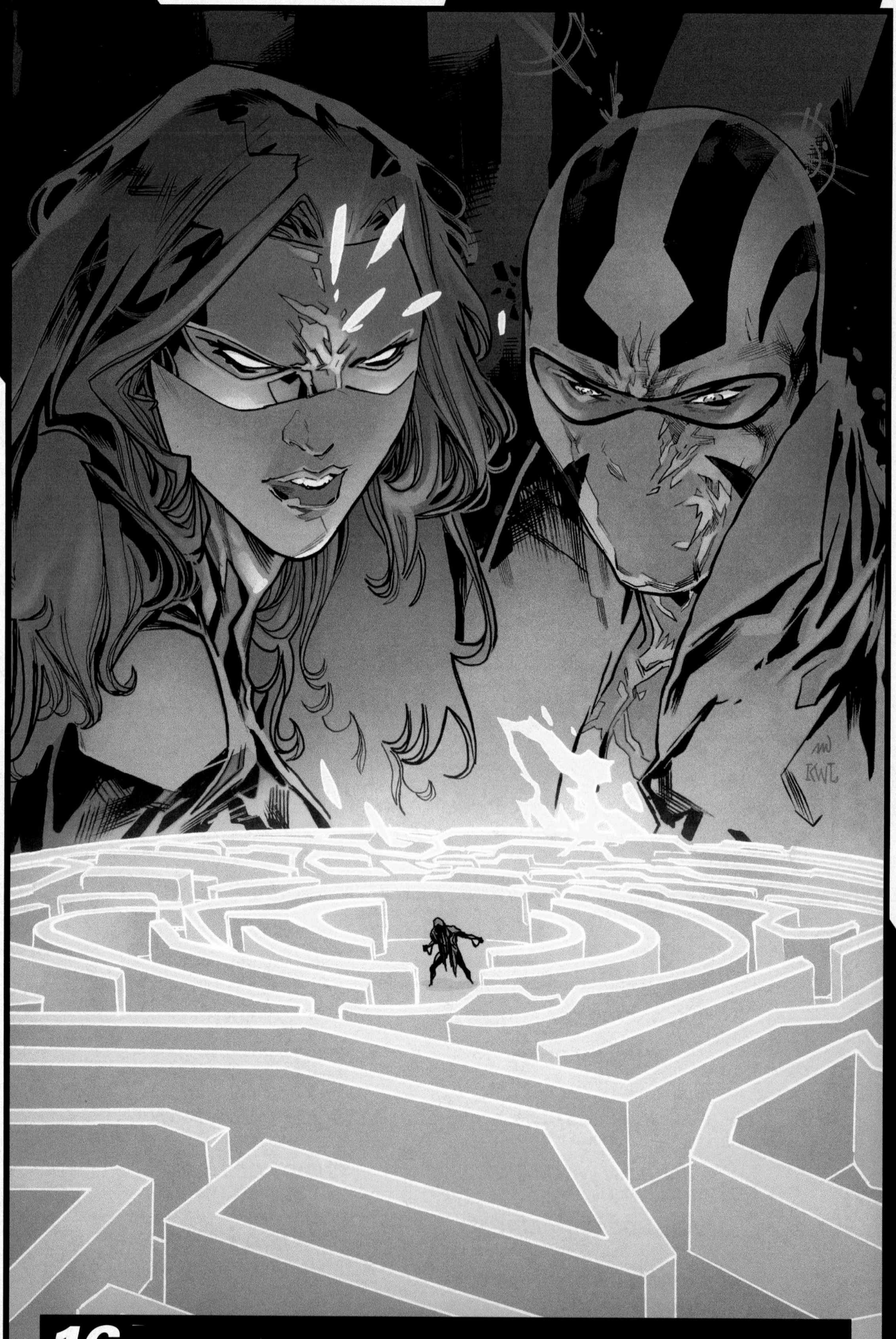
16

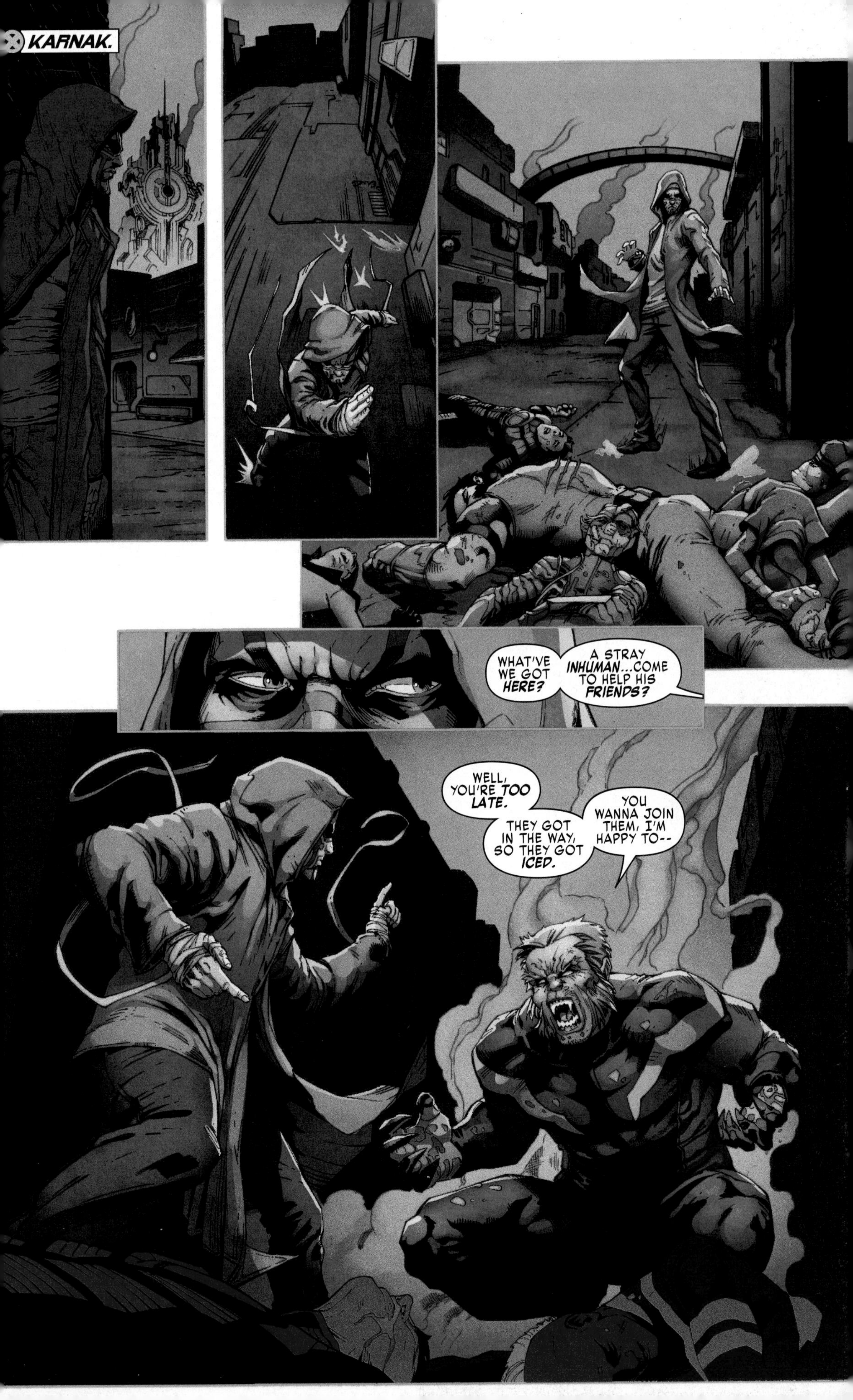
KARNAK.
WHAT'VE WE GOT HERE?
A STRAY INHUMAN...COME TO HELP HIS FRIENDS?
WELL, YOU'RE TOO LATE.
THEY GOT IN THE WAY, SO THEY GOT ICED.
YOU WANNA JOIN THEM, I'M HAPPY TO--

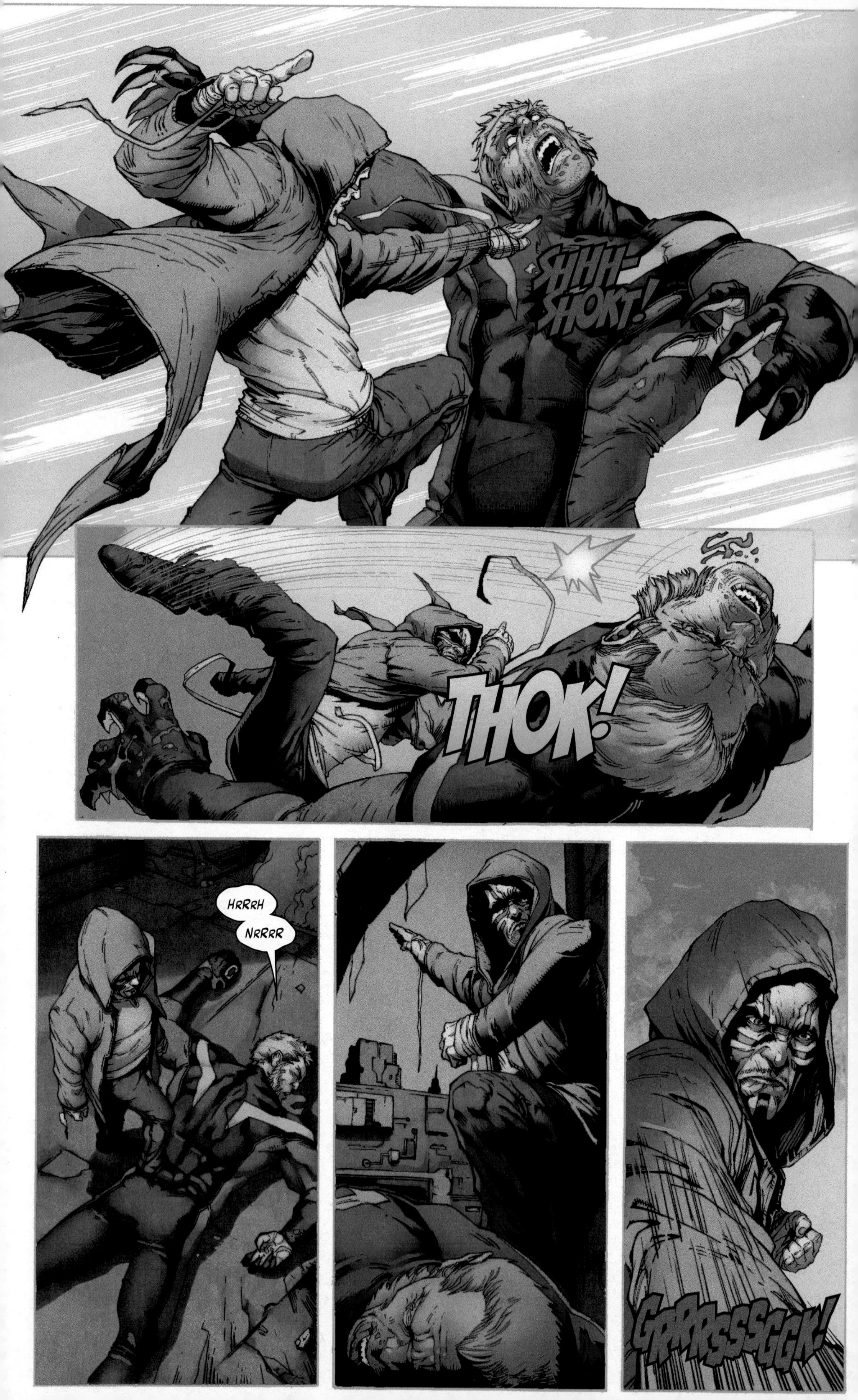
SHHH-SHOKT!
THOK!
HRRRH
NRRRR
GRRRSSSGGK!

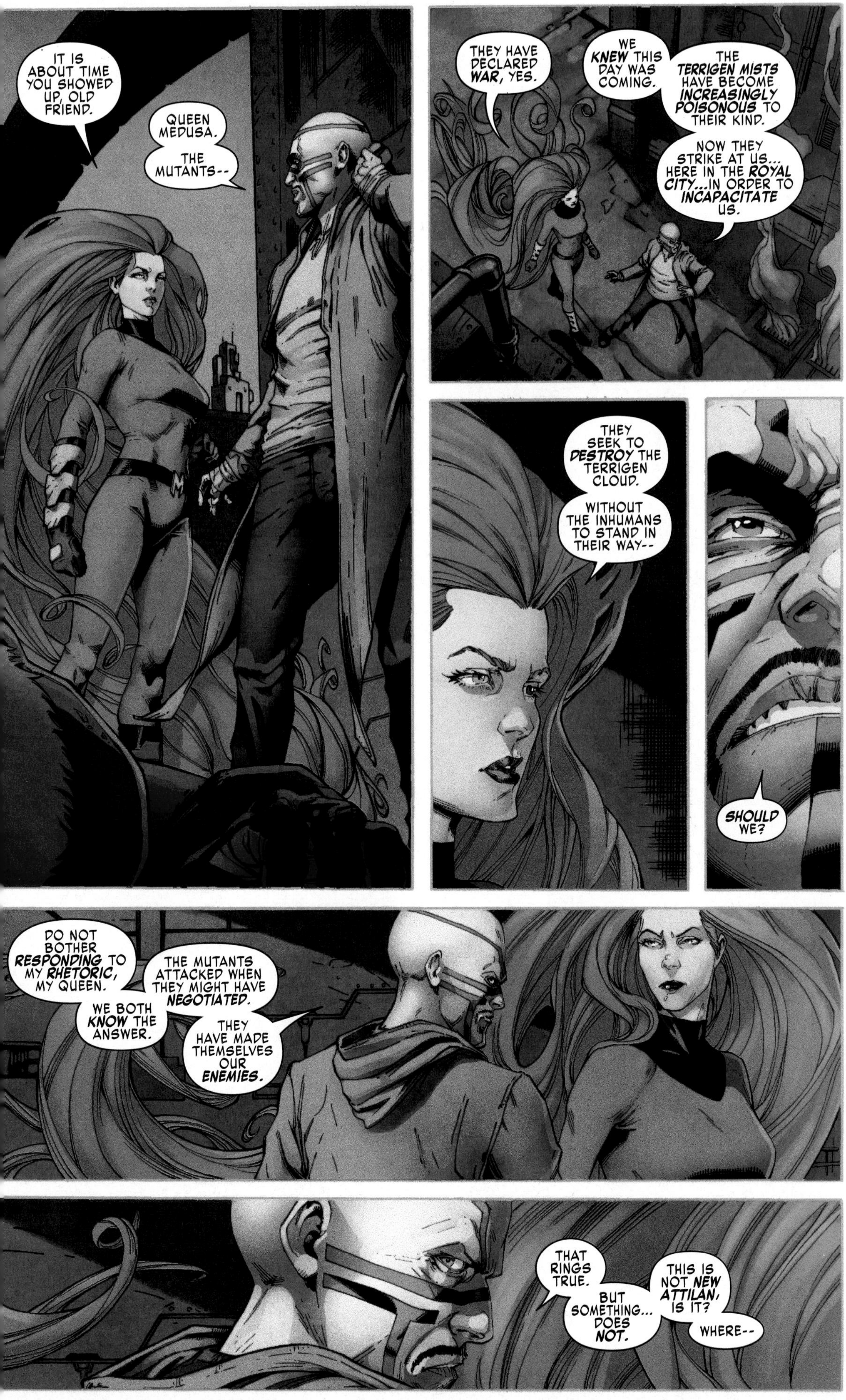
IT IS ABOUT TIME YOU SHOWED UP, OLD FRIEND.
QUEEN MEDUSA.
THE MUTANTS--
THEY HAVE DECLARED WAR, YES.
WE KNEW THIS DAY WAS COMING.
THE TERRIGEN MISTS HAVE BECOME INCREASINGLY POISONOUS TO THEIR KIND.
NOW THEY STRIKE AT US... HERE IN THE ROYAL CITY...IN ORDER TO INCAPACITATE US.
THEY SEEK TO DESTROY THE TERRIGEN CLOUD.
WITHOUT THE INHUMANS TO STAND IN THEIR WAY--
SHOULD WE?
DO NOT BOTHER RESPONDING TO MY RHETORIC, MY QUEEN.
WE BOTH KNOW THE ANSWER.
THE MUTANTS ATTACKED WHEN THEY MIGHT HAVE NEGOTIATED.
THEY HAVE MADE THEMSELVES OUR ENEMIES.
THAT RINGS TRUE.
BUT SOMETHING... DOES NOT.
THIS IS NOT NEW ATTILAN, IS IT?
WHERE--

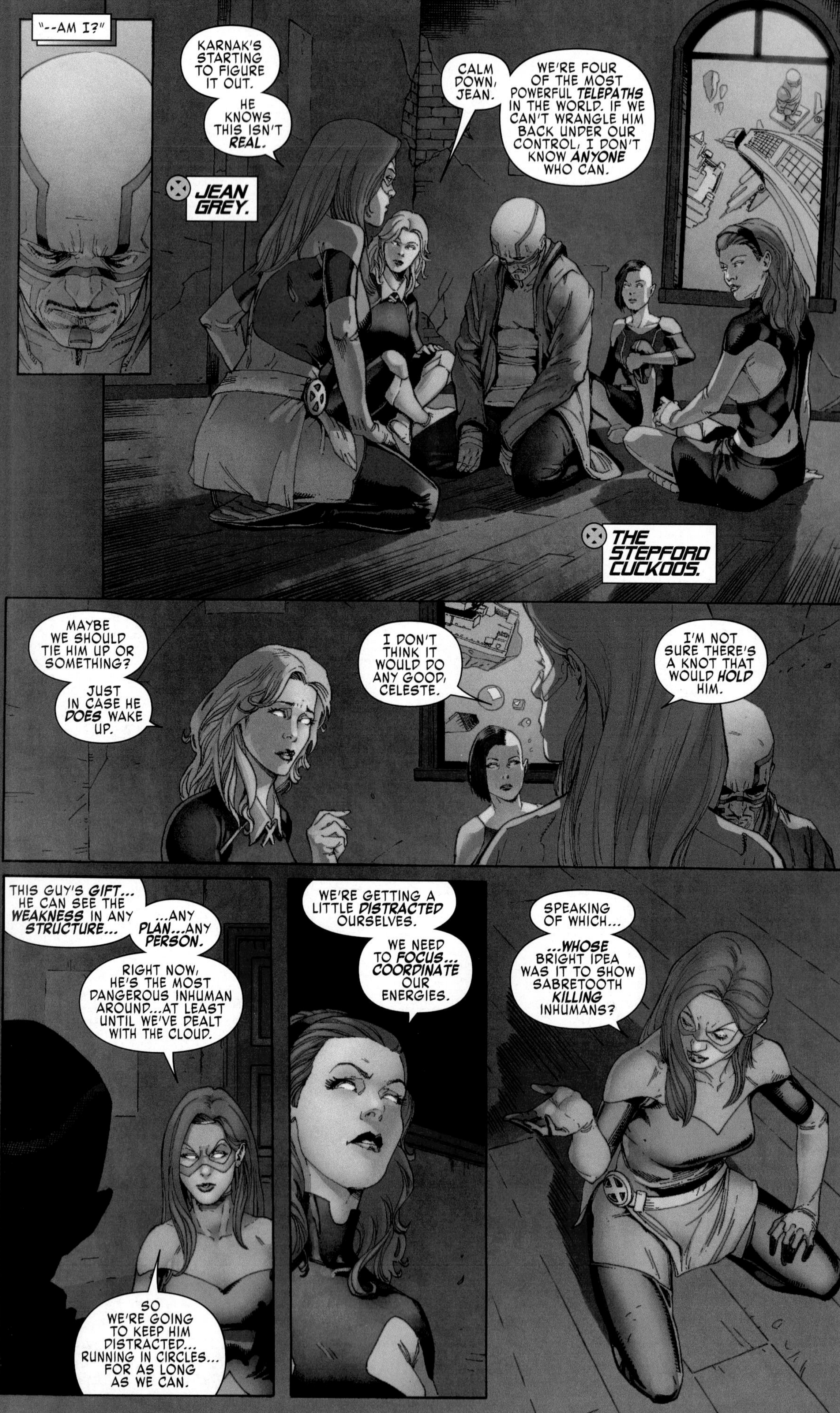
"--AM I?"
KARNAK'S STARTING TO FIGURE IT OUT.
HE KNOWS THIS ISN'T REAL.
JEAN GREY.
CALM DOWN, JEAN.
WE'RE FOUR OF THE MOST POWERFUL TELEPATHS IN THE WORLD. IF WE CAN'T WRANGLE HIM BACK UNDER OUR CONTROL, I DON'T KNOW ANYONE WHO CAN.
THE STEPFORD CUCKOOS.
MAYBE WE SHOULD TIE HIM UP OR SOMETHING?
JUST IN CASE HE DOES WAKE UP.
I DON'T THINK IT WOULD DO ANY GOOD, CELESTE.
I'M NOT SURE THERE'S A KNOT THAT WOULD HOLD HIM.
THIS GUY'S GIFT... HE CAN SEE THE WEAKNESS IN ANY STRUCTURE...
...ANY PLAN...ANY PERSON.
RIGHT NOW, HE'S THE MOST DANGEROUS INHUMAN AROUND...AT LEAST UNTIL WE'VE DEALT WITH THE CLOUD.
SO WE'RE GOING TO KEEP HIM DISTRACTED... RUNNING IN CIRCLES... FOR AS LONG AS WE CAN.
WE'RE GETTING A LITTLE DISTRACTED OURSELVES.
WE NEED TO FOCUS... COORDINATE OUR ENERGIES.
SPEAKING OF WHICH...
...WHOSE BRIGHT IDEA WAS IT TO SHOW SABRETOOTH KILLING INHUMANS?

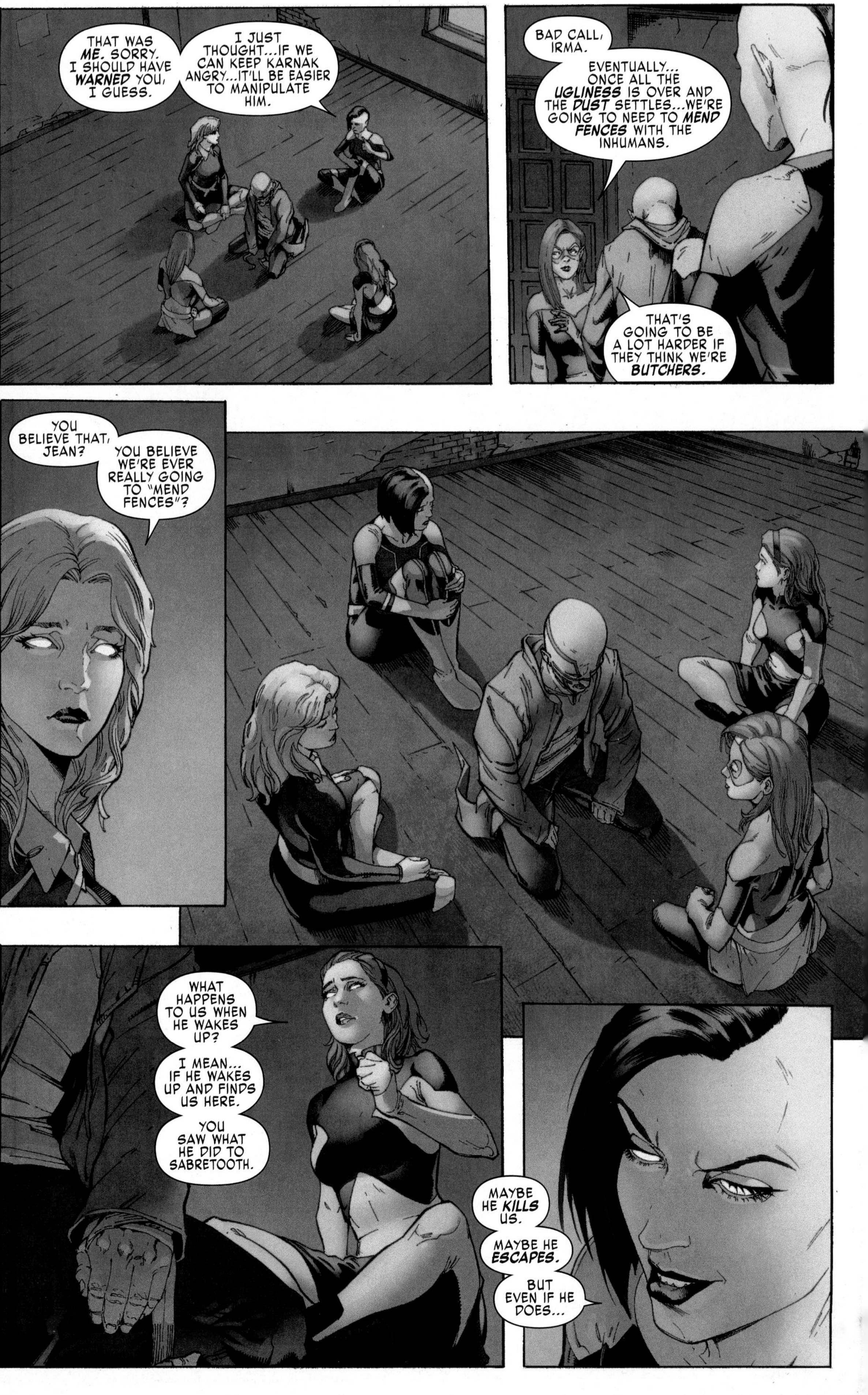
THAT WAS ME. SORRY. I SHOULD HAVE WARNED YOU, I GUESS.
I JUST THOUGHT...IF WE CAN KEEP KARNAK ANGRY...IT'LL BE EASIER TO MANIPULATE HIM.
BAD CALL, IRMA.
EVENTUALLY... ONCE ALL THE UGLINESS IS OVER AND THE DUST SETTLES...WE'RE GOING TO NEED TO MEND FENCES WITH THE INHUMANS.
THAT'S GOING TO BE A LOT HARDER IF THEY THINK WE'RE BUTCHERS.
YOU BELIEVE THAT, JEAN?
YOU BELIEVE WE'RE EVER REALLY GOING TO "MEND FENCES"?
WHAT HAPPENS TO US WHEN HE WAKES UP?
I MEAN... IF HE WAKES UP AND FINDS US HERE.
YOU SAW WHAT HE DID TO SABRETOOTH.
MAYBE HE KILLS US.
MAYBE HE ESCAPES.
BUT EVEN IF HE DOES...

...WHERE'S HE GOING TO GO?

HAVE A *CARE*, MADEMOISELLE.

IF WE LOST KARNAK IN HERE...

...WE MIGHT *NEVER* SEE HIM AGAIN.

THE WORLD IS A *BIG* PLACE. AND FULL OF VIOLENT, VIOLENT THINGS.

THE WORLD.
ARTIFICIAL REALITY
SUPER-SENTINEL FACTORY.

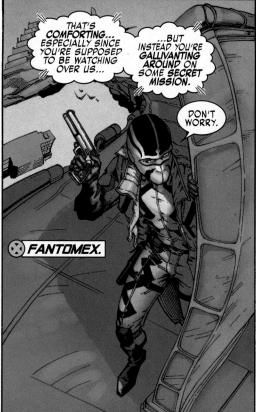

THAT'S COMFORTING... ESPECIALLY SINCE YOU'RE SUPPOSED TO BE WATCHING OVER US...

...BUT INSTEAD YOU'RE *GALLIVANTING* AROUND ON SOME *SECRET* MISSION.

DON'T WORRY.

(X) FANTOMEX.

ULTIMATON WILL NOT LET ANY HARM BEFALL YOU.

BESIDES...IF WE WANT KARNAK OFF THE PLAYING FIELD, WHY NOT LET HIM GO?

SOUNDS LIKE CUTTING HIM LOOSE MIGHT BE GOOD FOR ALL OF MUTANTKIND.

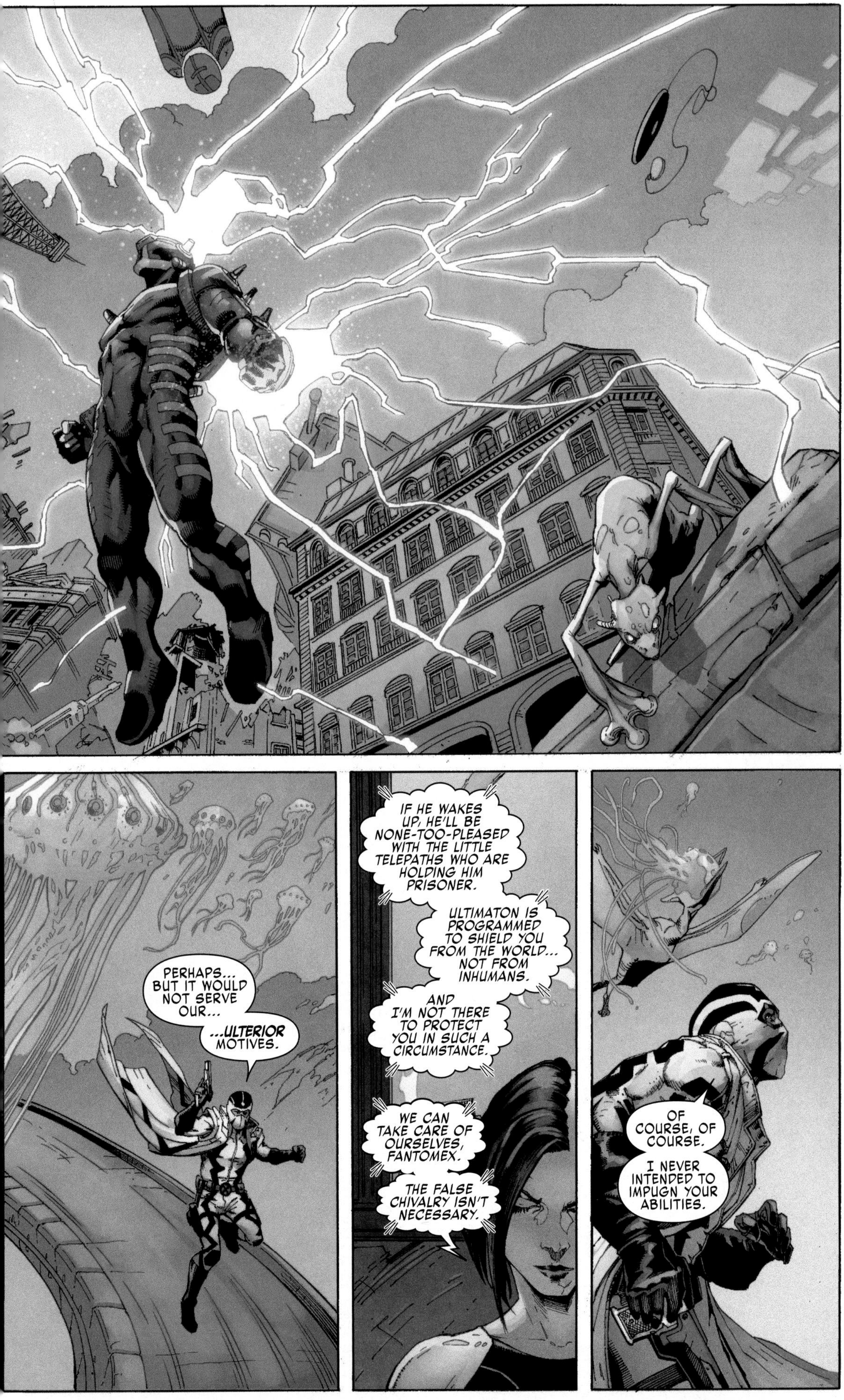
PERHAPS... BUT IT WOULD NOT SERVE OUR...
...ULTERIOR MOTIVES.
IF HE WAKES UP, HE'LL BE NONE-TOO-PLEASED WITH THE LITTLE TELEPATHS WHO ARE HOLDING HIM PRISONER.
ULTIMATON IS PROGRAMMED TO SHIELD YOU FROM THE WORLD... NOT FROM INHUMANS.
AND I'M NOT THERE TO PROTECT YOU IN SUCH A CIRCUMSTANCE.
WE CAN TAKE CARE OF OURSELVES, FANTOMEX.
THE FALSE CHIVALRY ISN'T NECESSARY.
OF COURSE, OF COURSE.
I NEVER INTENDED TO IMPUGN YOUR ABILITIES.

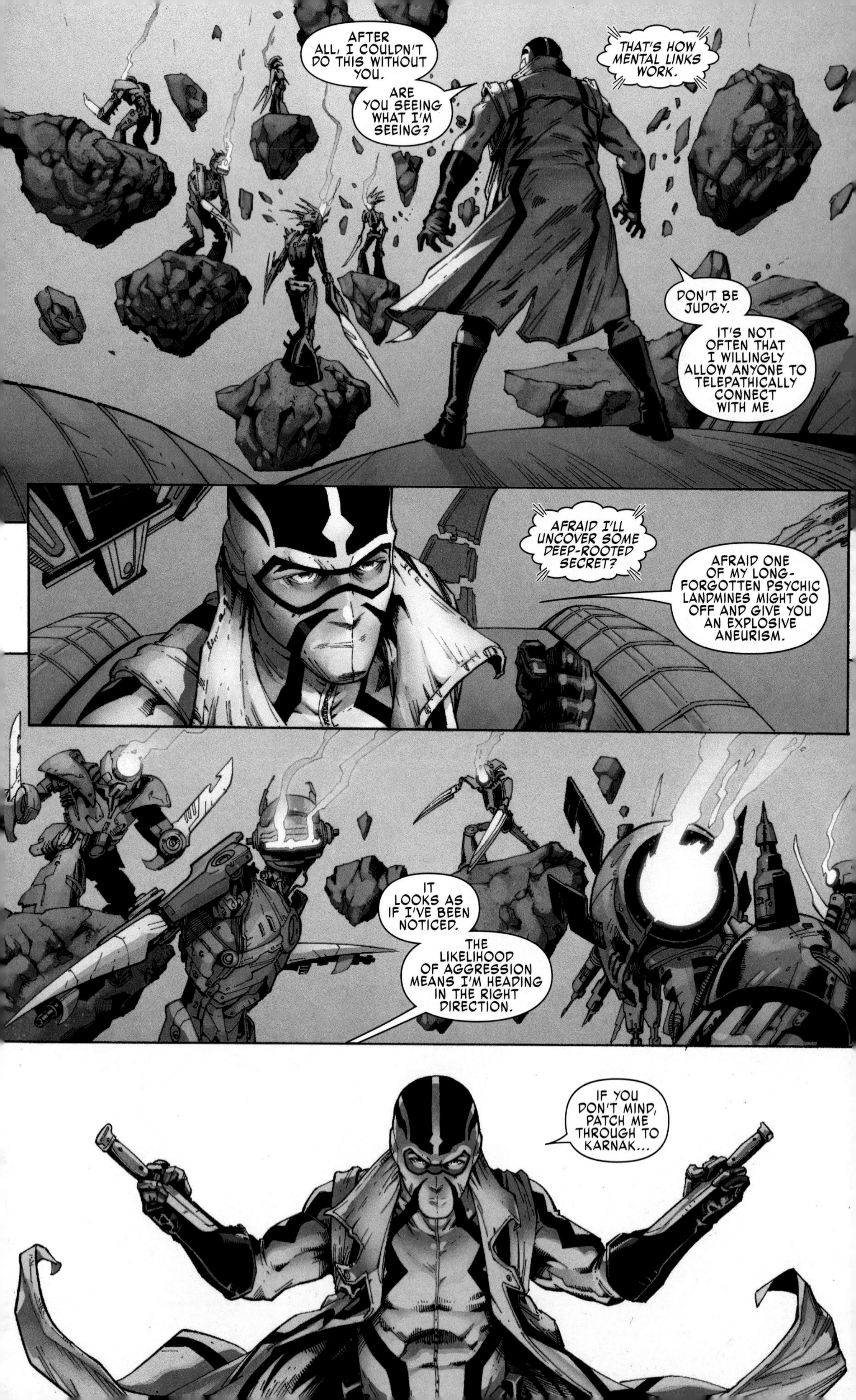
AFTER ALL, I COULDN'T DO THIS WITHOUT YOU.
ARE YOU SEEING WHAT I'M SEEING?
THAT'S HOW MENTAL LINKS WORK.
DON'T BE JUDGY.
IT'S NOT OFTEN THAT I WILLINGLY ALLOW ANYONE TO TELEPATHICALLY CONNECT WITH ME.
AFRAID I'LL UNCOVER SOME DEEP-ROOTED SECRET?
AFRAID ONE OF MY LONG-FORGOTTEN PSYCHIC LANDMINES MIGHT GO OFF AND GIVE YOU AN EXPLOSIVE ANEURISM.
IT LOOKS AS IF I'VE BEEN NOTICED.
THE LIKELIHOOD OF AGGRESSION MEANS I'M HEADING IN THE RIGHT DIRECTION.
IF YOU DON'T MIND, PATCH ME THROUGH TO KARNAK...

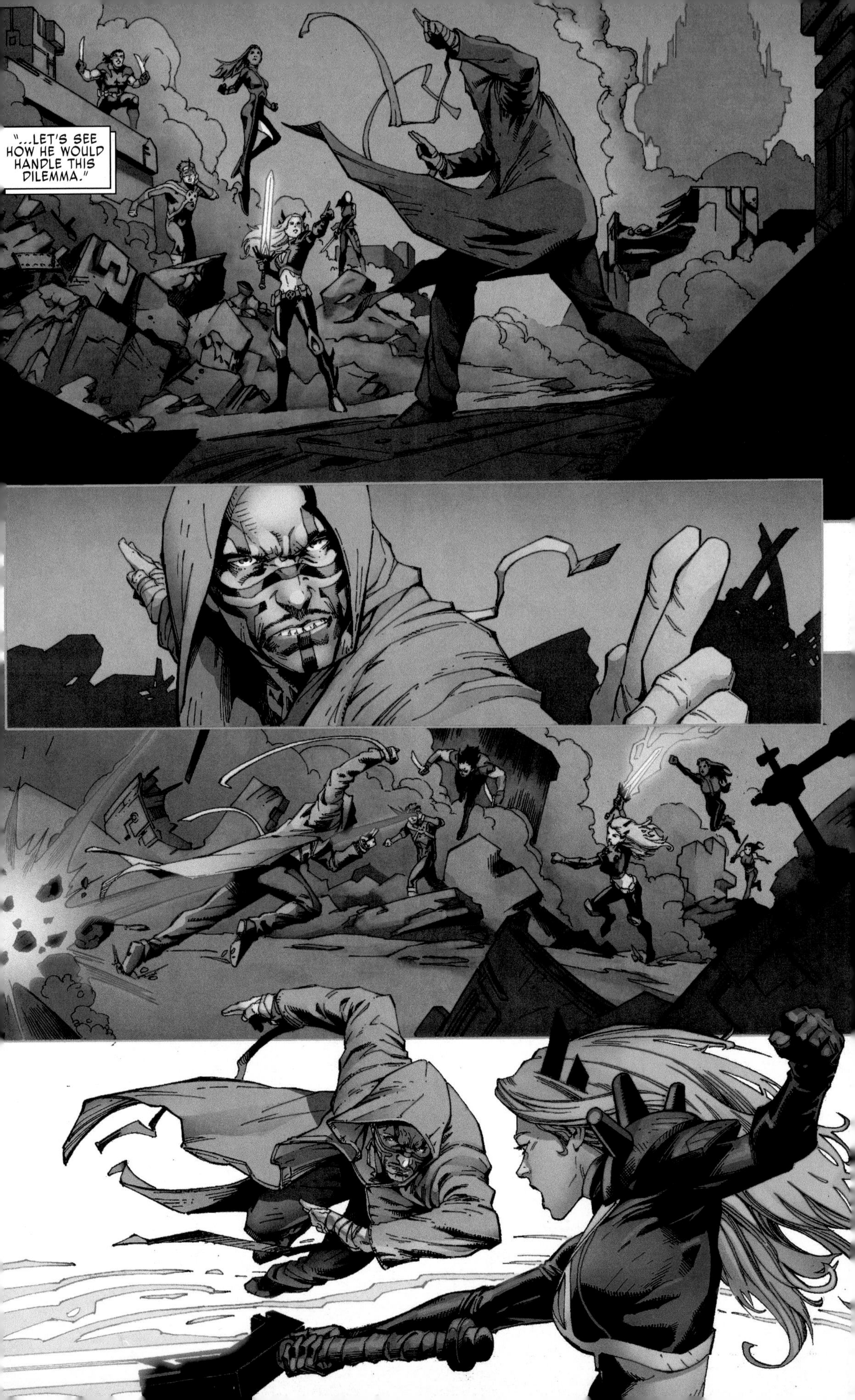
"...LET'S SEE HOW HE WOULD HANDLE THIS DILEMMA."

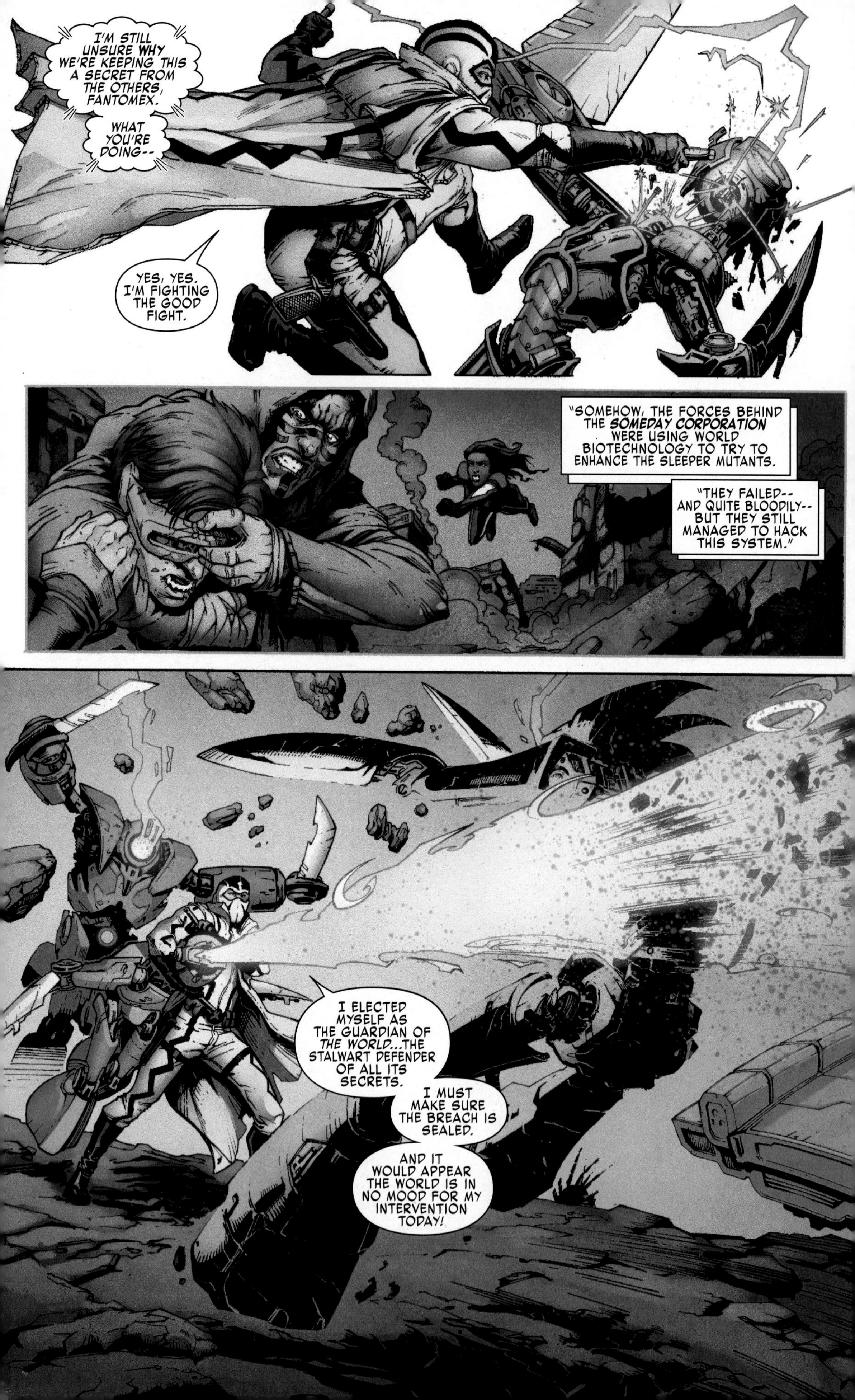
I'M STILL UNSURE WHY WE'RE KEEPING THIS A SECRET FROM THE OTHERS, FANTOMEX.
WHAT YOU'RE DOING--
YES, YES. I'M FIGHTING THE GOOD FIGHT.
"SOMEHOW, THE FORCES BEHIND THE SOMEDAY CORPORATION WERE USING WORLD BIOTECHNOLOGY TO TRY TO ENHANCE THE SLEEPER MUTANTS.
"THEY FAILED-- AND QUITE BLOODILY-- BUT THEY STILL MANAGED TO HACK THIS SYSTEM."
I ELECTED MYSELF AS THE GUARDIAN OF THE WORLD...THE STALWART DEFENDER OF ALL ITS SECRETS.
I MUST MAKE SURE THE BREACH IS SEALED.
AND IT WOULD APPEAR THE WORLD IS IN NO MOOD FOR MY INTERVENTION TODAY!

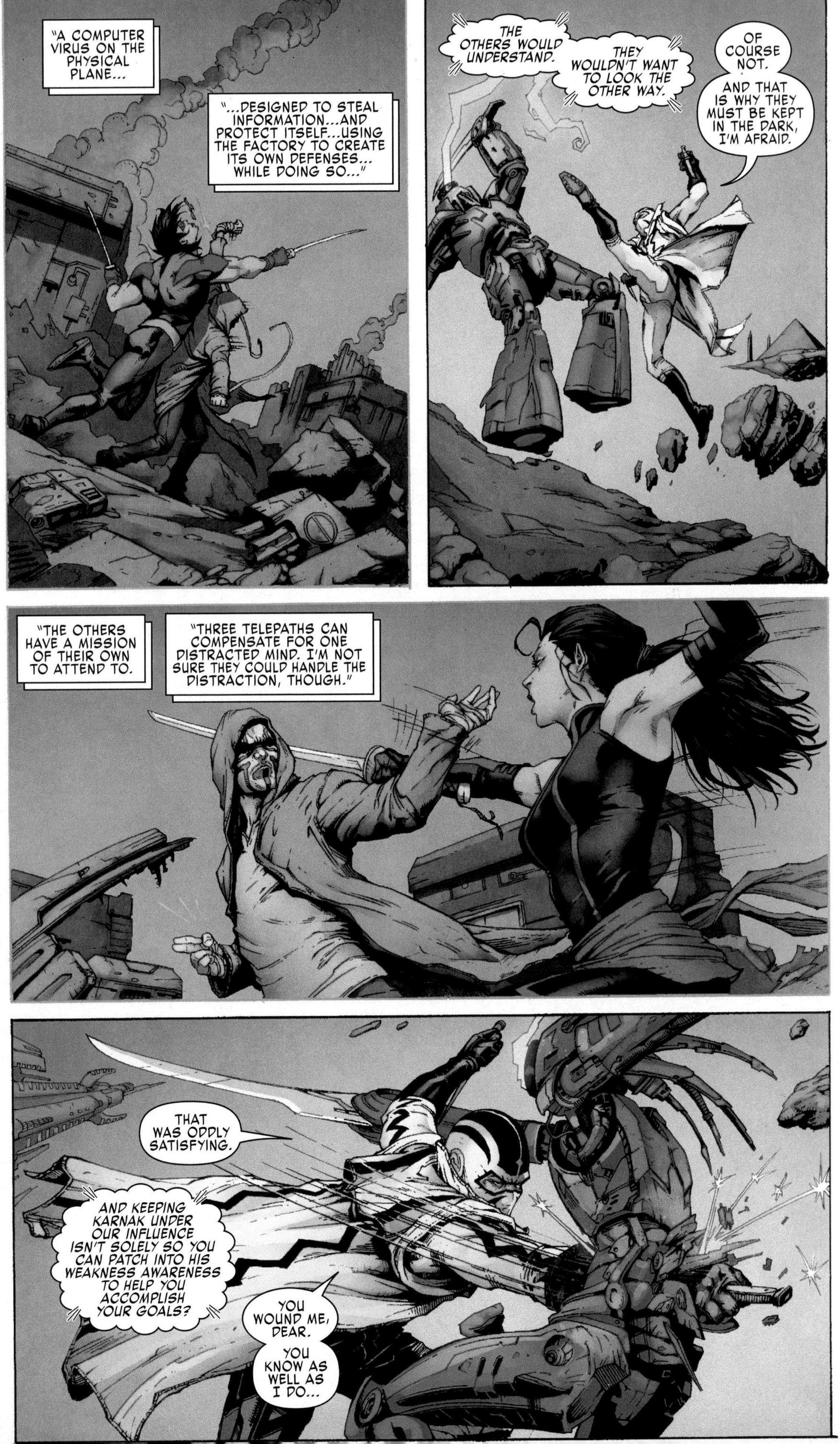
"A COMPUTER VIRUS ON THE PHYSICAL PLANE...
"...DESIGNED TO STEAL INFORMATION...AND PROTECT ITSELF...USING THE FACTORY TO CREATE ITS OWN DEFENSES... WHILE DOING SO..."
THE OTHERS WOULD UNDERSTAND.
THEY WOULDN'T WANT TO LOOK THE OTHER WAY.
OF COURSE NOT.
AND THAT IS WHY THEY MUST BE KEPT IN THE DARK, I'M AFRAID.
"THE OTHERS HAVE A MISSION OF THEIR OWN TO ATTEND TO.
"THREE TELEPATHS CAN COMPENSATE FOR ONE DISTRACTED MIND. I'M NOT SURE THEY COULD HANDLE THE DISTRACTION, THOUGH."
THAT WAS ODDLY SATISFYING.
AND KEEPING KARNAK UNDER OUR INFLUENCE ISN'T SOLELY SO YOU CAN PATCH INTO HIS WEAKNESS AWARENESS TO HELP YOU ACCOMPLISH YOUR GOALS?
YOU WOUND ME, DEAR.
YOU KNOW AS WELL AS I DO...

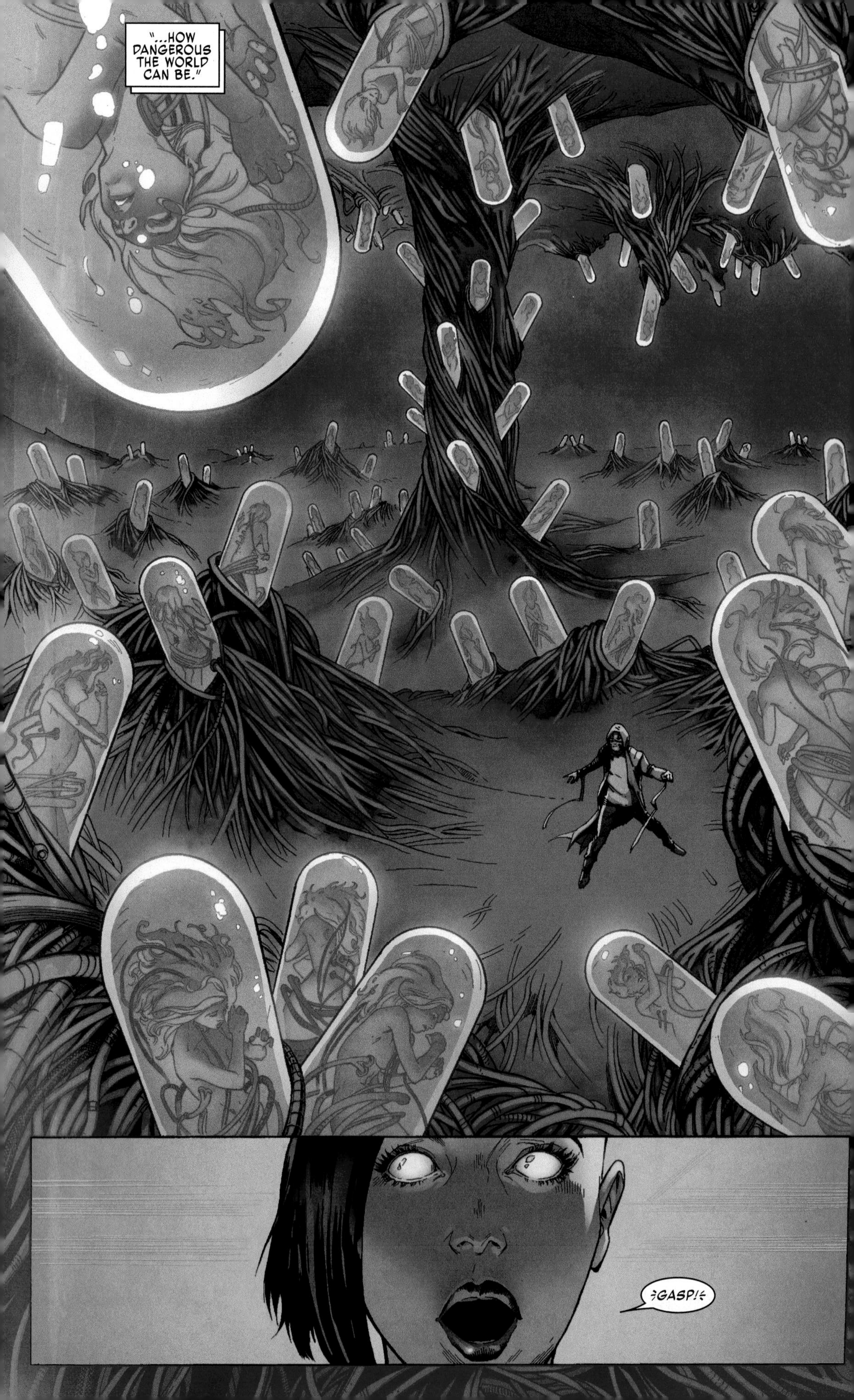
"...HOW DANGEROUS THE WORLD CAN BE."
GASP!

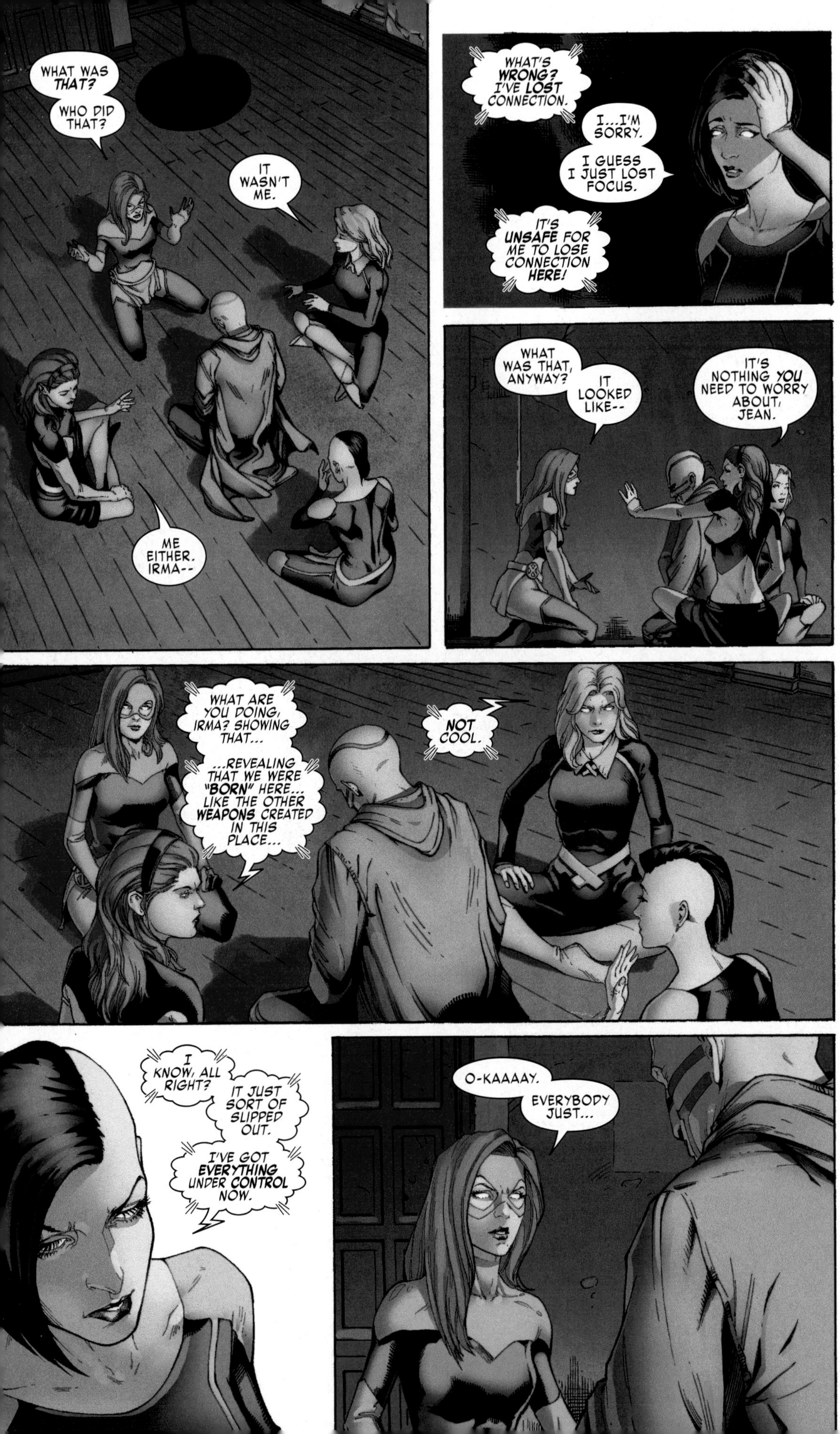

WHAT WAS THAT?
WHO DID THAT?
IT WASN'T ME.
ME EITHER. IRMA--
WHAT'S WRONG? I'VE LOST CONNECTION.
I...I'M SORRY.
I GUESS I JUST LOST FOCUS.
IT'S UNSAFE FOR ME TO LOSE CONNECTION HERE!
WHAT WAS THAT, ANYWAY?
IT LOOKED LIKE--
IT'S NOTHING YOU NEED TO WORRY ABOUT, JEAN.
WHAT ARE YOU DOING, IRMA? SHOWING THAT...
...REVEALING THAT WE WERE "BORN" HERE... LIKE THE OTHER WEAPONS CREATED IN THIS PLACE...
NOT COOL.
I KNOW, ALL RIGHT?
IT JUST SORT OF SLIPPED OUT.
I'VE GOT EVERYTHING UNDER CONTROL NOW.
O-KAAAAY.
EVERYBODY JUST...

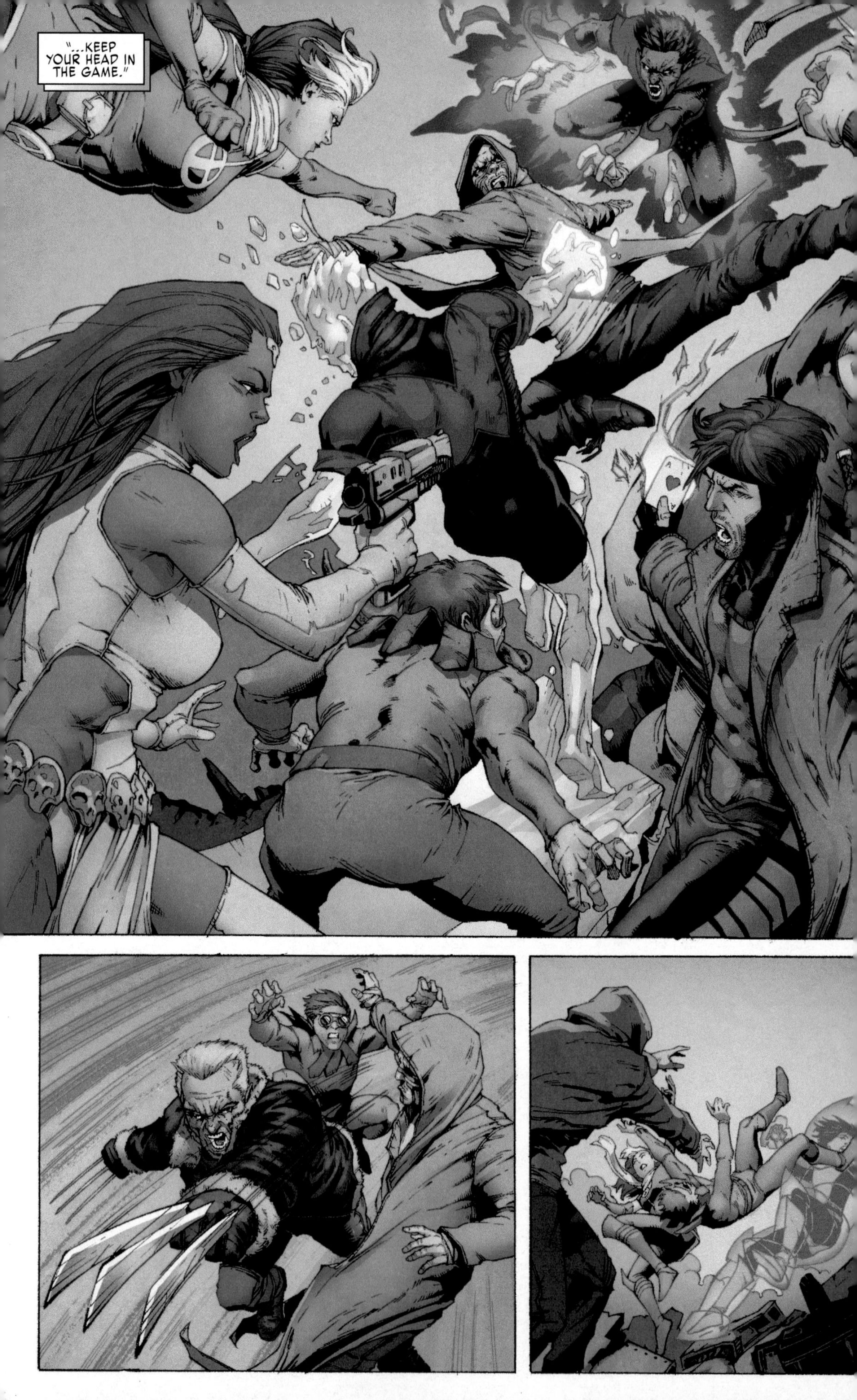
"...KEEP YOUR HEAD IN THE GAME."

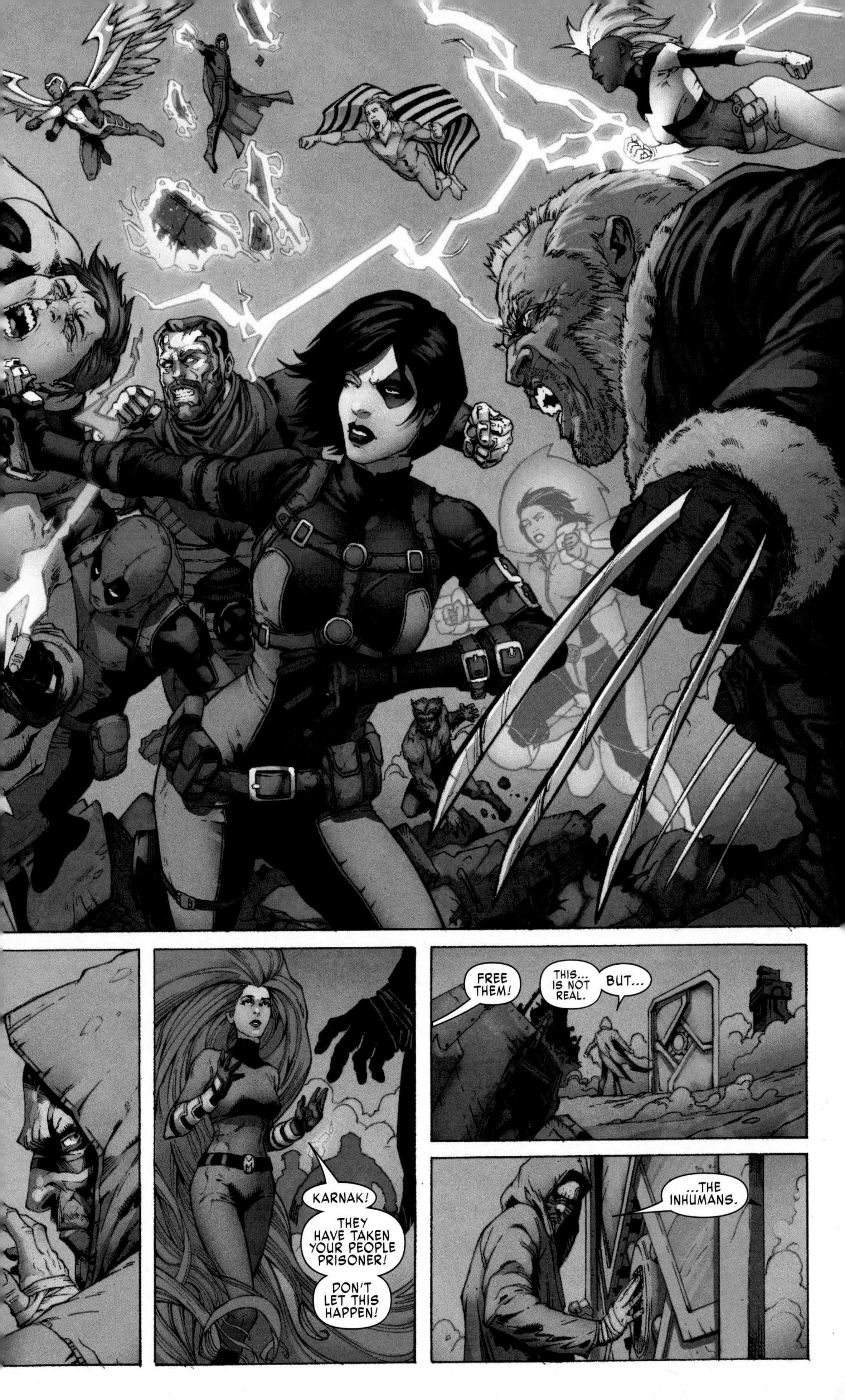

KARNAK!
THEY HAVE TAKEN YOUR PEOPLE PRISONER!
DON'T LET THIS HAPPEN!
FREE THEM!
THIS... IS NOT REAL.
BUT...
...THE INHUMANS.

YES, YES. WE *ALL* HAVE SPECIES TO SAVE.

INHUMAN...

...MUTANT...

...AND WHATEVER IS BEYOND.

THE VIRUS...

...LIKE A FLOWER...

...ITS PETALS OPENING...

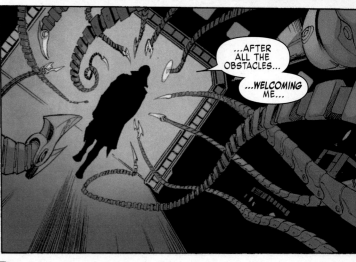

...AFTER ALL THE OBSTACLES...

...WELCOMING ME...

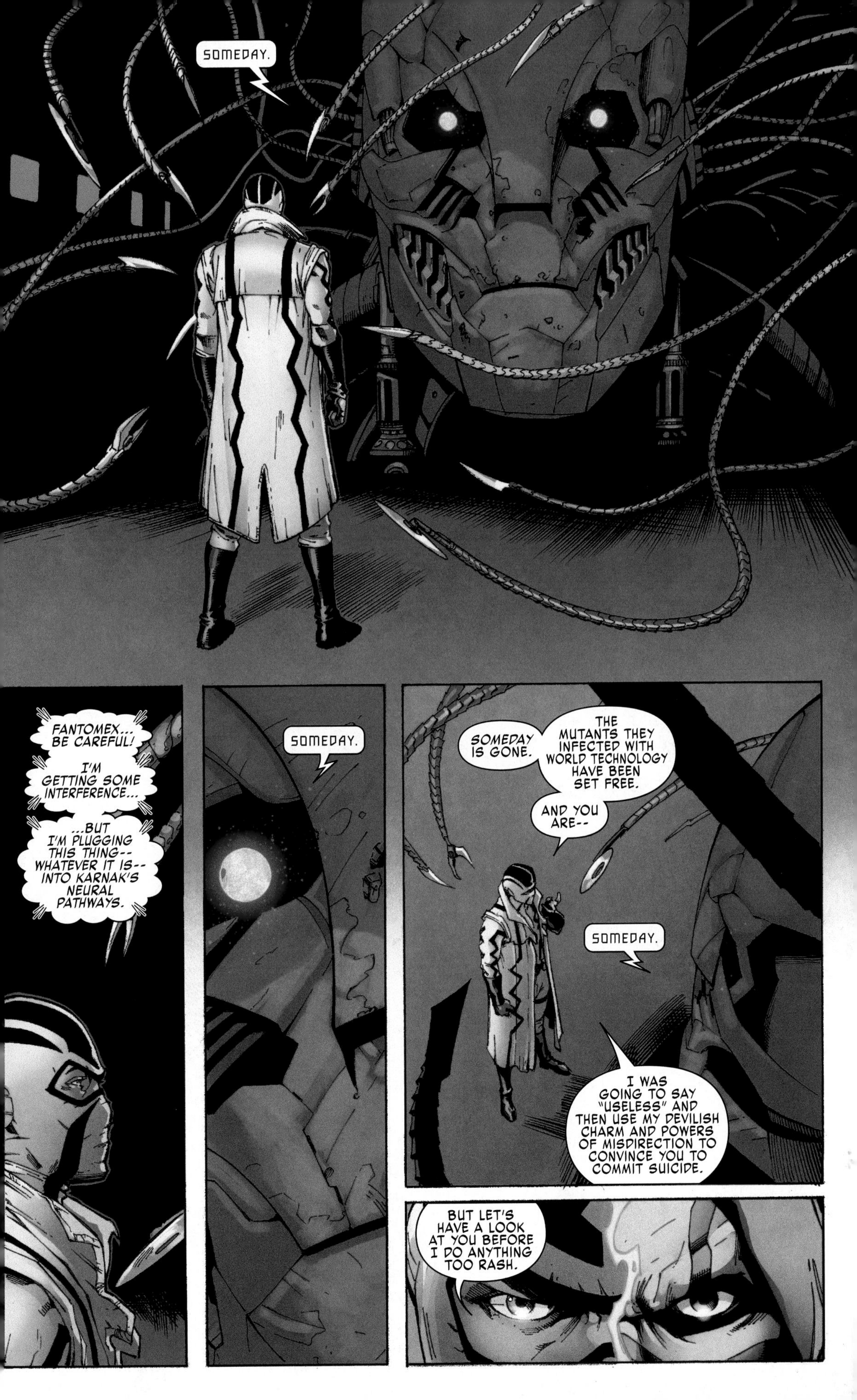
SOMEDAY.
FANTOMEX... BE CAREFUL!
I'M GETTING SOME INTERFERENCE...
...BUT I'M PLUGGING THIS THING-- WHATEVER IT IS-- INTO KARNAK'S NEURAL PATHWAYS.
SOMEDAY.
SOMEDAY IS GONE.
THE MUTANTS THEY INFECTED WITH WORLD TECHNOLOGY HAVE BEEN SET FREE.
AND YOU ARE--
SOMEDAY.
I WAS GOING TO SAY "USELESS" AND THEN USE MY DEVILISH CHARM AND POWERS OF MISDIRECTION TO CONVINCE YOU TO COMMIT SUICIDE.
BUT LET'S HAVE A LOOK AT YOU BEFORE I DO ANYTHING TOO RASH.

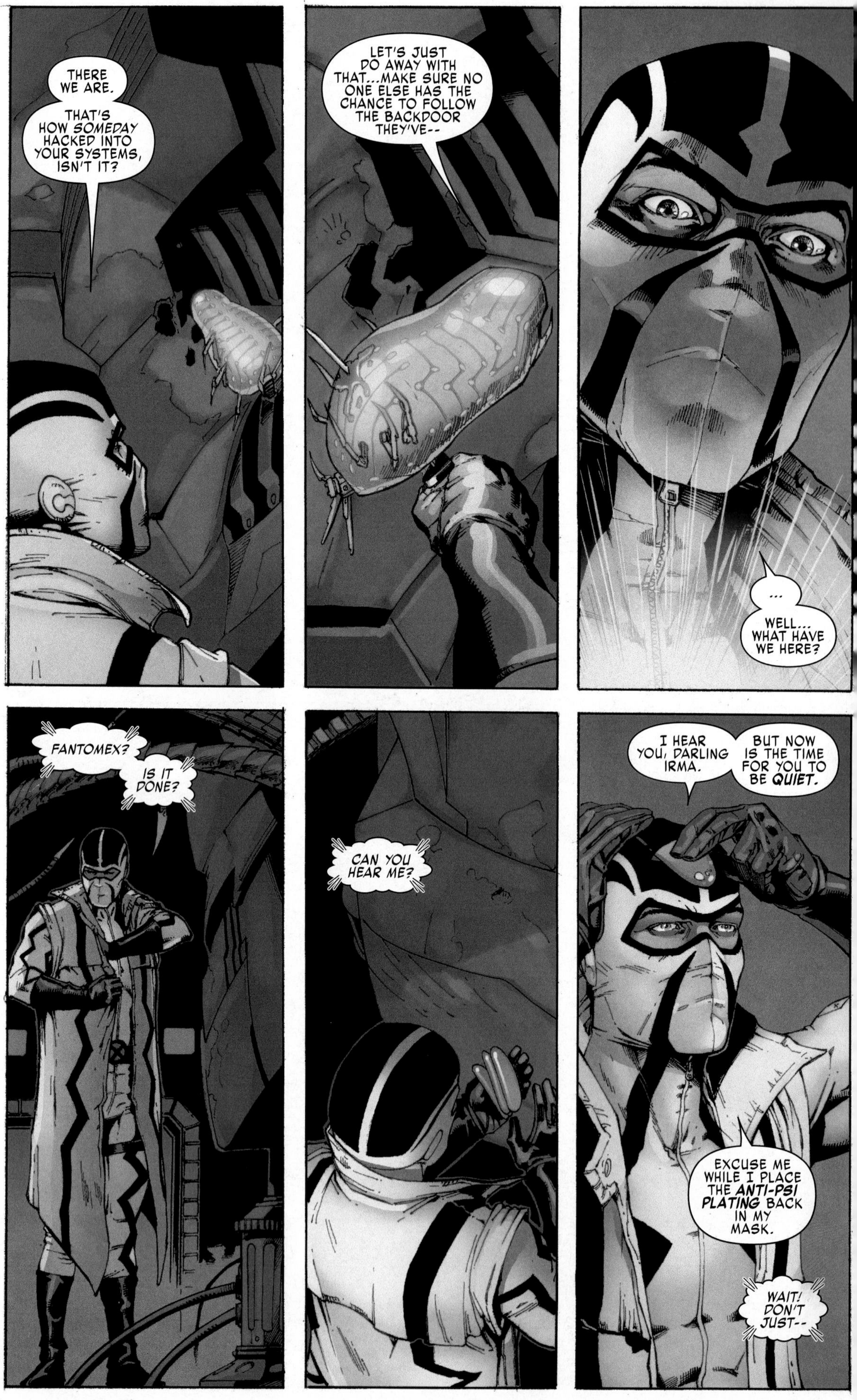
THERE WE ARE.
THAT'S HOW SOMEDAY HACKED INTO YOUR SYSTEMS, ISN'T IT?
LET'S JUST DO AWAY WITH THAT...MAKE SURE NO ONE ELSE HAS THE CHANCE TO FOLLOW THE BACKDOOR THEY'VE--
...
WELL... WHAT HAVE WE HERE?
FANTOMEX?
IS IT DONE?
CAN YOU HEAR ME?
I HEAR YOU, DARLING IRMA.
BUT NOW IS THE TIME FOR YOU TO BE QUIET.
EXCUSE ME WHILE I PLACE THE ANTI-PSI PLATING BACK IN MY MASK.
WAIT! DON'T JUST--

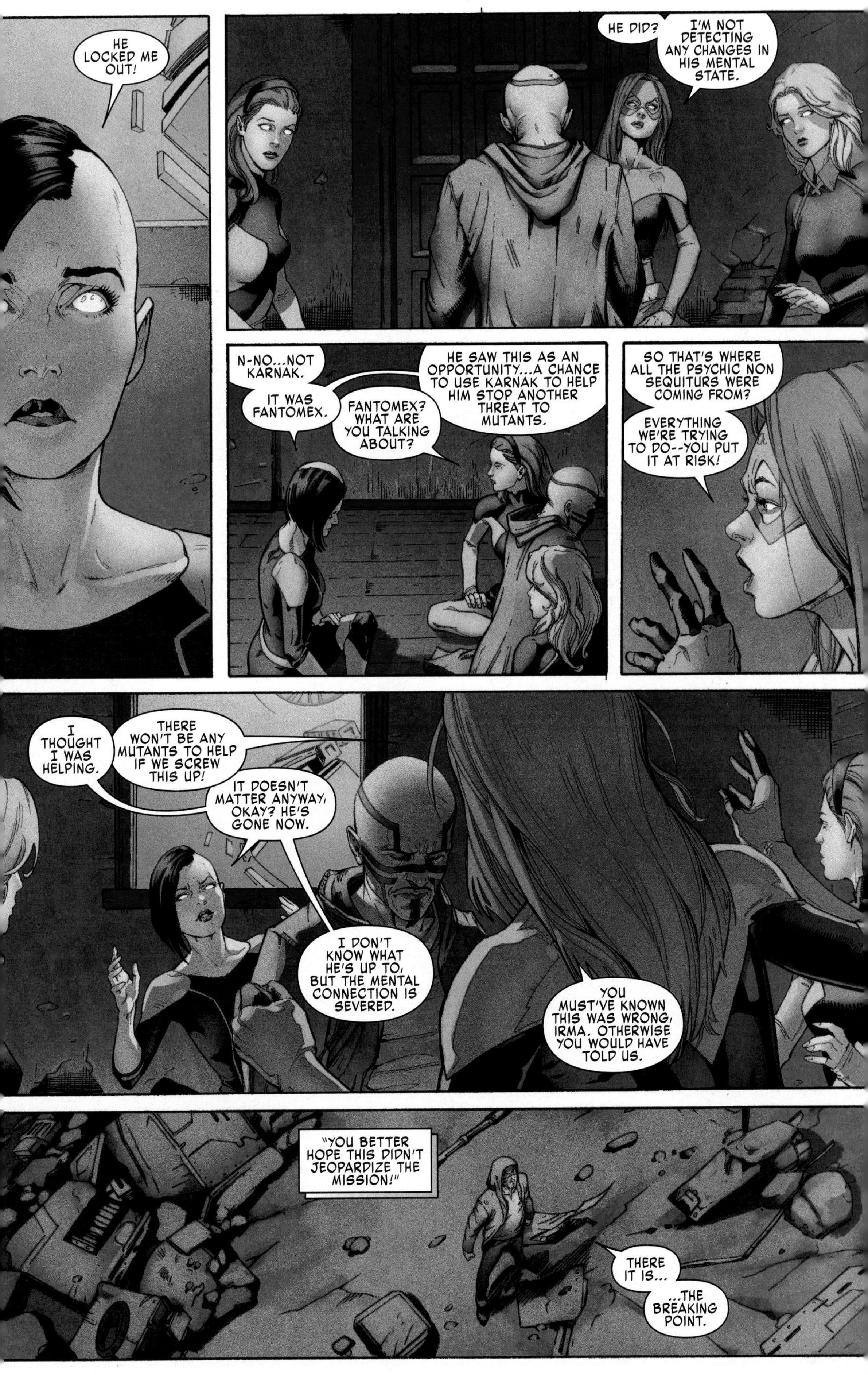
HE LOCKED ME OUT!
HE DID?
I'M NOT DETECTING ANY CHANGES IN HIS MENTAL STATE.
N-NO...NOT KARNAK.
IT WAS FANTOMEX.
FANTOMEX? WHAT ARE YOU TALKING ABOUT?
HE SAW THIS AS AN OPPORTUNITY...A CHANCE TO USE KARNAK TO HELP HIM STOP ANOTHER THREAT TO MUTANTS.
SO THAT'S WHERE ALL THE PSYCHIC NON SEQUITURS WERE COMING FROM?
EVERYTHING WE'RE TRYING TO DO--YOU PUT IT AT RISK!
I THOUGHT I WAS HELPING.
THERE WON'T BE ANY MUTANTS TO HELP IF WE SCREW THIS UP!
IT DOESN'T MATTER ANYWAY, OKAY? HE'S GONE NOW.
I DON'T KNOW WHAT HE'S UP TO, BUT THE MENTAL CONNECTION IS SEVERED.
YOU MUST'VE KNOWN THIS WAS WRONG, IRMA. OTHERWISE YOU WOULD HAVE TOLD US.
"YOU BETTER HOPE THIS DIDN'T JEOPARDIZE THE MISSION!"
THERE IT IS...
...THE BREAKING POINT.

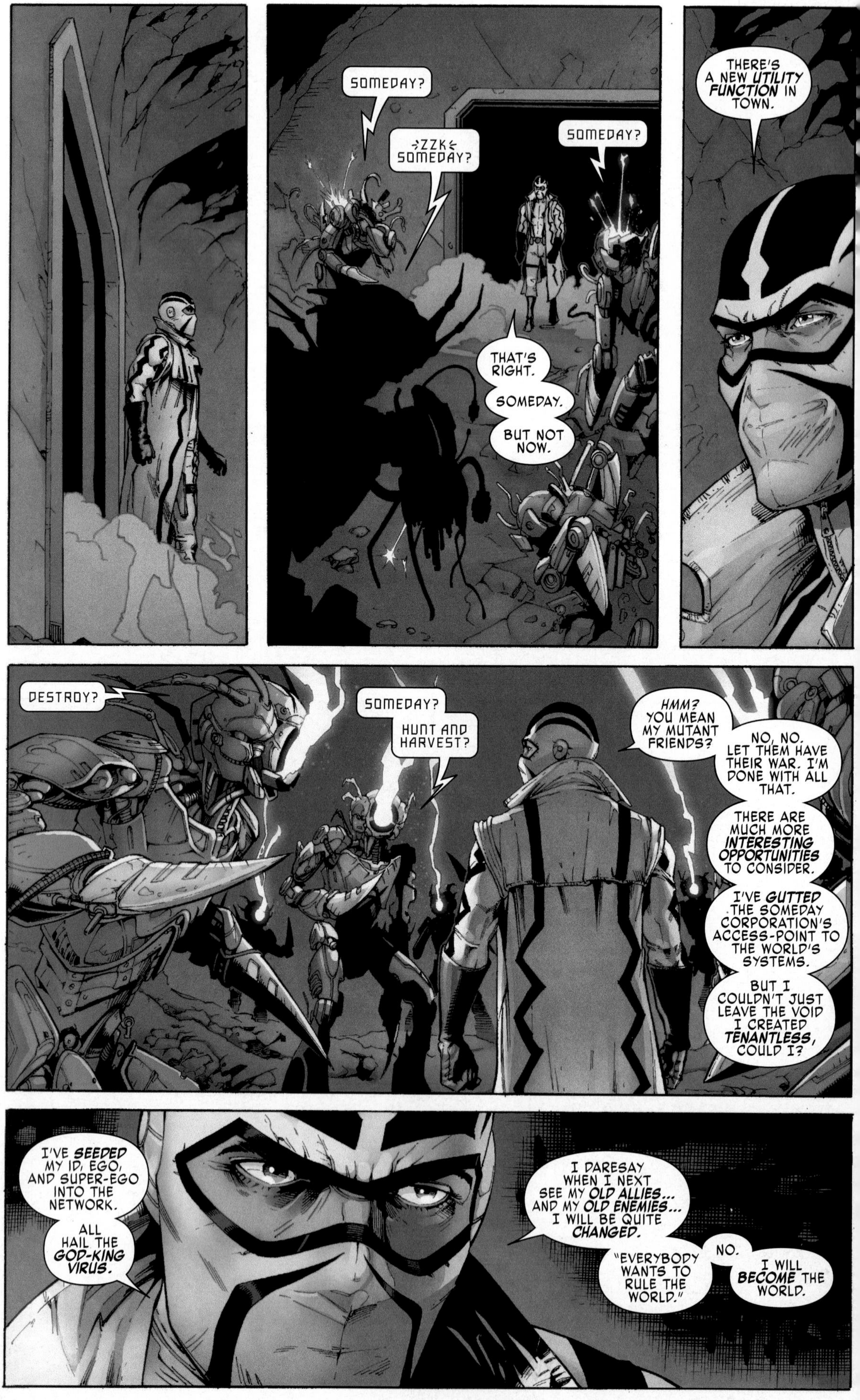
SOMEDAY?
ZZK SOMEDAY?
SOMEDAY?
THAT'S RIGHT.
SOMEDAY.
BUT NOT NOW.
THERE'S A NEW UTILITY FUNCTION IN TOWN.
DESTROY?
SOMEDAY?
HUNT AND HARVEST?
HMM? YOU MEAN MY MUTANT FRIENDS?
NO, NO. LET THEM HAVE THEIR WAR. I'M DONE WITH ALL THAT.
THERE ARE MUCH MORE INTERESTING OPPORTUNITIES TO CONSIDER.
I'VE GUTTED THE SOMEDAY CORPORATION'S ACCESS-POINT TO THE WORLD'S SYSTEMS.
BUT I COULDN'T JUST LEAVE THE VOID I CREATED TENANTLESS, COULD I?
I'VE SEEDED MY ID, EGO, AND SUPER-EGO INTO THE NETWORK.
ALL HAIL THE GOD-KING VIRUS.
I DARESAY WHEN I NEXT SEE MY OLD ALLIES... AND MY OLD ENEMIES... I WILL BE QUITE CHANGED.
"EVERYBODY WANTS TO RULE THE WORLD."
NO.
I WILL BECOME THE WORLD.

17

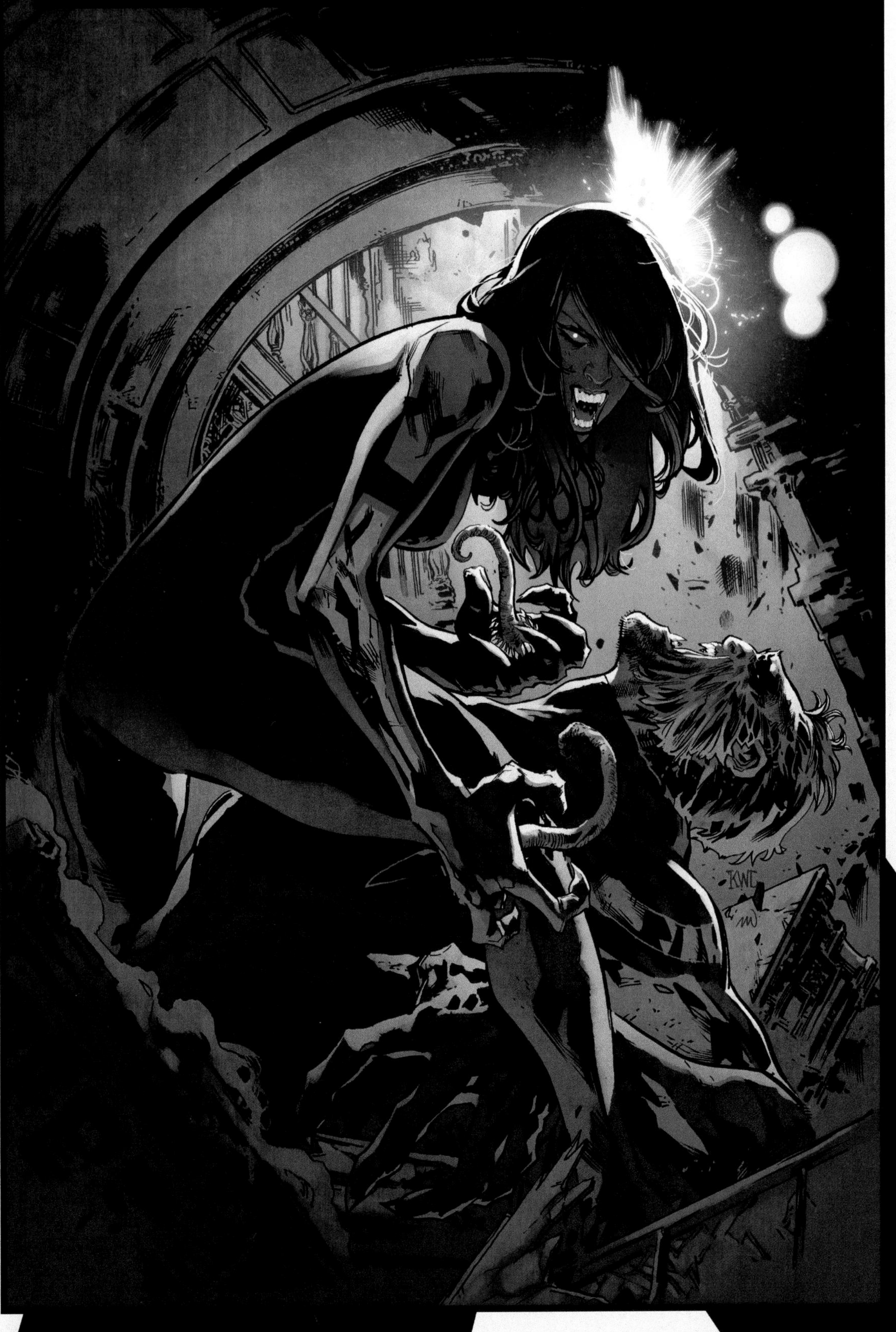

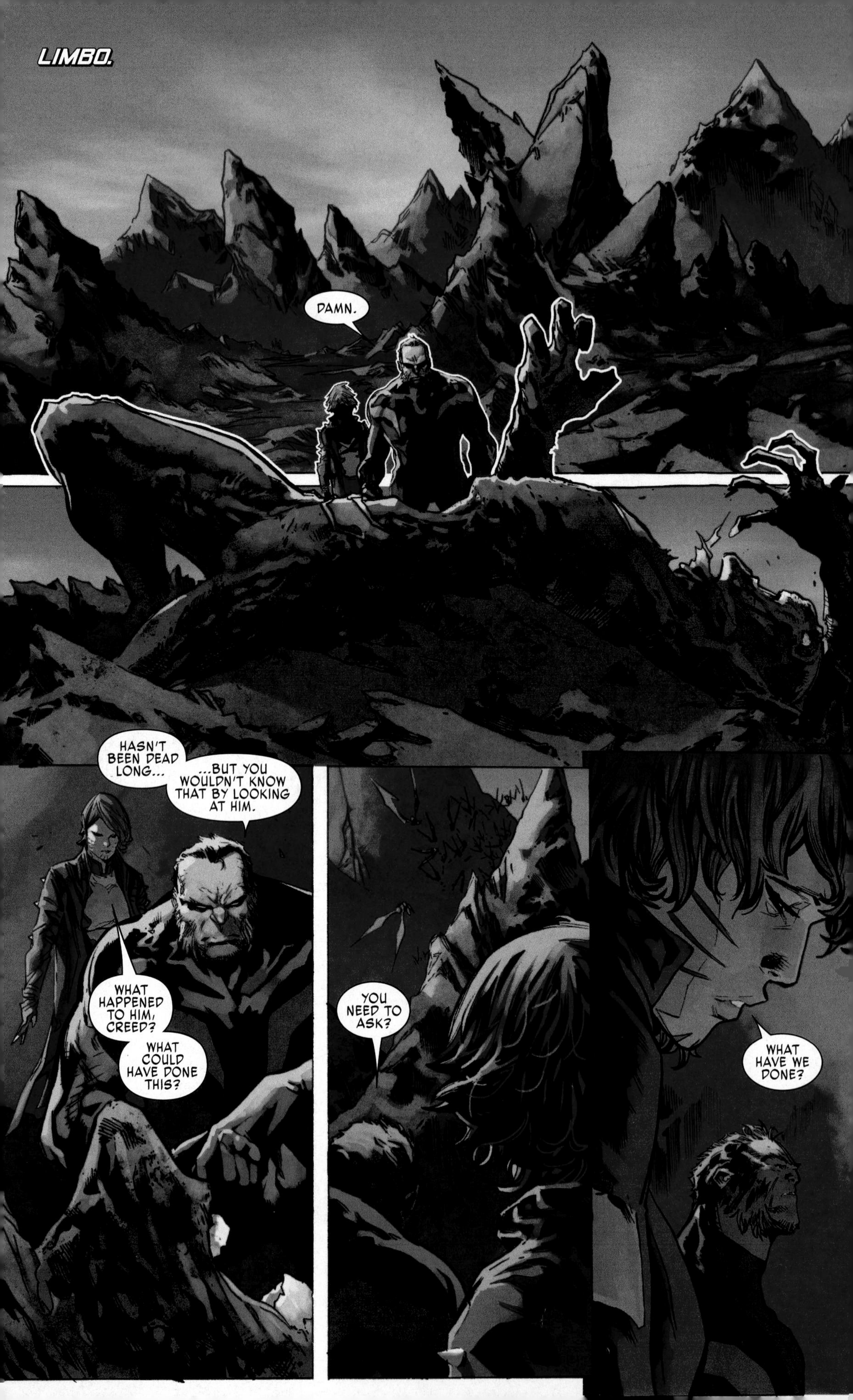
LIMBO.
DAMN.
HASN'T BEEN DEAD LONG...
...BUT YOU WOULDN'T KNOW THAT BY LOOKING AT HIM.
WHAT HAPPENED TO HIM, CREED?
WHAT COULD HAVE DONE THIS?
YOU NEED TO ASK?
WHAT HAVE WE DONE?

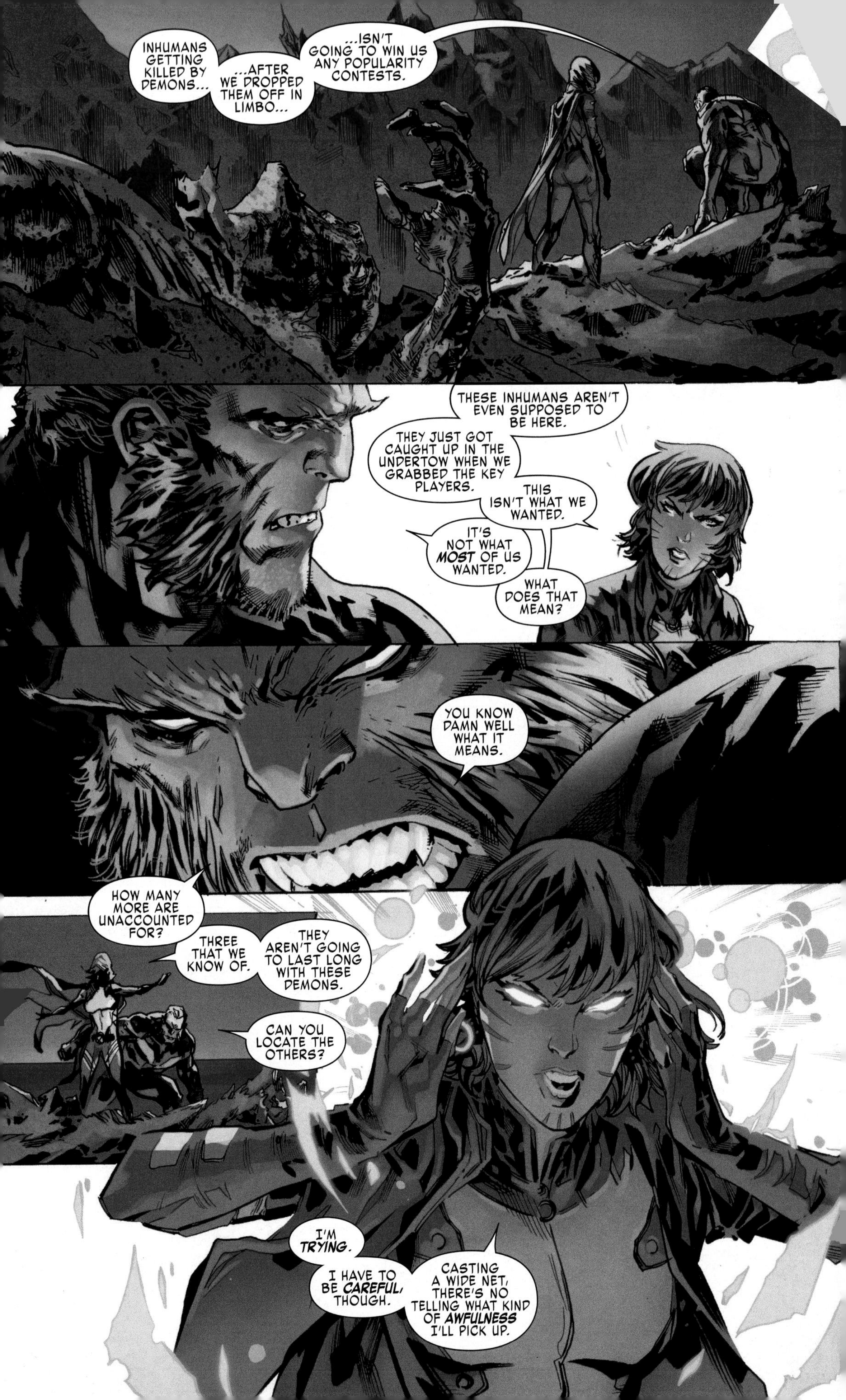
INHUMANS GETTING KILLED BY DEMONS...
...AFTER WE DROPPED THEM OFF IN LIMBO...
...ISN'T GOING TO WIN US ANY POPULARITY CONTESTS.
THESE INHUMANS AREN'T EVEN SUPPOSED TO BE HERE.
THEY JUST GOT CAUGHT UP IN THE UNDERTOW WHEN WE GRABBED THE KEY PLAYERS.
THIS ISN'T WHAT WE WANTED.
IT'S NOT WHAT *MOST* OF US WANTED.
WHAT DOES THAT MEAN?
YOU KNOW DAMN WELL WHAT IT MEANS.
HOW MANY MORE ARE UNACCOUNTED FOR?
THREE THAT WE KNOW OF.
THEY AREN'T GOING TO LAST LONG WITH THESE DEMONS.
CAN YOU LOCATE THE OTHERS?
I'M *TRYING*.
I HAVE TO BE *CAREFUL*, THOUGH.
CASTING A WIDE NET, THERE'S NO TELLING WHAT KIND OF *AWFULNESS* I'LL PICK UP.

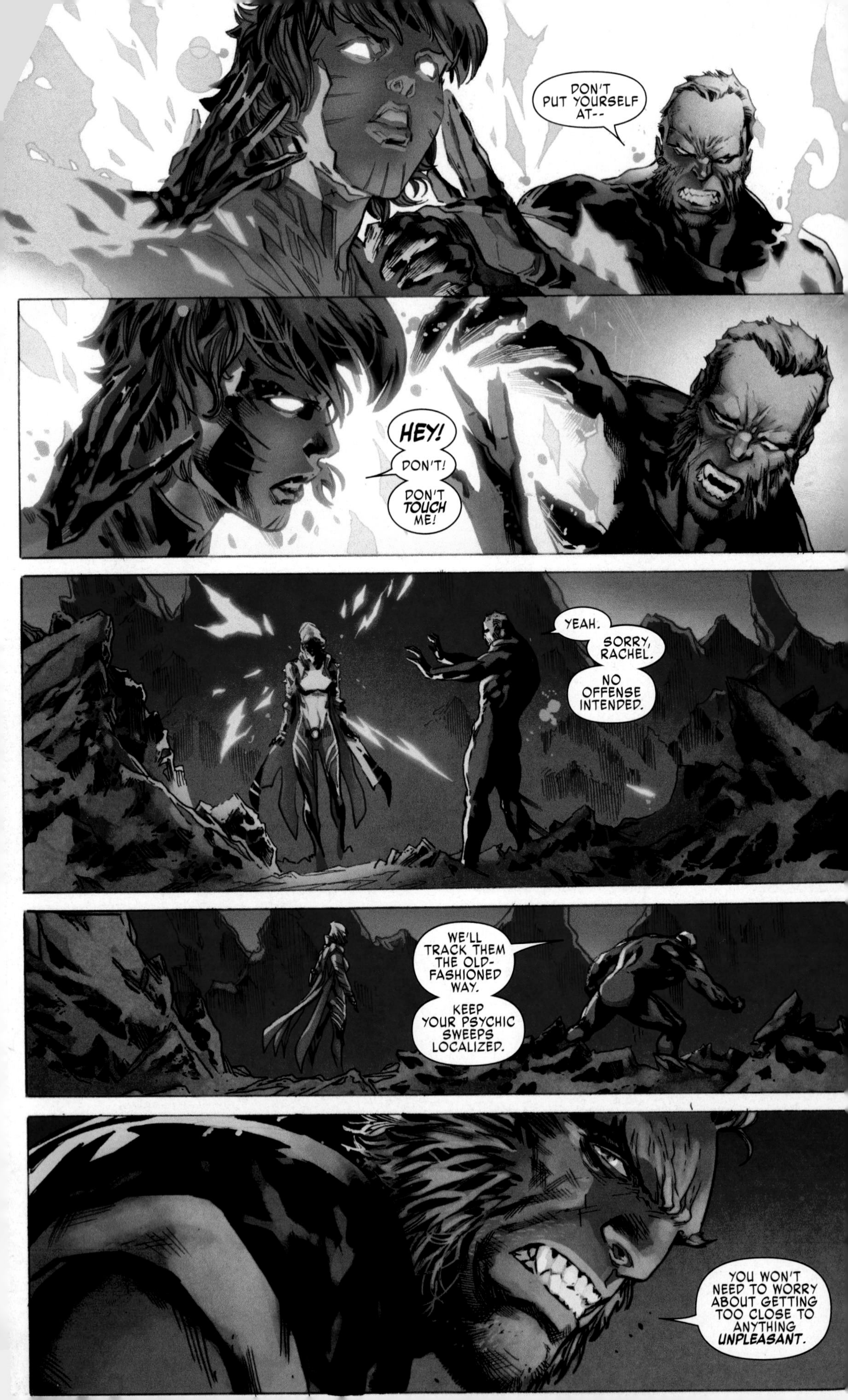
DON'T PUT YOURSELF AT--
HEY!
DON'T!
DON'T TOUCH ME!
YEAH.
SORRY, RACHEL.
NO OFFENSE INTENDED.
WE'LL TRACK THEM THE OLD-FASHIONED WAY.
KEEP YOUR PSYCHIC SWEEPS LOCALIZED.
YOU WON'T NEED TO WORRY ABOUT GETTING TOO CLOSE TO ANYTHING UNPLEASANT.

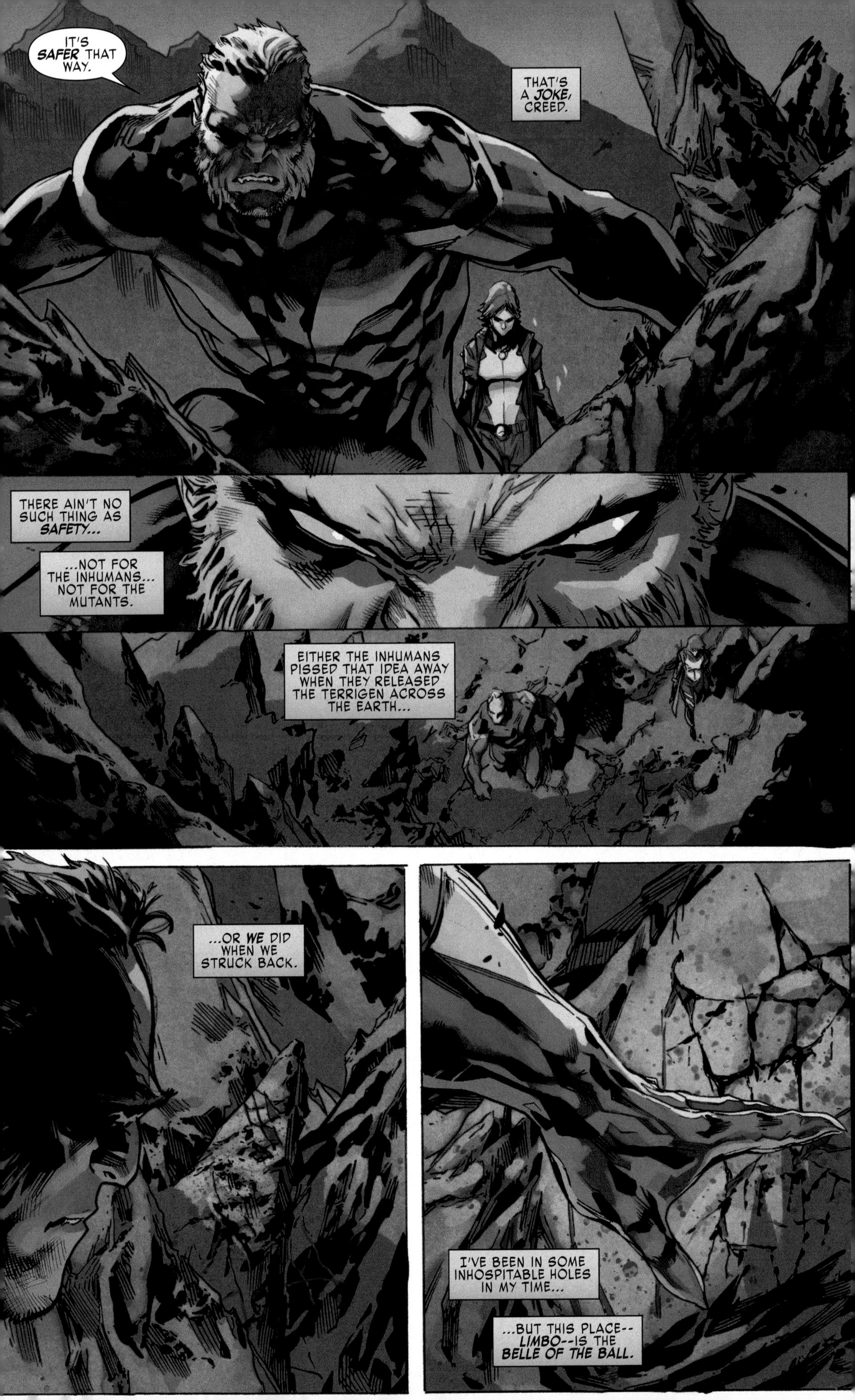
IT'S SAFER THAT WAY.
THAT'S A JOKE, CREED.
THERE AIN'T NO SUCH THING AS SAFETY...
...NOT FOR THE INHUMANS... NOT FOR THE MUTANTS.
EITHER THE INHUMANS PISSED THAT IDEA AWAY WHEN THEY RELEASED THE TERRIGEN ACROSS THE EARTH...
...OR WE DID WHEN WE STRUCK BACK.
I'VE BEEN IN SOME INHOSPITABLE HOLES IN MY TIME...
...BUT THIS PLACE--LIMBO--IS THE BELLE OF THE BALL.

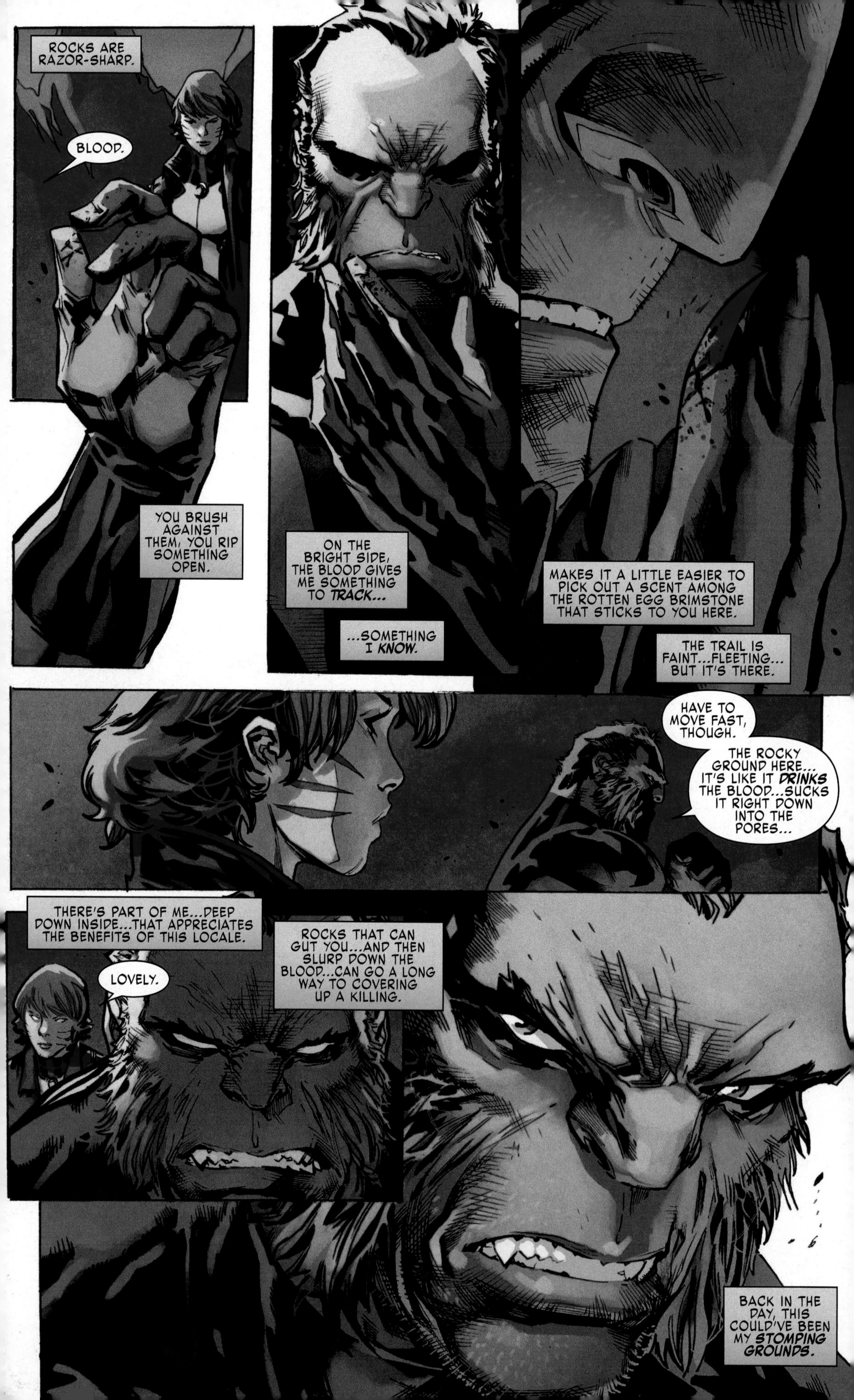
ROCKS ARE RAZOR-SHARP.
BLOOD.
YOU BRUSH AGAINST THEM, YOU RIP SOMETHING OPEN.
ON THE BRIGHT SIDE, THE BLOOD GIVES ME SOMETHING TO TRACK...
...SOMETHING I KNOW.
MAKES IT A LITTLE EASIER TO PICK OUT A SCENT AMONG THE ROTTEN EGG BRIMSTONE THAT STICKS TO YOU HERE.
THE TRAIL IS FAINT...FLEETING... BUT IT'S THERE.
HAVE TO MOVE FAST, THOUGH.
THE ROCKY GROUND HERE... IT'S LIKE IT DRINKS THE BLOOD...SUCKS IT RIGHT DOWN INTO THE PORES...
THERE'S PART OF ME...DEEP DOWN INSIDE...THAT APPRECIATES THE BENEFITS OF THIS LOCALE.
LOVELY.
ROCKS THAT CAN GUT YOU...AND THEN SLURP DOWN THE BLOOD...CAN GO A LONG WAY TO COVERING UP A KILLING.
BACK IN THE DAY, THIS COULD'VE BEEN MY STOMPING GROUNDS.

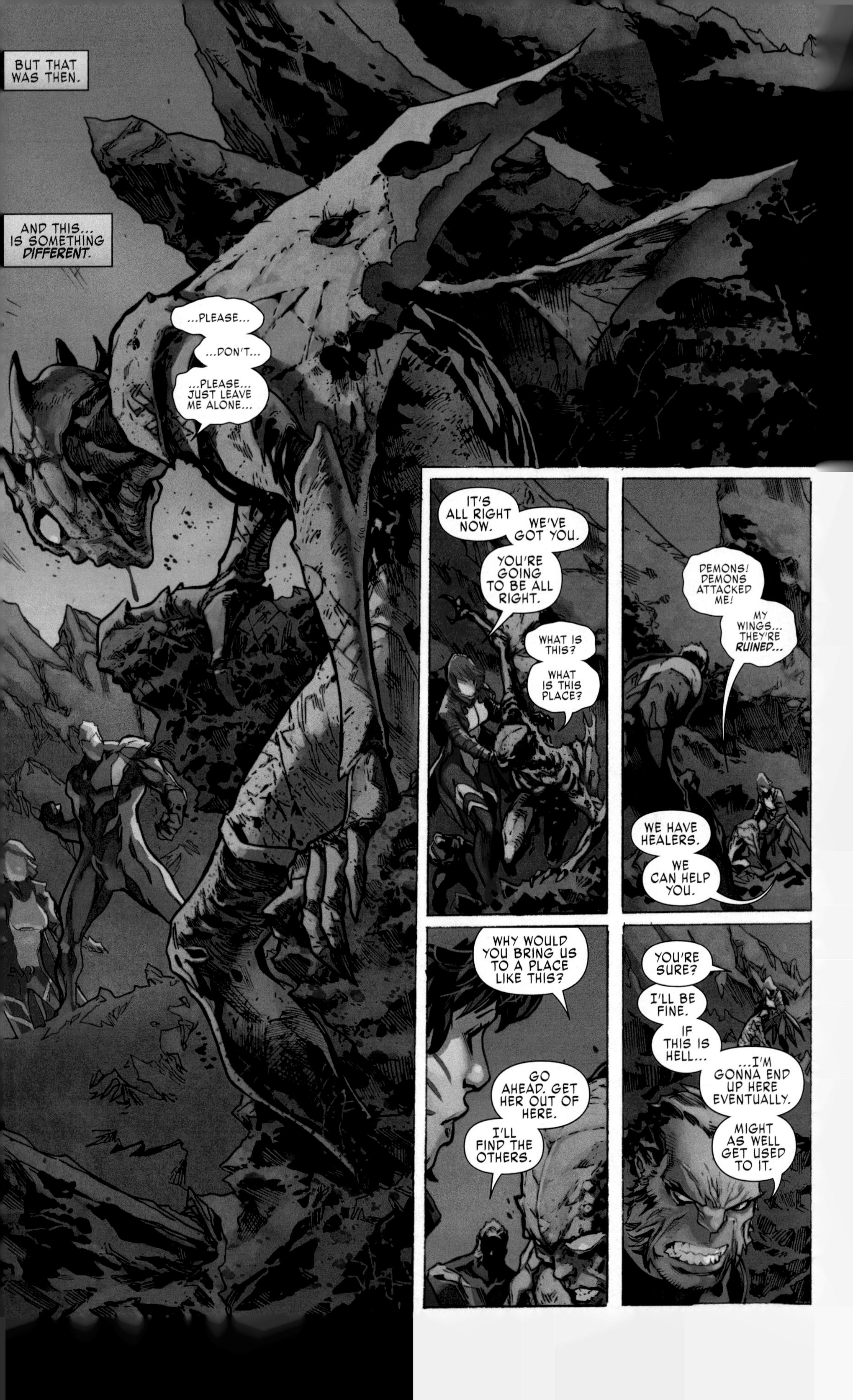
BUT THAT WAS THEN.
AND THIS... IS SOMETHING *DIFFERENT*.
...PLEASE...
...DON'T...
...PLEASE... JUST LEAVE ME ALONE...
IT'S ALL RIGHT NOW.
WE'VE GOT YOU.
YOU'RE GOING TO BE ALL RIGHT.
WHAT IS THIS?
WHAT IS THIS PLACE?
DEMONS! DEMONS ATTACKED ME!
MY WINGS... THEY'RE *RUINED*...
WE HAVE HEALERS.
WE CAN HELP YOU.
WHY WOULD YOU BRING US TO A PLACE LIKE THIS?
GO AHEAD. GET HER OUT OF HERE.
I'LL FIND THE OTHERS.
YOU'RE SURE?
I'LL BE FINE.
IF THIS IS HELL...
...I'M GONNA END UP HERE EVENTUALLY.
MIGHT AS WELL GET USED TO IT.

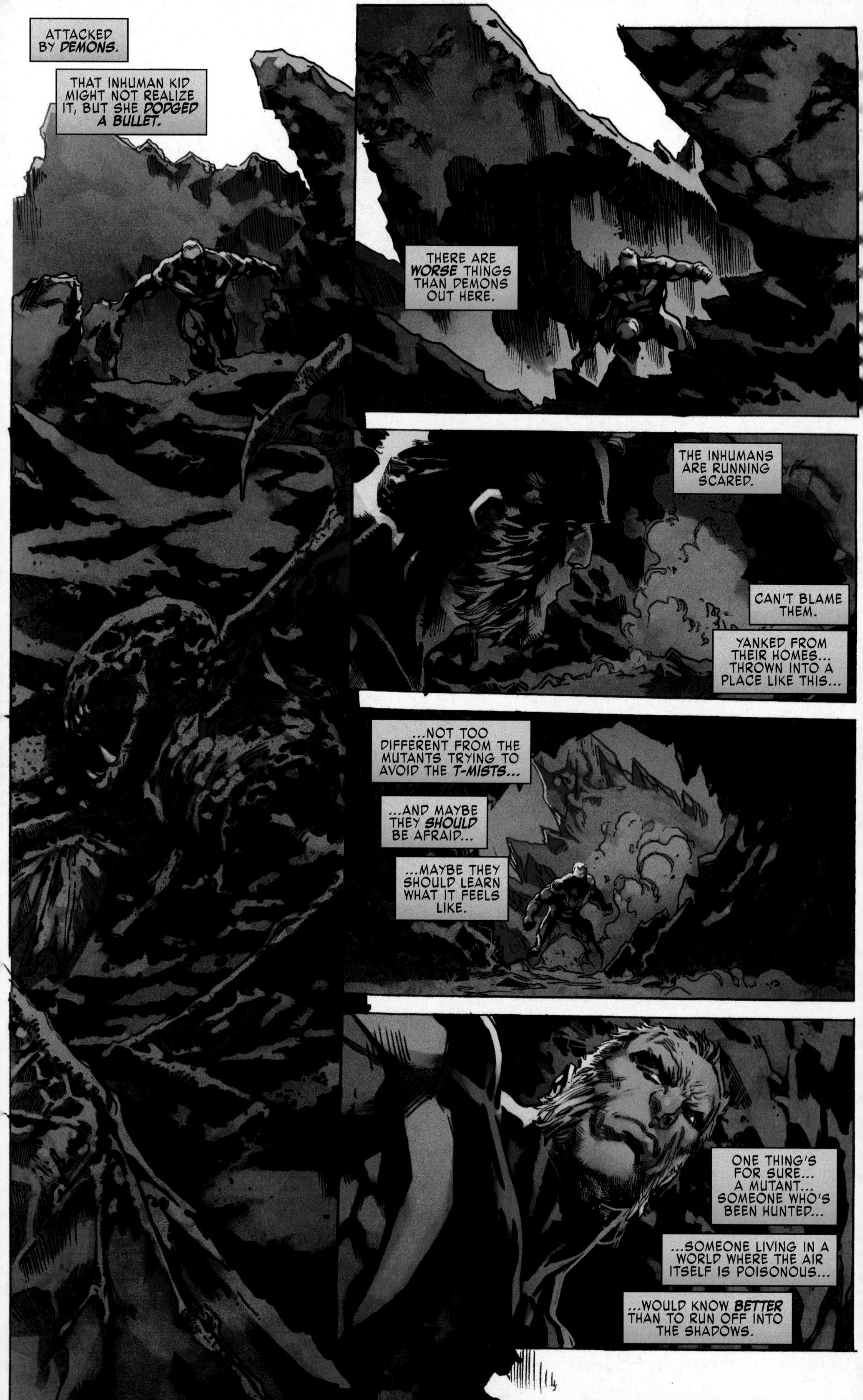
ATTACKED BY DEMONS.
THAT INHUMAN KID MIGHT NOT REALIZE IT, BUT SHE DODGED A BULLET.
THERE ARE WORSE THINGS THAN DEMONS OUT HERE.
THE INHUMANS ARE RUNNING SCARED.
CAN'T BLAME THEM.
YANKED FROM THEIR HOMES... THROWN INTO A PLACE LIKE THIS...
...NOT TOO DIFFERENT FROM THE MUTANTS TRYING TO AVOID THE T-MISTS...
...AND MAYBE THEY SHOULD BE AFRAID...
...MAYBE THEY SHOULD LEARN WHAT IT FEELS LIKE.
ONE THING'S FOR SURE... A MUTANT... SOMEONE WHO'S BEEN HUNTED...
...SOMEONE LIVING IN A WORLD WHERE THE AIR ITSELF IS POISONOUS...
...WOULD KNOW BETTER THAN TO RUN OFF INTO THE SHADOWS.

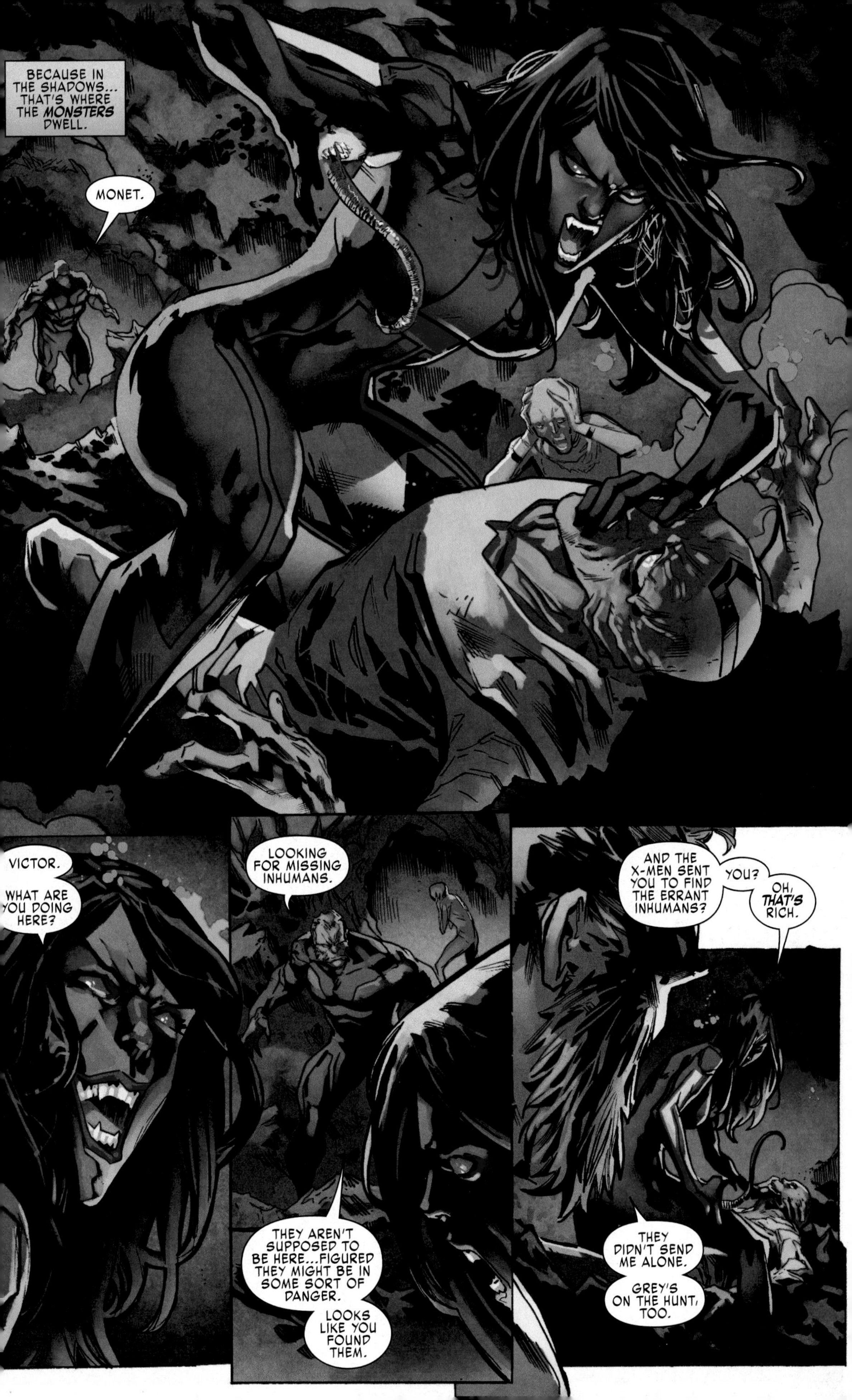
BECAUSE IN THE SHADOWS... THAT'S WHERE THE *MONSTERS* DWELL.
MONET.
VICTOR.
WHAT ARE YOU DOING HERE?
LOOKING FOR MISSING INHUMANS.
THEY AREN'T SUPPOSED TO BE HERE...FIGURED THEY MIGHT BE IN SOME SORT OF DANGER.
LOOKS LIKE YOU FOUND THEM.
AND THE X-MEN SENT YOU TO FIND THE ERRANT INHUMANS?
YOU?
OH, *THAT'S* RICH.
THEY DIDN'T SEND ME ALONE.
GREY'S ON THE HUNT, TOO.

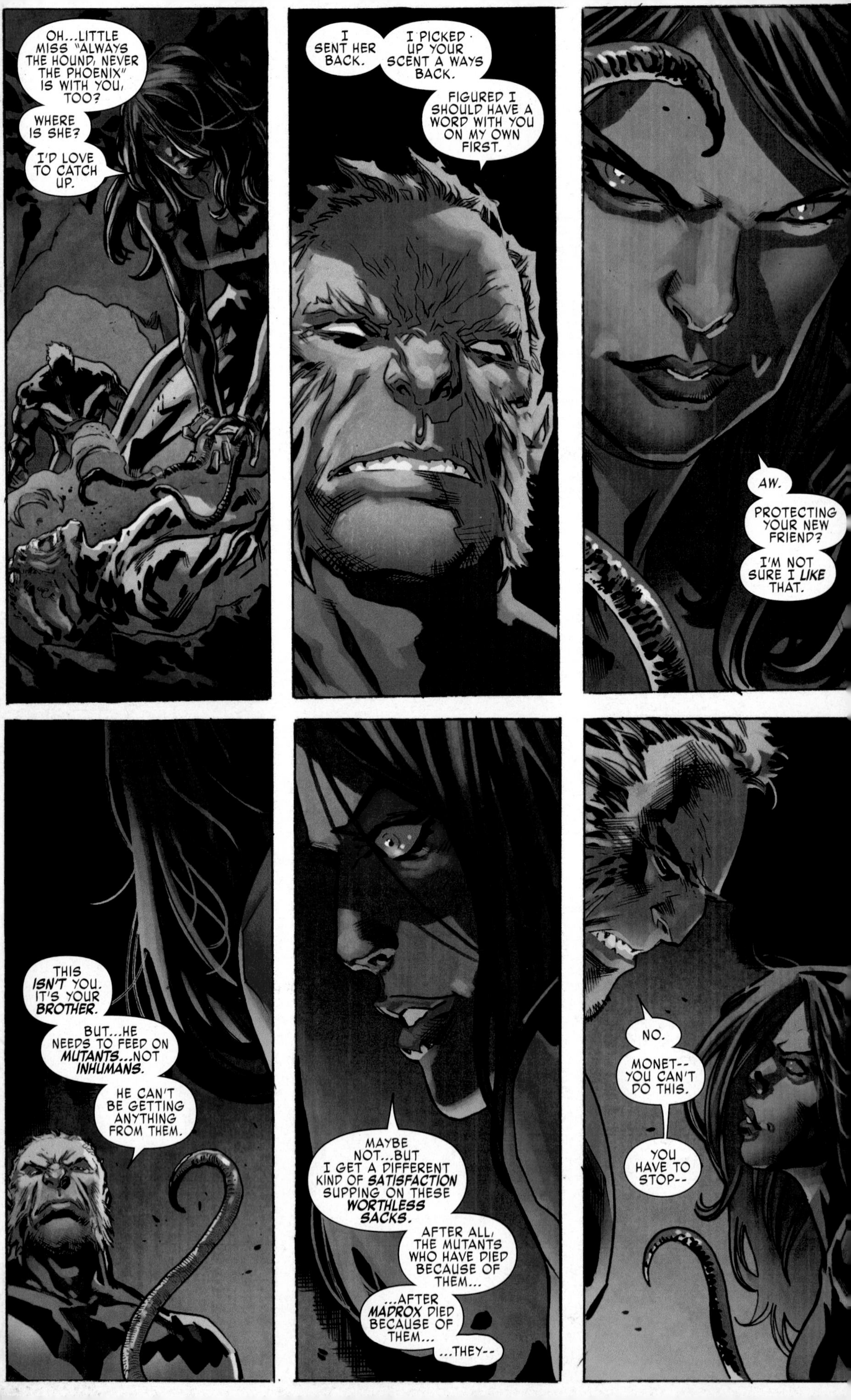
OH...LITTLE MISS "ALWAYS THE HOUND, NEVER THE PHOENIX" IS WITH YOU, TOO?
WHERE IS SHE?
I'D LOVE TO CATCH UP.
I SENT HER BACK.
I PICKED UP YOUR SCENT A WAYS BACK.
FIGURED I SHOULD HAVE A WORD WITH YOU ON MY OWN FIRST.
AW.
PROTECTING YOUR NEW FRIEND?
I'M NOT SURE I *LIKE* THAT.
THIS *ISN'T* YOU. IT'S YOUR *BROTHER*.
BUT...HE NEEDS TO FEED ON *MUTANTS*...NOT *INHUMANS*.
HE CAN'T BE GETTING ANYTHING FROM THEM.
MAYBE NOT...BUT I GET A DIFFERENT KIND OF *SATISFACTION* SUPPING ON THESE *WORTHLESS SACKS*.
AFTER ALL, THE MUTANTS WHO HAVE DIED BECAUSE OF THEM...
...AFTER *MADROX* DIED BECAUSE OF THEM...
...THEY--
NO.
MONET-- YOU CAN'T DO THIS.
YOU HAVE TO STOP--

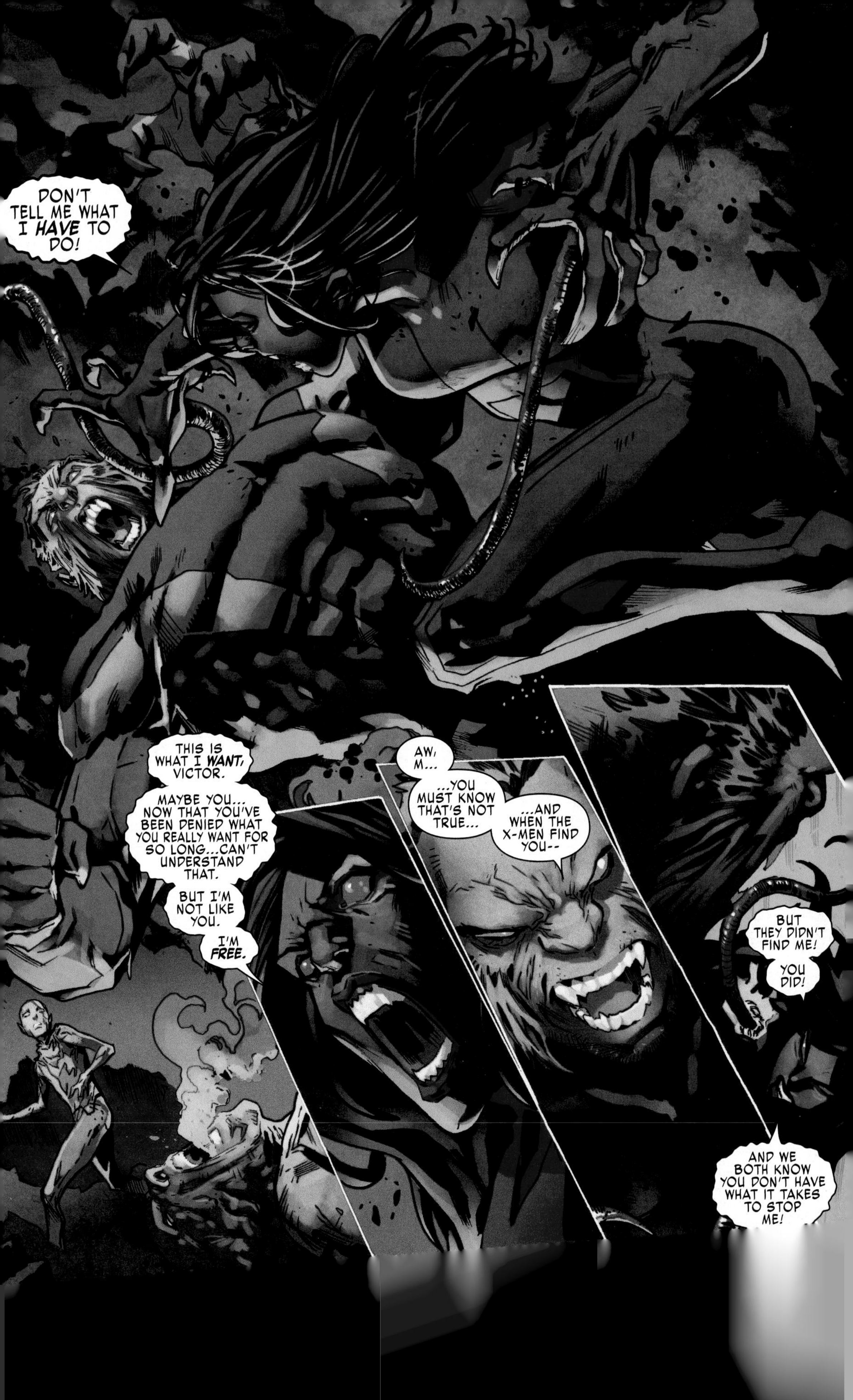
DON'T TELL ME WHAT I *HAVE* TO DO!
THIS IS WHAT I *WANT*, VICTOR.
MAYBE YOU... NOW THAT YOU'VE BEEN DENIED WHAT YOU REALLY WANT FOR SO LONG...CAN'T UNDERSTAND THAT.
BUT I'M NOT LIKE YOU.
I'M *FREE.*
AW, M...
...YOU MUST KNOW THAT'S NOT TRUE...
...AND WHEN THE X-MEN FIND YOU--
BUT THEY DIDN'T FIND ME!
YOU DID!
AND WE BOTH KNOW YOU DON'T HAVE WHAT IT TAKES TO STOP ME!

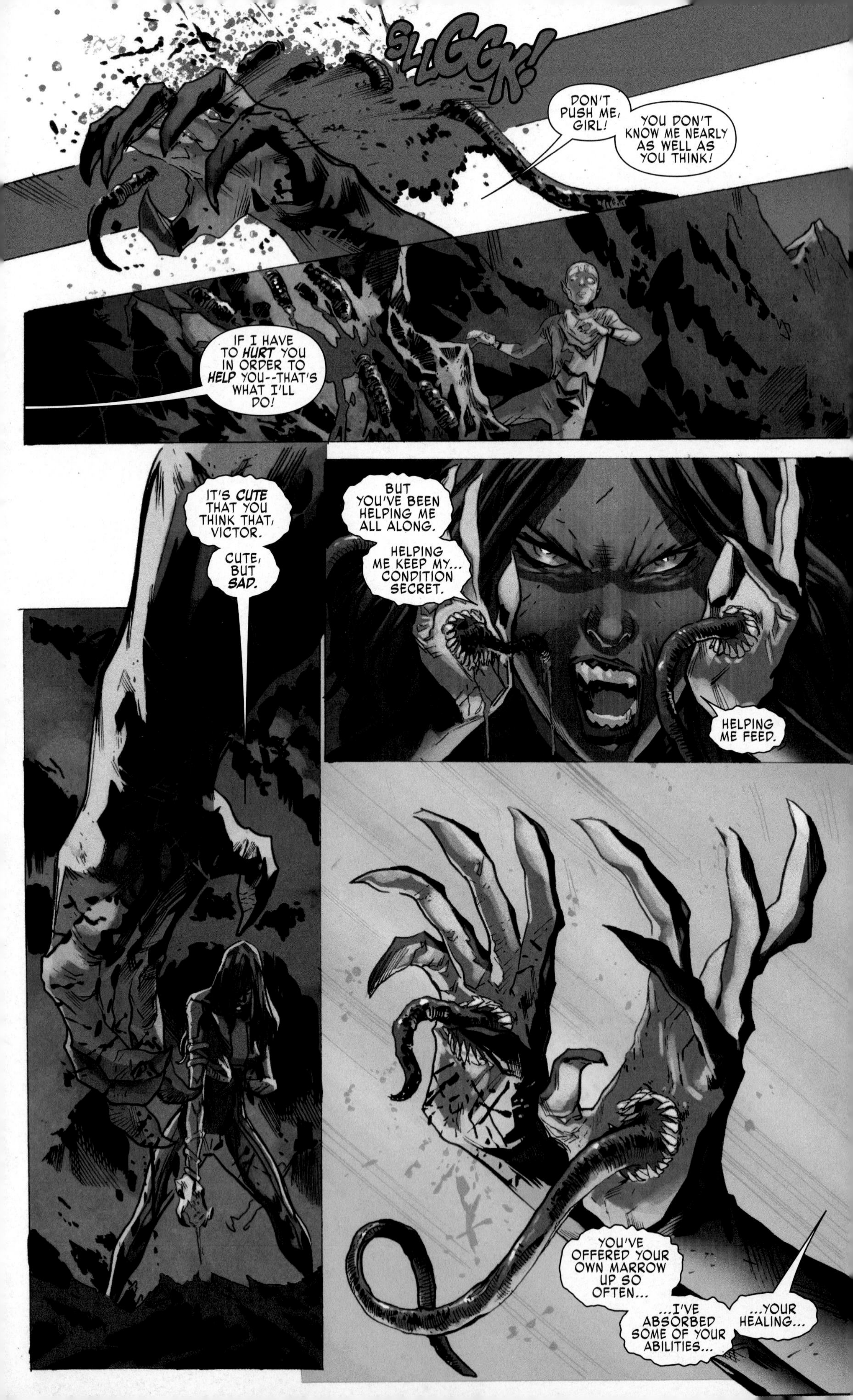
SLLGGK!
DON'T PUSH ME, GIRL!
YOU DON'T KNOW ME NEARLY AS WELL AS YOU THINK!
IF I HAVE TO HURT YOU IN ORDER TO HELP YOU--THAT'S WHAT I'LL DO!
IT'S CUTE THAT YOU THINK THAT, VICTOR.
CUTE, BUT SAD.
BUT YOU'VE BEEN HELPING ME ALL ALONG.
HELPING ME KEEP MY... CONDITION SECRET.
HELPING ME FEED.
YOU'VE OFFERED YOUR OWN MARROW UP SO OFTEN...
...I'VE ABSORBED SOME OF YOUR ABILITIES...
...YOUR HEALING...

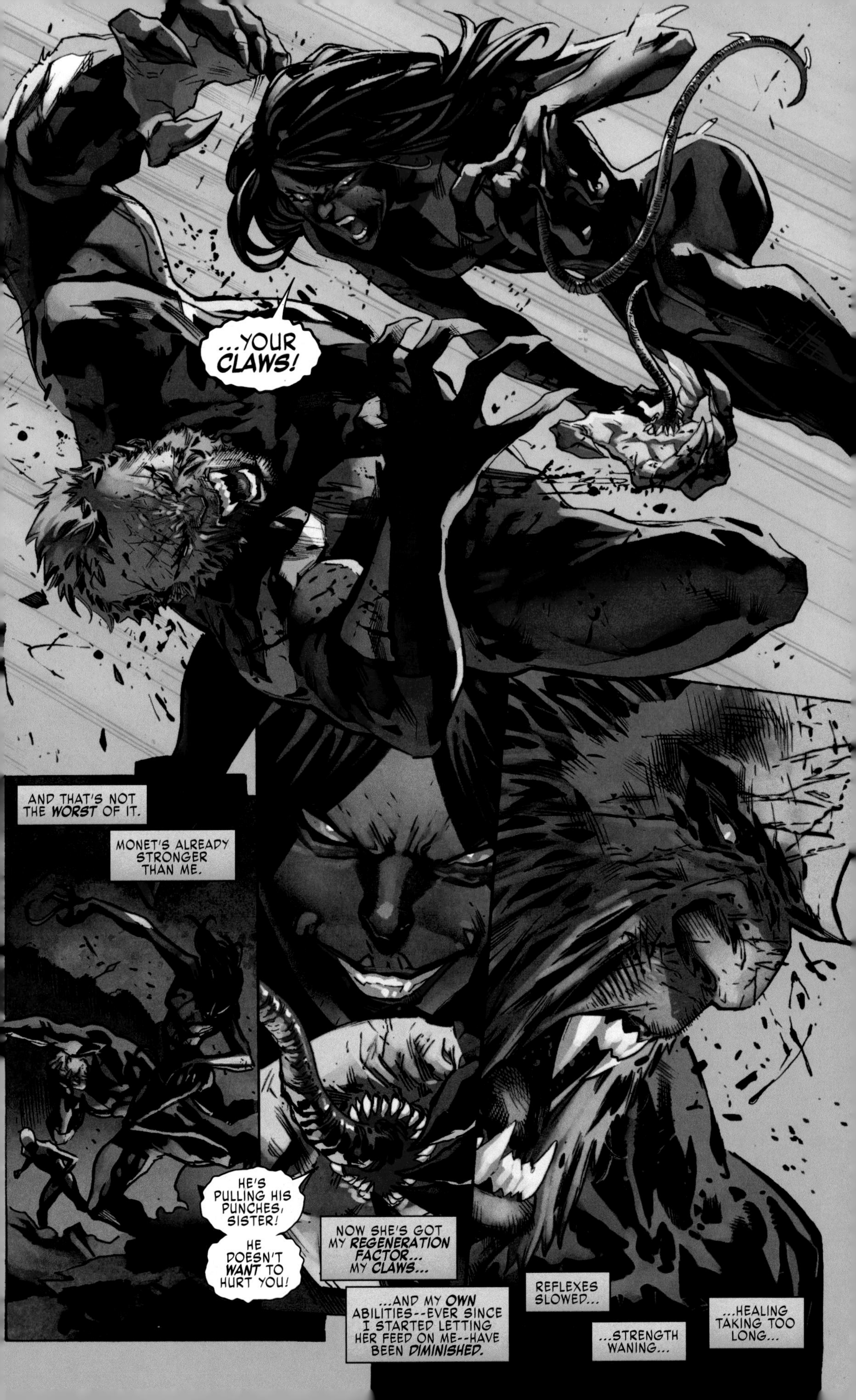
...YOUR CLAWS!
AND THAT'S NOT THE WORST OF IT.
MONET'S ALREADY STRONGER THAN ME.
HE'S PULLING HIS PUNCHES, SISTER!
HE DOESN'T WANT TO HURT YOU!
NOW SHE'S GOT MY REGENERATION FACTOR... MY CLAWS...
...AND MY OWN ABILITIES--EVER SINCE I STARTED LETTING HER FEED ON ME--HAVE BEEN DIMINISHED.
REFLEXES SLOWED...
...STRENGTH WANING...
...HEALING TAKING TOO LONG...

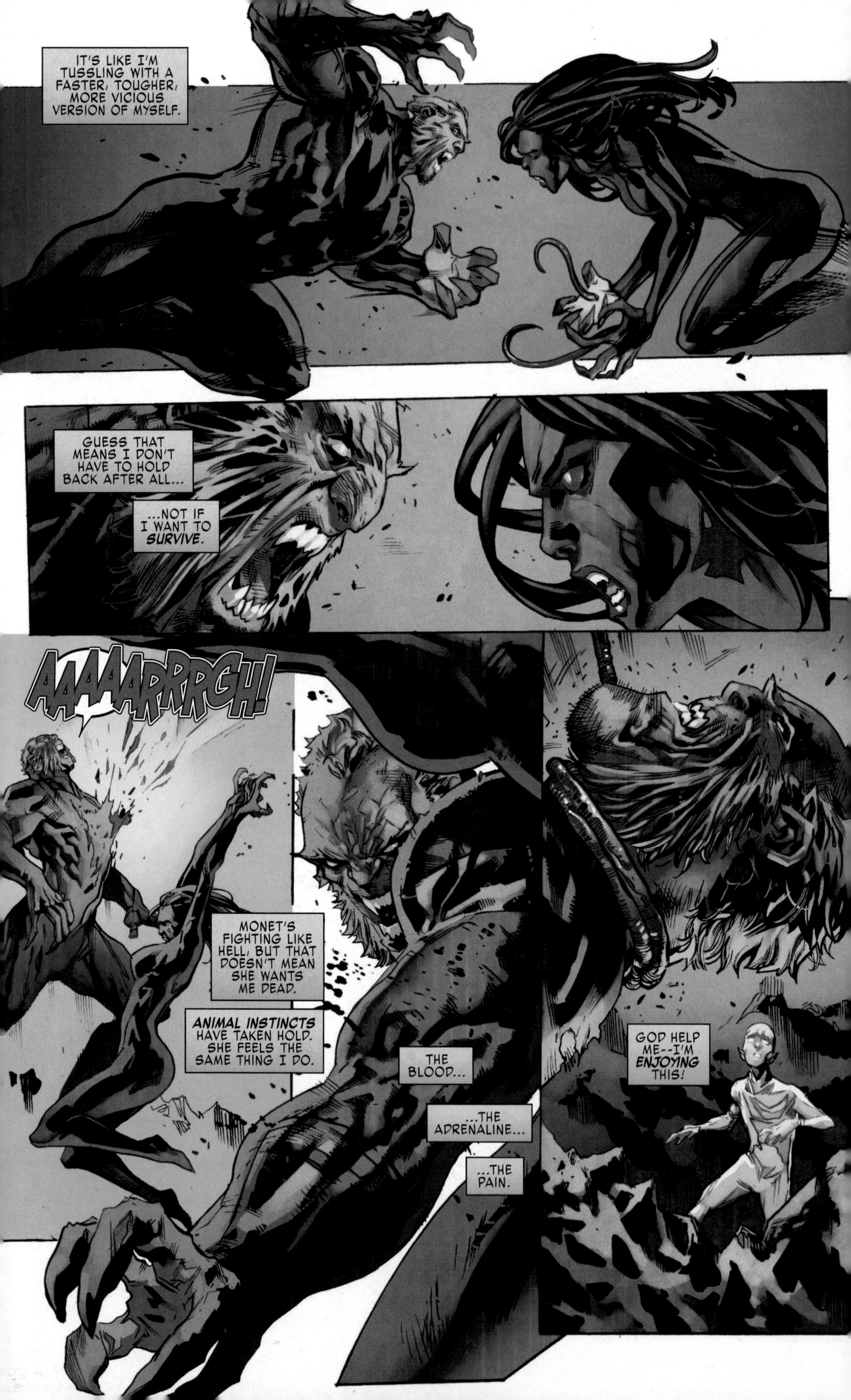
IT'S LIKE I'M TUSSLING WITH A FASTER, TOUGHER, MORE VICIOUS VERSION OF MYSELF.
GUESS THAT MEANS I DON'T HAVE TO HOLD BACK AFTER ALL...
...NOT IF I WANT TO SURVIVE.
AAAAARRRGH!
MONET'S FIGHTING LIKE HELL, BUT THAT DOESN'T MEAN SHE WANTS ME DEAD.
ANIMAL INSTINCTS HAVE TAKEN HOLD. SHE FEELS THE SAME THING I DO.
THE BLOOD...
...THE ADRENALINE...
...THE PAIN.
GOD HELP ME--I'M ENJOYING THIS!

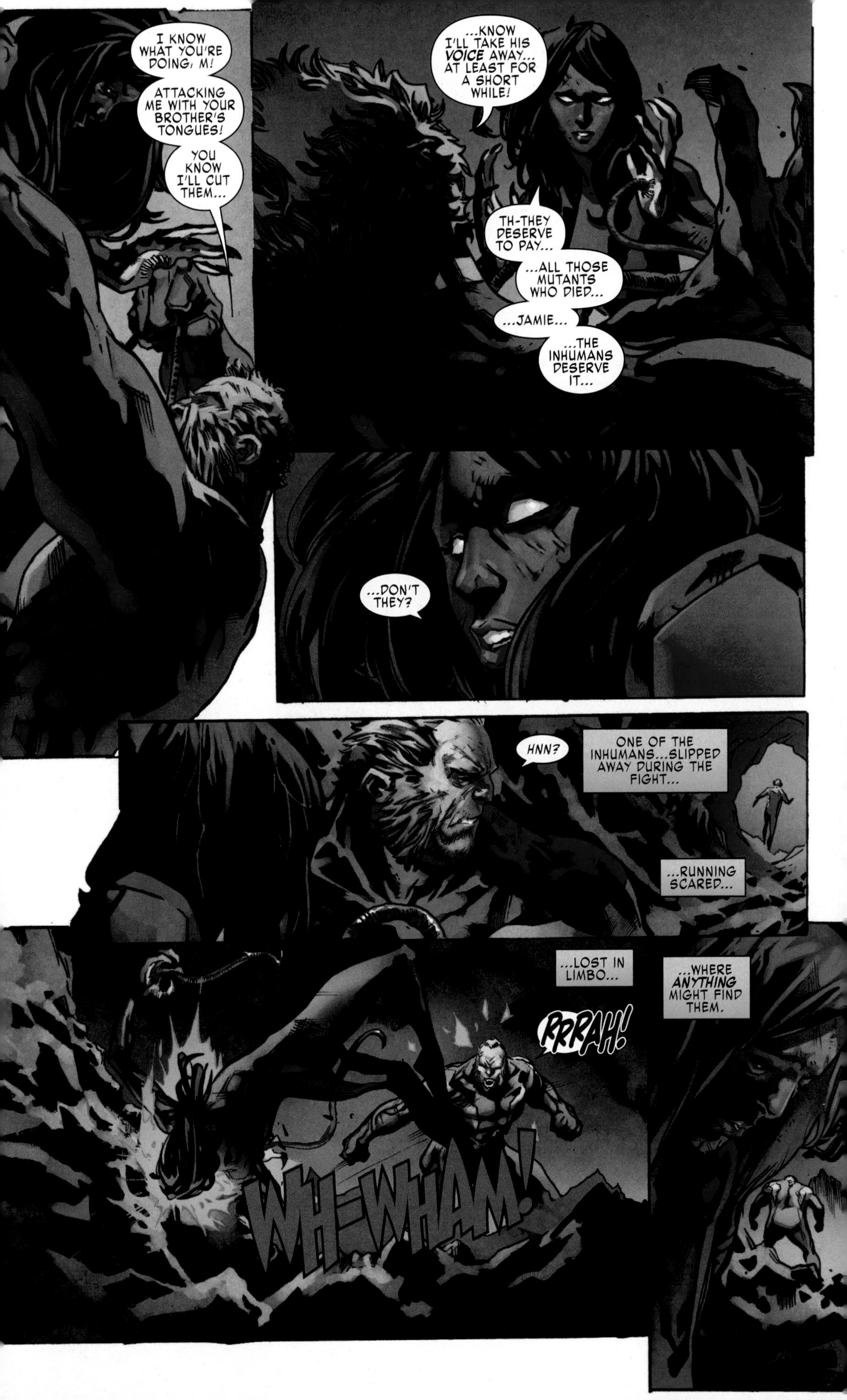
I KNOW WHAT YOU'RE DOING, M!
ATTACKING ME WITH YOUR BROTHER'S TONGUES!
YOU KNOW I'LL CUT THEM...
...KNOW I'LL TAKE HIS VOICE AWAY... AT LEAST FOR A SHORT WHILE!
TH-THEY DESERVE TO PAY...
...ALL THOSE MUTANTS WHO DIED...
...JAMIE...
...THE INHUMANS DESERVE IT...
...DON'T THEY?
HNN?
ONE OF THE INHUMANS...SLIPPED AWAY DURING THE FIGHT...
...RUNNING SCARED...
...LOST IN LIMBO...
...WHERE ANYTHING MIGHT FIND THEM.
RRRAH!
WH-WHAM!

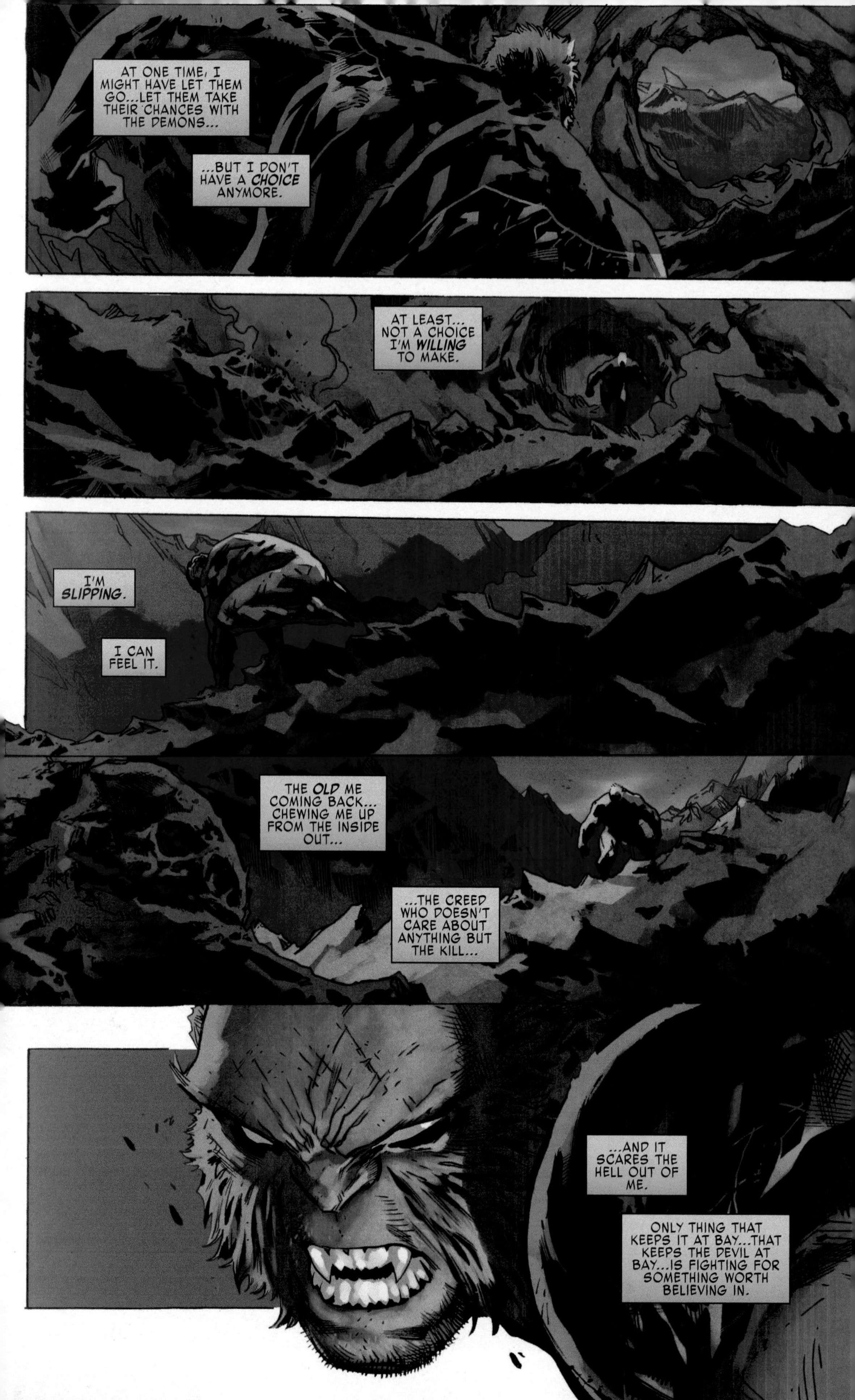
AT ONE TIME, I MIGHT HAVE LET THEM GO...LET THEM TAKE THEIR CHANCES WITH THE DEMONS...
...BUT I DON'T HAVE A CHOICE ANYMORE.
AT LEAST... NOT A CHOICE I'M WILLING TO MAKE.
I'M SLIPPING.
I CAN FEEL IT.
THE OLD ME COMING BACK... CHEWING ME UP FROM THE INSIDE OUT...
...THE CREED WHO DOESN'T CARE ABOUT ANYTHING BUT THE KILL...
...AND IT SCARES THE HELL OUT OF ME.
ONLY THING THAT KEEPS IT AT BAY...THAT KEEPS THE DEVIL AT BAY...IS FIGHTING FOR SOMETHING WORTH BELIEVING IN.

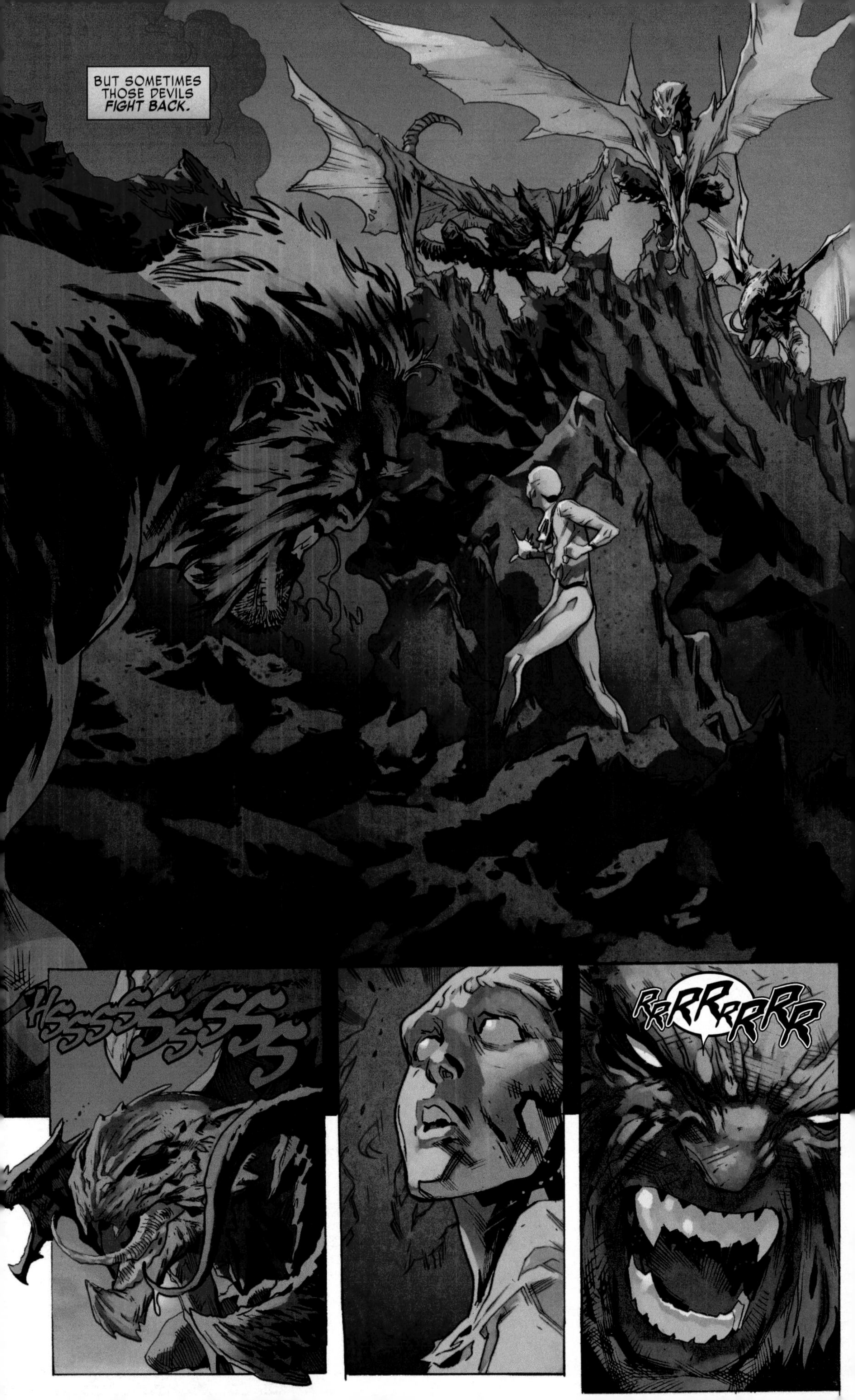
BUT SOMETIMES THOSE DEVILS *FIGHT BACK*.
HSSSSSSSS
RRRRRRRRR

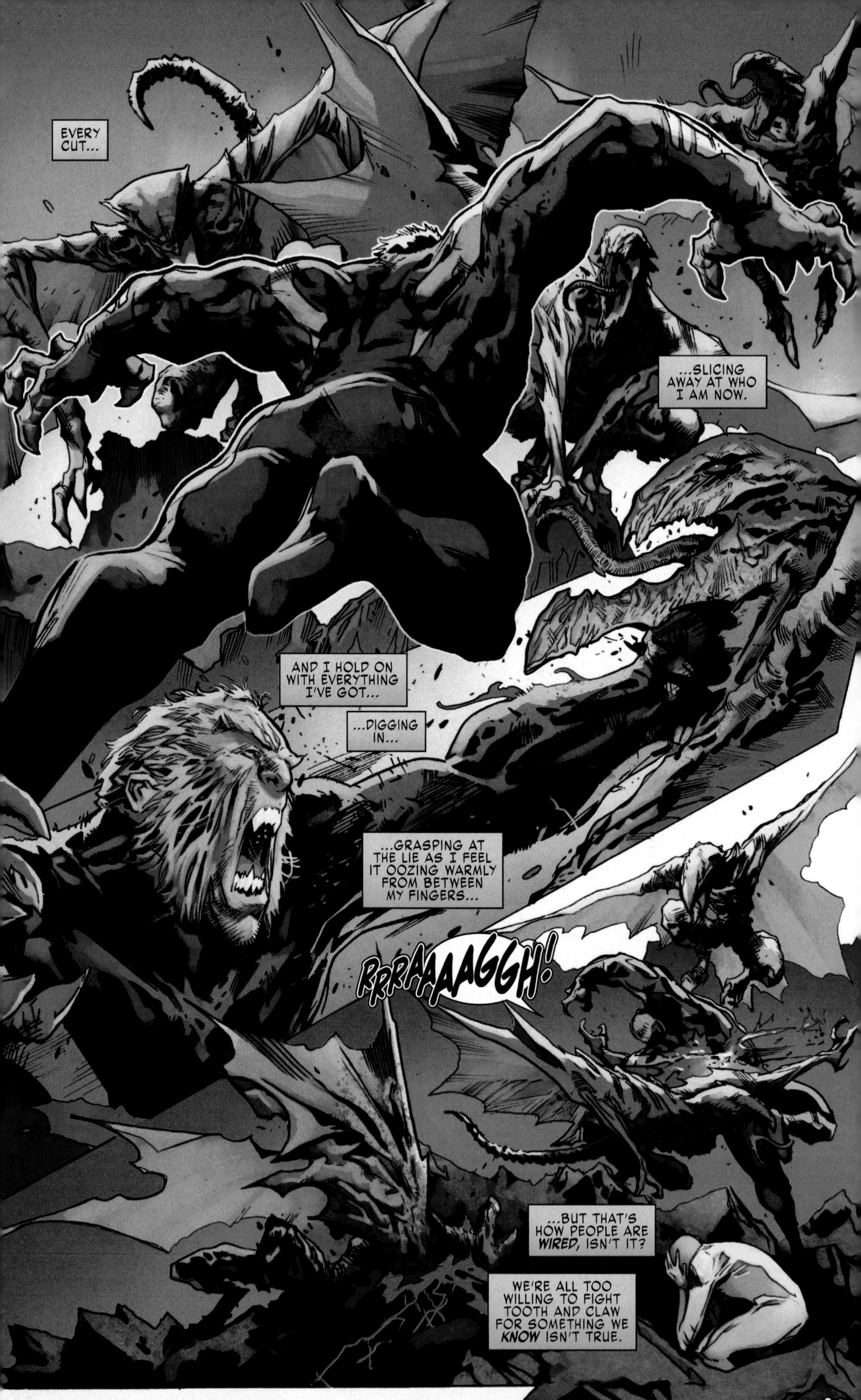
EVERY CUT...
...SLICING AWAY AT WHO I AM NOW.
AND I HOLD ON WITH EVERYTHING I'VE GOT...
...DIGGING IN...
...GRASPING AT THE LIE AS I FEEL IT OOZING WARMLY FROM BETWEEN MY FINGERS...
RRRAAAAGGH!
...BUT THAT'S HOW PEOPLE ARE WIRED, ISN'T IT?
WE'RE ALL TOO WILLING TO FIGHT TOOTH AND CLAW FOR SOMETHING WE KNOW ISN'T TRUE.

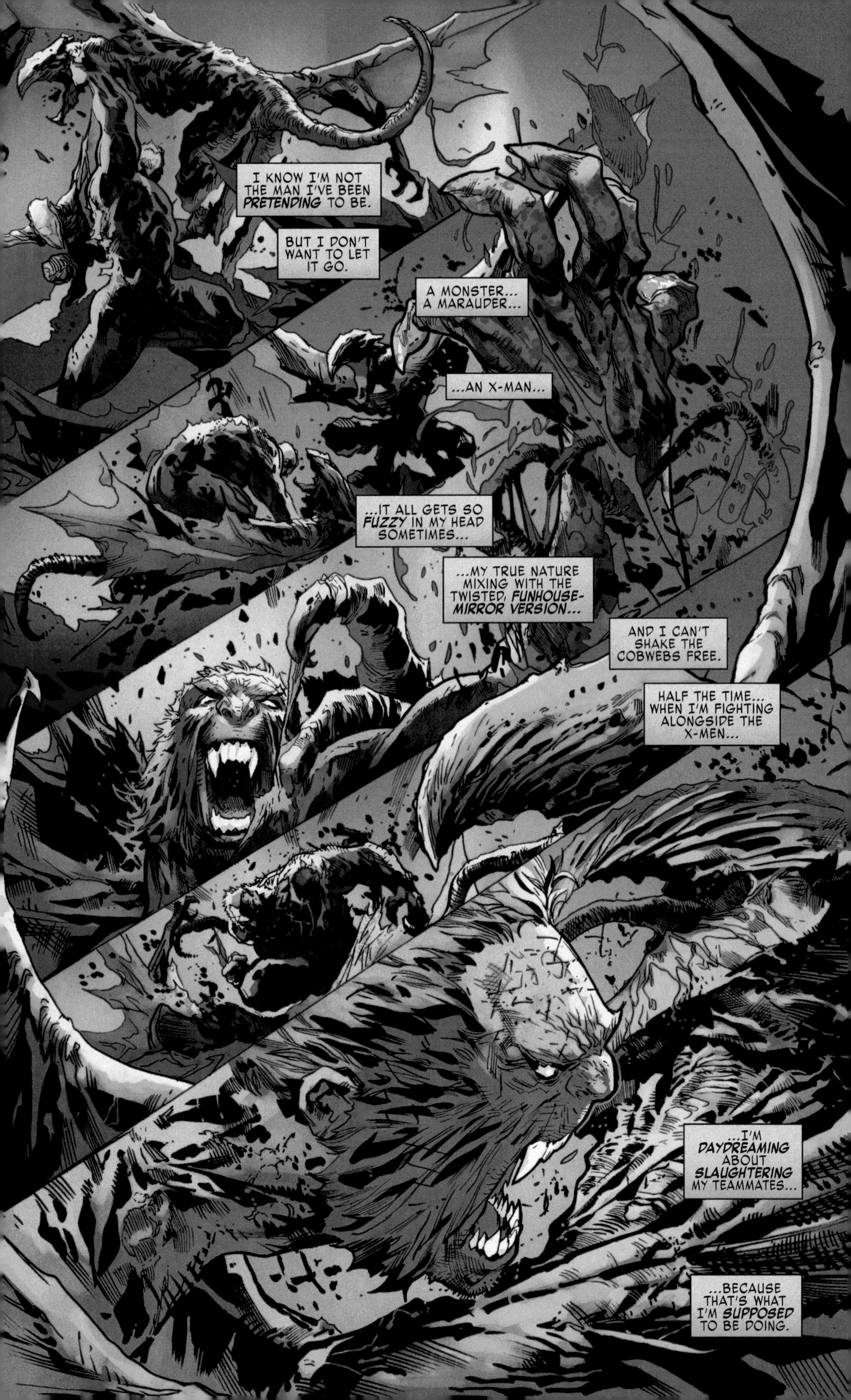
I KNOW I'M NOT THE MAN I'VE BEEN PRETENDING TO BE.
BUT I DON'T WANT TO LET IT GO.
A MONSTER... A MARAUDER...
...AN X-MAN...
...IT ALL GETS SO FUZZY IN MY HEAD SOMETIMES...
...MY TRUE NATURE MIXING WITH THE TWISTED, FUNHOUSE-MIRROR VERSION...
AND I CAN'T SHAKE THE COBWEBS FREE.
HALF THE TIME... WHEN I'M FIGHTING ALONGSIDE THE X-MEN...
...I'M DAYDREAMING ABOUT SLAUGHTERING MY TEAMMATES...
...BECAUSE THAT'S WHAT I'M SUPPOSED TO BE DOING.

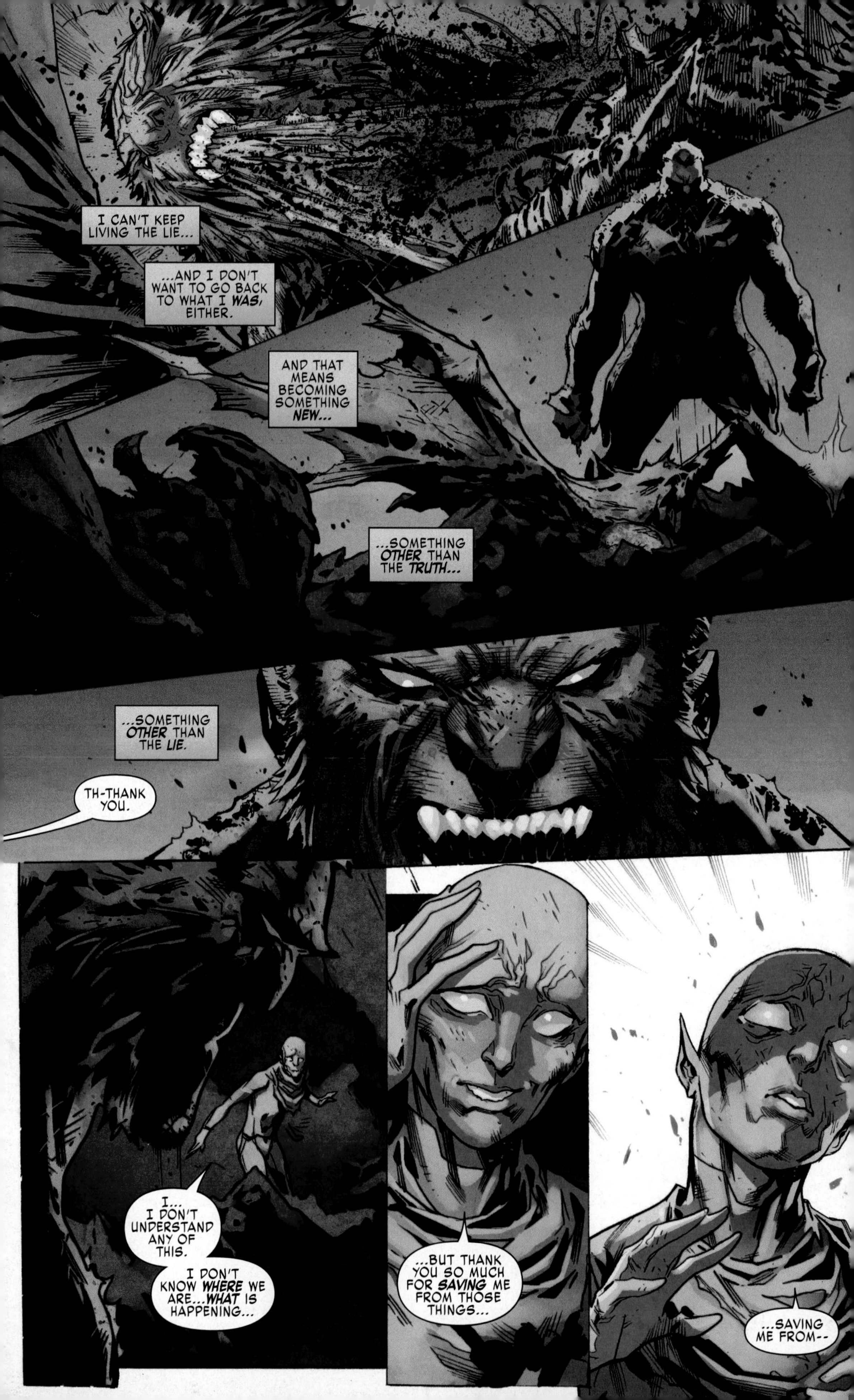
I CAN'T KEEP LIVING THE LIE...
...AND I DON'T WANT TO GO BACK TO WHAT I *WAS*, EITHER.
AND THAT MEANS BECOMING SOMETHING *NEW...*
...SOMETHING *OTHER* THAN THE *TRUTH...*
...SOMETHING *OTHER* THAN THE *LIE.*
TH-THANK YOU.
I... I DON'T UNDERSTAND ANY OF THIS.
I DON'T KNOW *WHERE* WE ARE... *WHAT* IS HAPPENING...
...BUT THANK YOU SO MUCH FOR *SAVING* ME FROM THOSE THINGS...
...SAVING ME FROM--

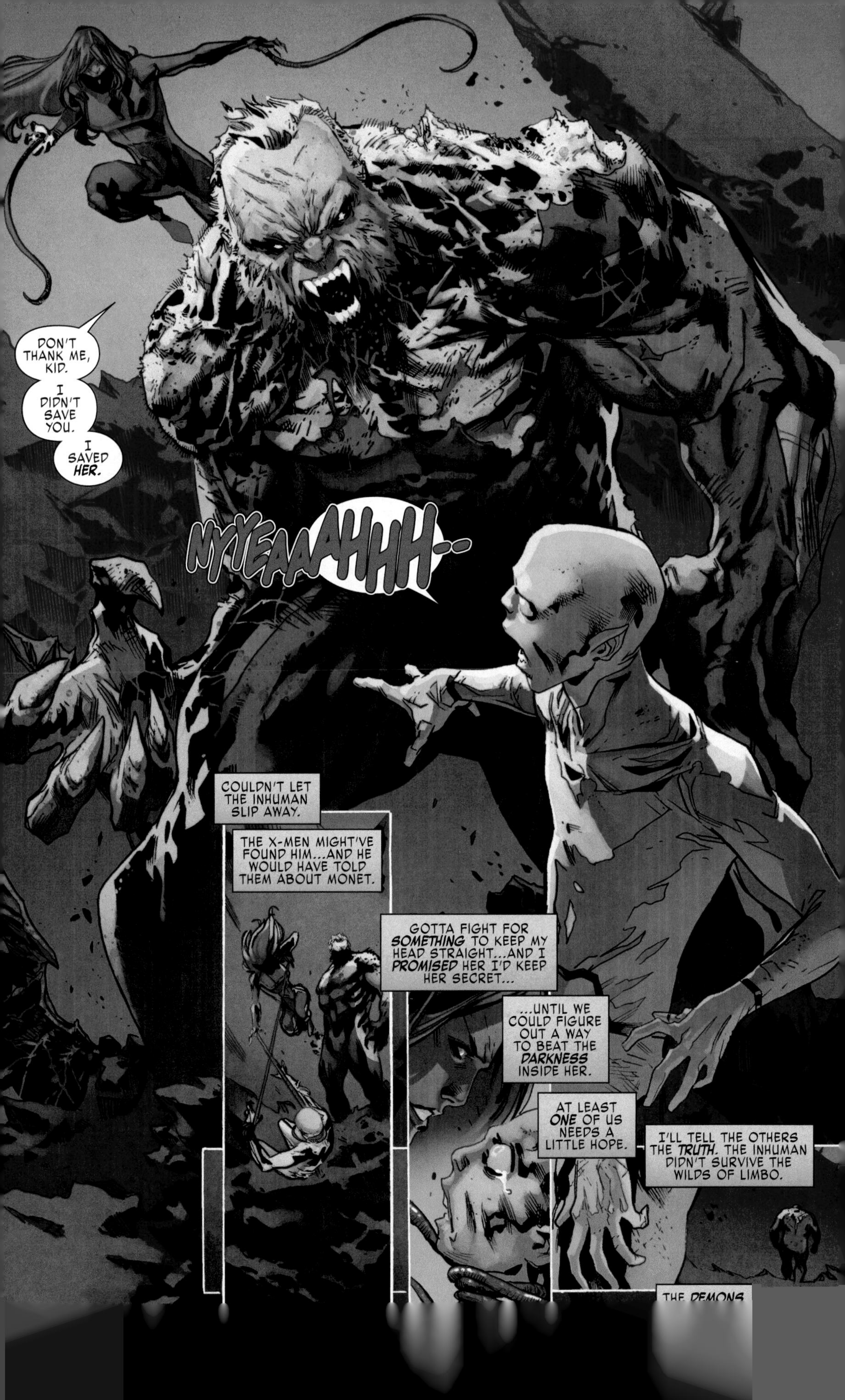

DON'T THANK ME, KID.
I DIDN'T SAVE YOU.
I SAVED HER.
NYYEAAAHHH--
COULDN'T LET THE INHUMAN SLIP AWAY.
THE X-MEN MIGHT'VE FOUND HIM...AND HE WOULD HAVE TOLD THEM ABOUT MONET.
GOTTA FIGHT FOR SOMETHING TO KEEP MY HEAD STRAIGHT...AND I PROMISED HER I'D KEEP HER SECRET...
...UNTIL WE COULD FIGURE OUT A WAY TO BEAT THE DARKNESS INSIDE HER.
AT LEAST ONE OF US NEEDS A LITTLE HOPE.
I'LL TELL THE OTHERS THE TRUTH. THE INHUMAN DIDN'T SURVIVE THE WILDS OF LIMBO.
THE DEMONS

18

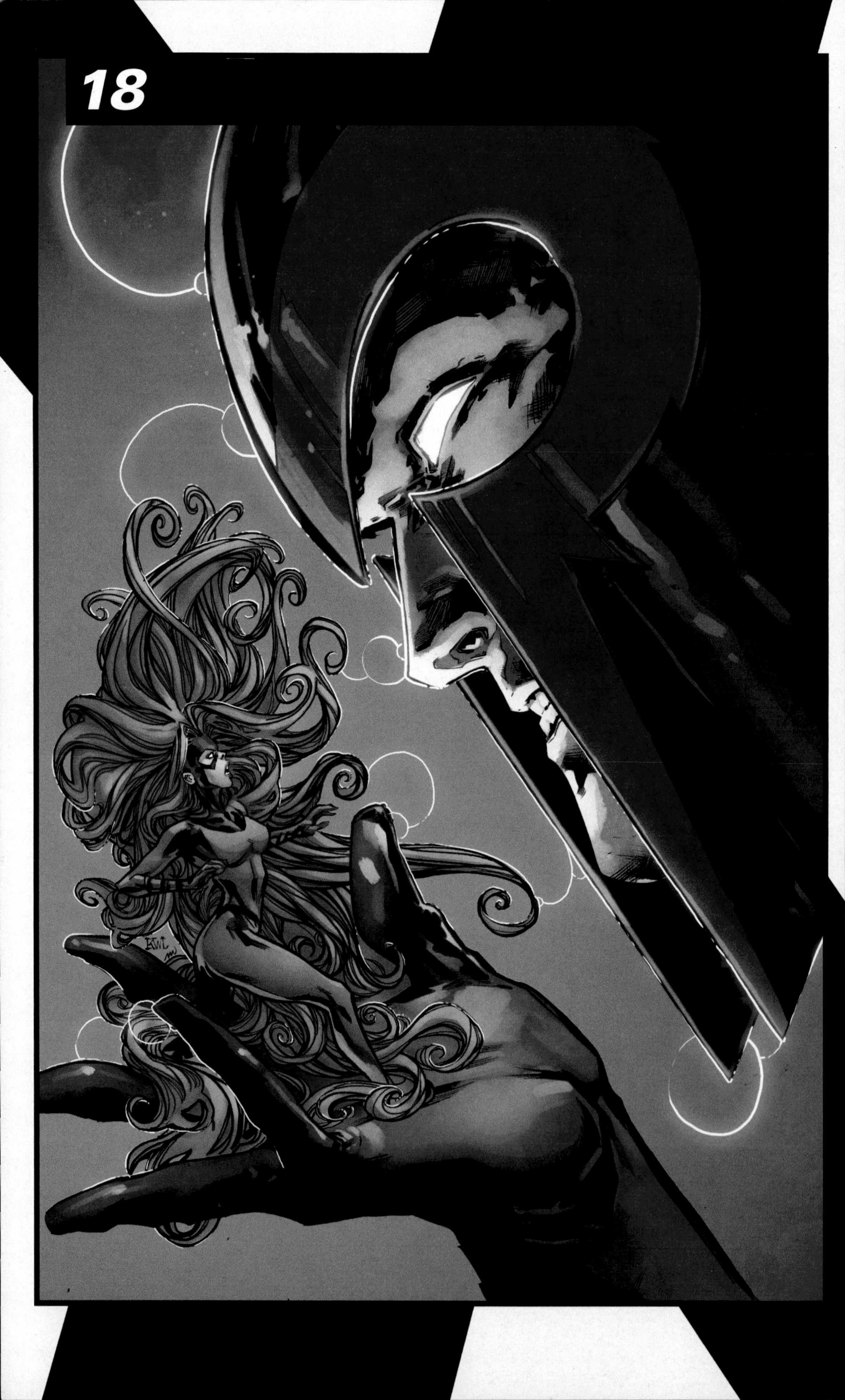

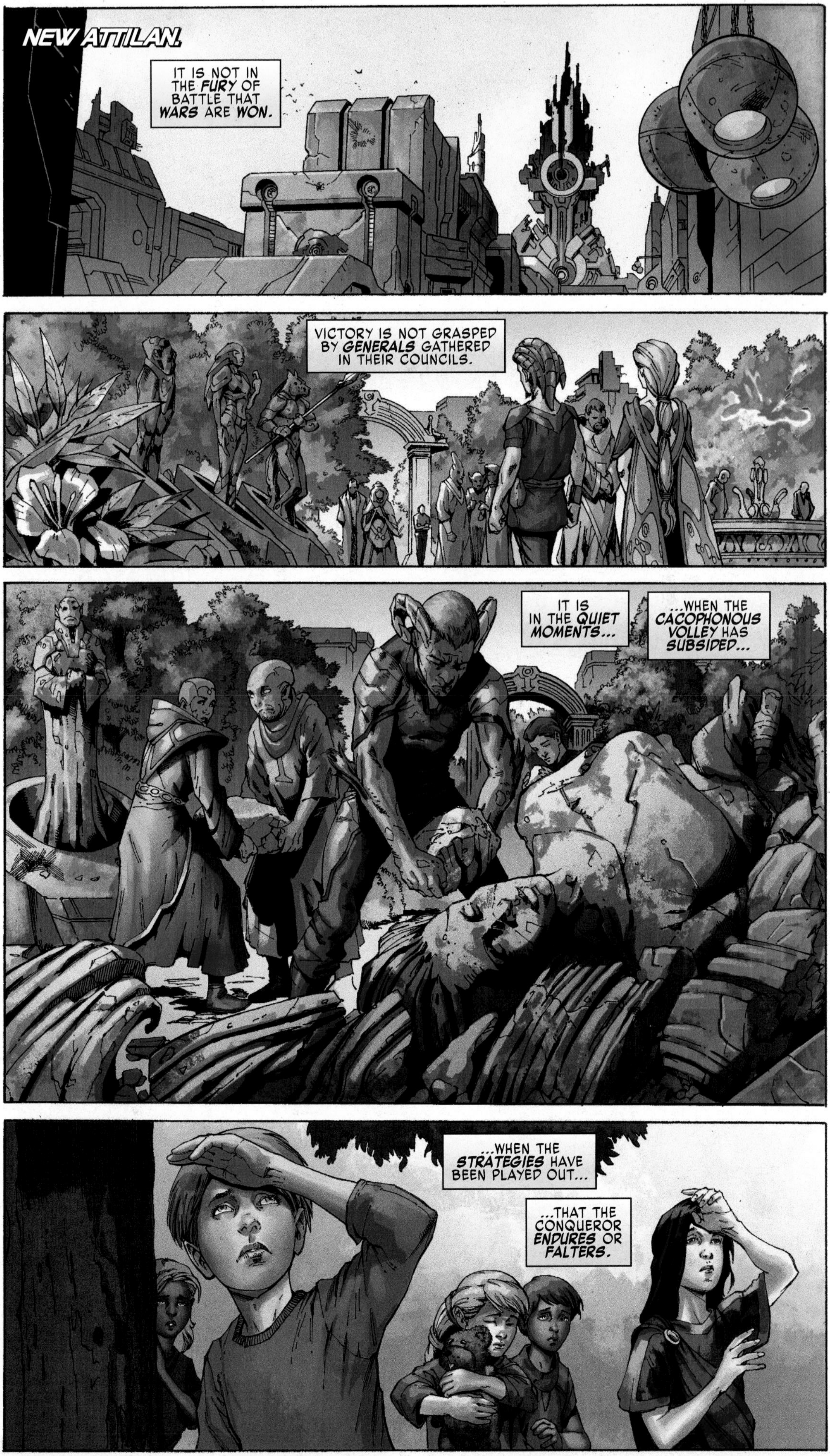
NEW ATTILAN.
IT IS NOT IN THE FURY OF BATTLE THAT WARS ARE WON.
VICTORY IS NOT GRASPED BY GENERALS GATHERED IN THEIR COUNCILS.
IT IS IN THE QUIET MOMENTS...
...WHEN THE CACOPHONOUS VOLLEY HAS SUBSIDED...
...WHEN THE STRATEGIES HAVE BEEN PLAYED OUT...
...THAT THE CONQUEROR ENDURES OR FALTERS.

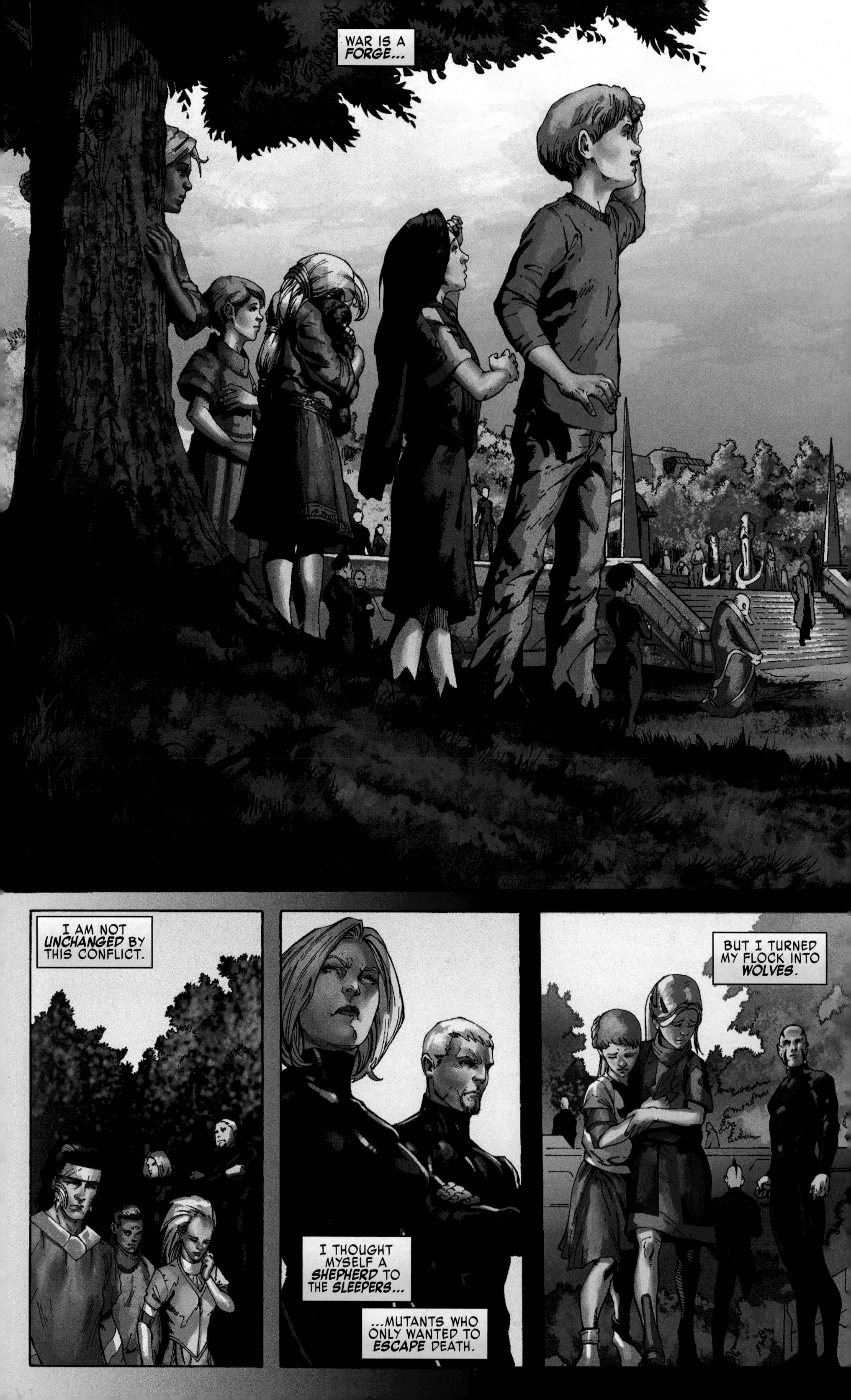
WAR IS A FORGE...
I AM NOT UNCHANGED BY THIS CONFLICT.
I THOUGHT MYSELF A SHEPHERD TO THE SLEEPERS...
...MUTANTS WHO ONLY WANTED TO ESCAPE DEATH.
BUT I TURNED MY FLOCK INTO WOLVES.

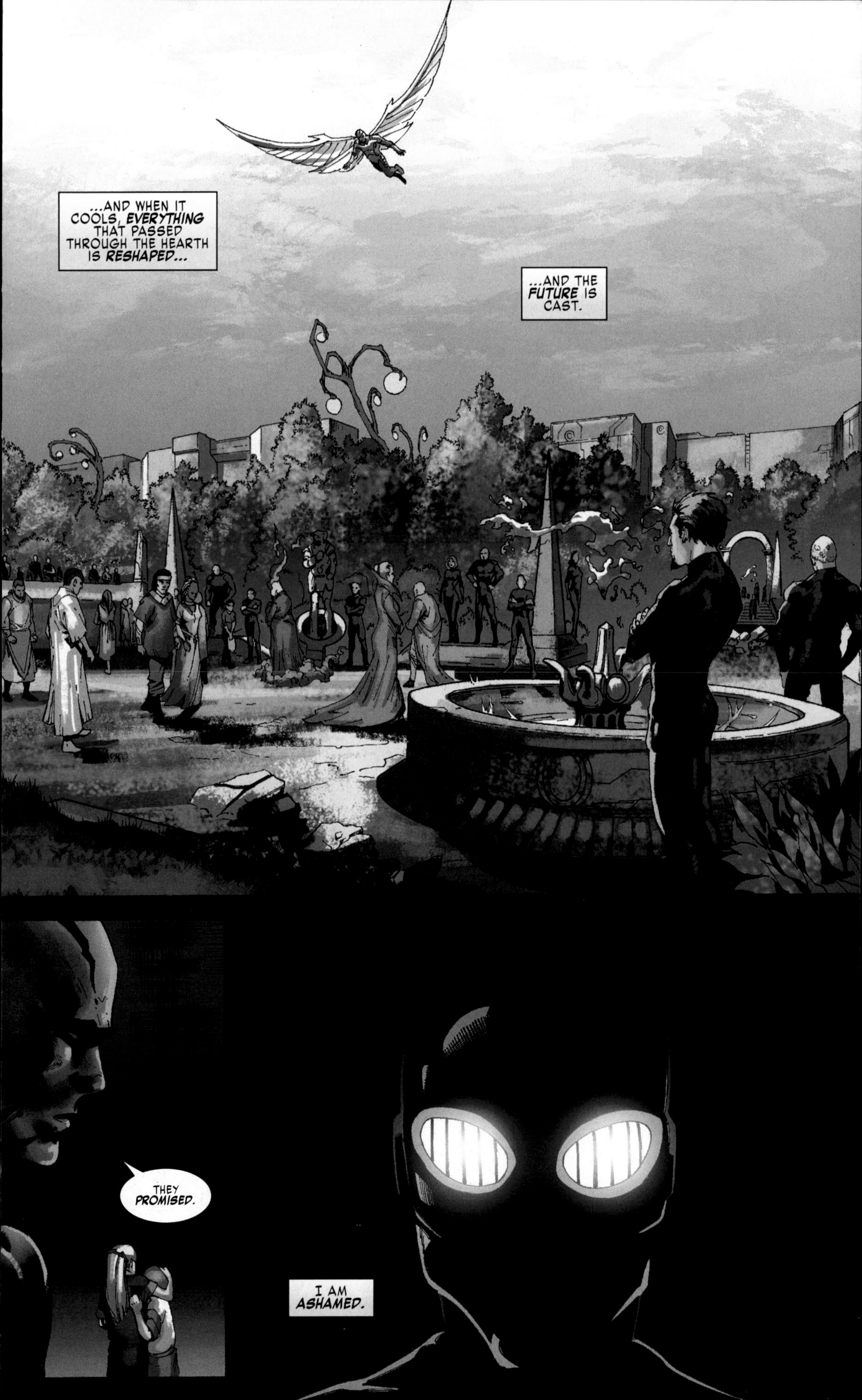
...AND WHEN IT COOLS, EVERYTHING THAT PASSED THROUGH THE HEARTH IS RESHAPED...
...AND THE FUTURE IS CAST.
THEY PROMISED.
I AM ASHAMED.

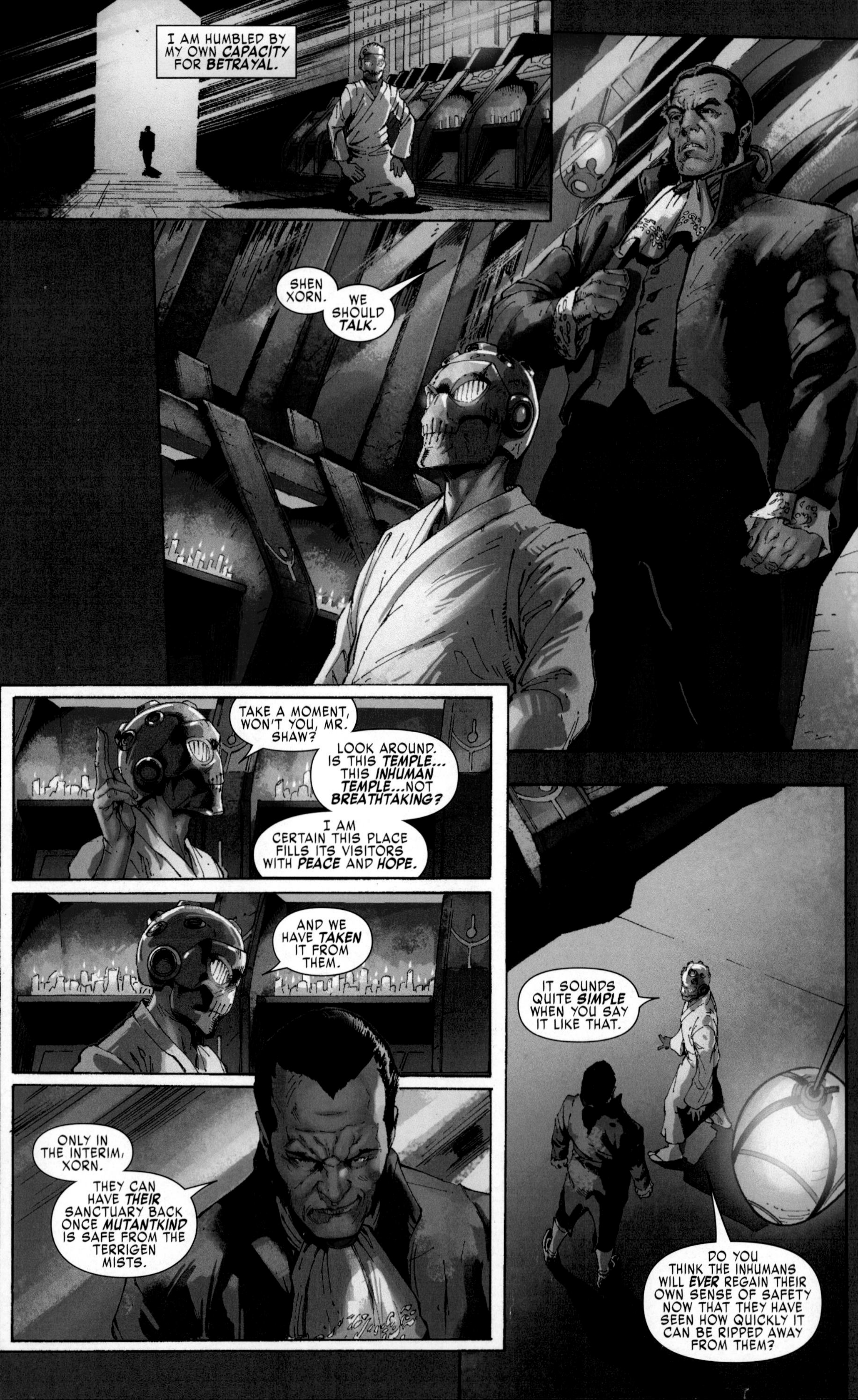
I AM HUMBLED BY MY OWN CAPACITY FOR BETRAYAL.
SHEN XORN.
WE SHOULD TALK.
TAKE A MOMENT, WON'T YOU, MR. SHAW?
LOOK AROUND. IS THIS TEMPLE... THIS INHUMAN TEMPLE...NOT BREATHTAKING?
I AM CERTAIN THIS PLACE FILLS ITS VISITORS WITH PEACE AND HOPE.
AND WE HAVE TAKEN IT FROM THEM.
ONLY IN THE INTERIM, XORN.
THEY CAN HAVE THEIR SANCTUARY BACK ONCE MUTANTKIND IS SAFE FROM THE TERRIGEN MISTS.
IT SOUNDS QUITE SIMPLE WHEN YOU SAY IT LIKE THAT.
DO YOU THINK THE INHUMANS WILL EVER REGAIN THEIR OWN SENSE OF SAFETY NOW THAT THEY HAVE SEEN HOW QUICKLY IT CAN BE RIPPED AWAY FROM THEM?

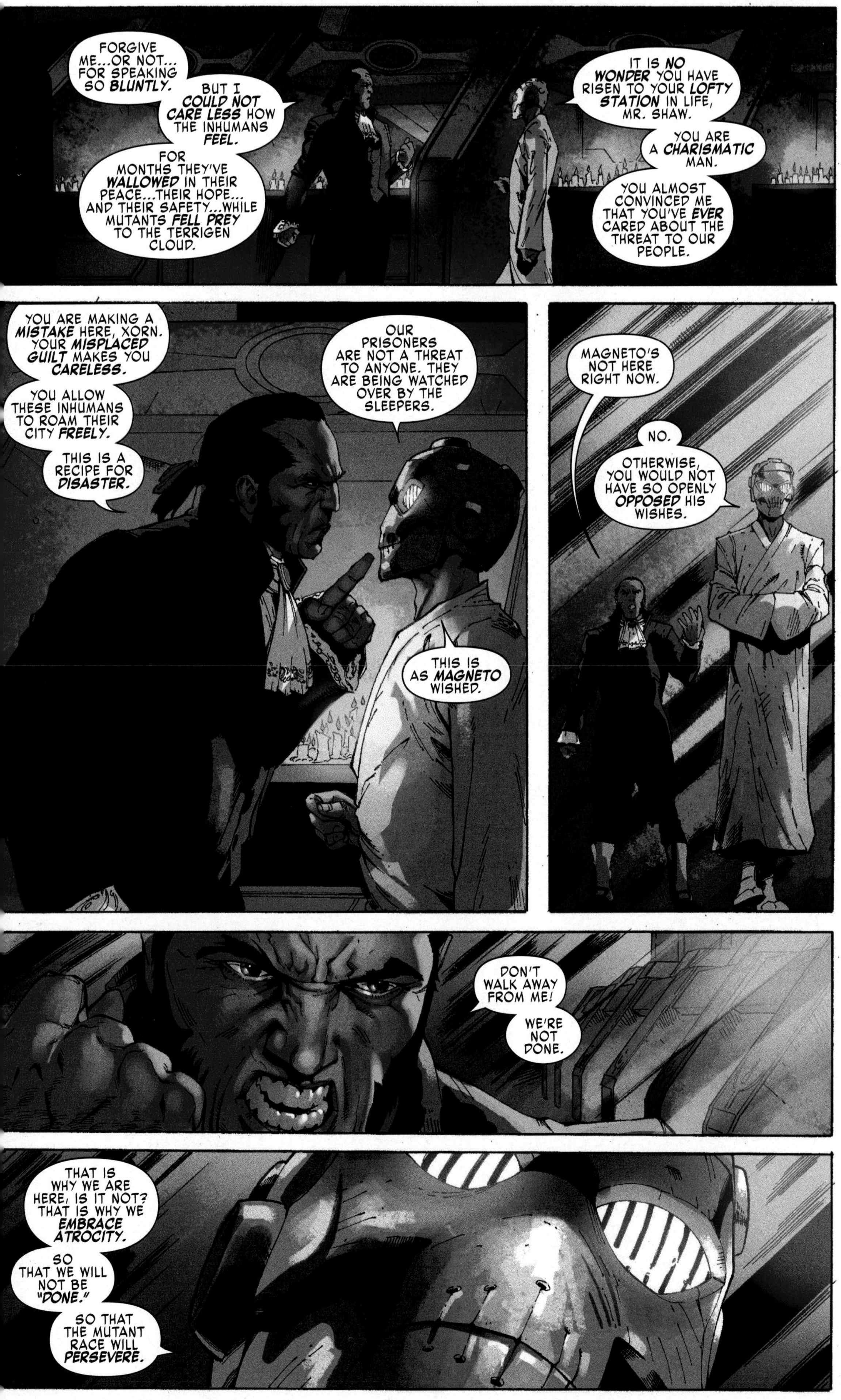
FORGIVE ME...OR NOT... FOR SPEAKING SO BLUNTLY.
BUT I COULD NOT CARE LESS HOW THE INHUMANS FEEL.
FOR MONTHS THEY'VE WALLOWED IN THEIR PEACE...THEIR HOPE... AND THEIR SAFETY...WHILE MUTANTS FELL PREY TO THE TERRIGEN CLOUD.
IT IS NO WONDER YOU HAVE RISEN TO YOUR LOFTY STATION IN LIFE, MR. SHAW.
YOU ARE A CHARISMATIC MAN.
YOU ALMOST CONVINCED ME THAT YOU'VE EVER CARED ABOUT THE THREAT TO OUR PEOPLE.
YOU ARE MAKING A MISTAKE HERE, XORN. YOUR MISPLACED GUILT MAKES YOU CARELESS.
YOU ALLOW THESE INHUMANS TO ROAM THEIR CITY FREELY.
THIS IS A RECIPE FOR DISASTER.
OUR PRISONERS ARE NOT A THREAT TO ANYONE. THEY ARE BEING WATCHED OVER BY THE SLEEPERS.
THIS IS AS MAGNETO WISHED.
MAGNETO'S NOT HERE RIGHT NOW.
NO.
OTHERWISE, YOU WOULD NOT HAVE SO OPENLY OPPOSED HIS WISHES.
DON'T WALK AWAY FROM ME!
WE'RE NOT DONE.
THAT IS WHY WE ARE HERE, IS IT NOT? THAT IS WHY WE EMBRACE ATROCITY.
SO THAT WE WILL NOT BE "DONE."
SO THAT THE MUTANT RACE WILL PERSEVERE.

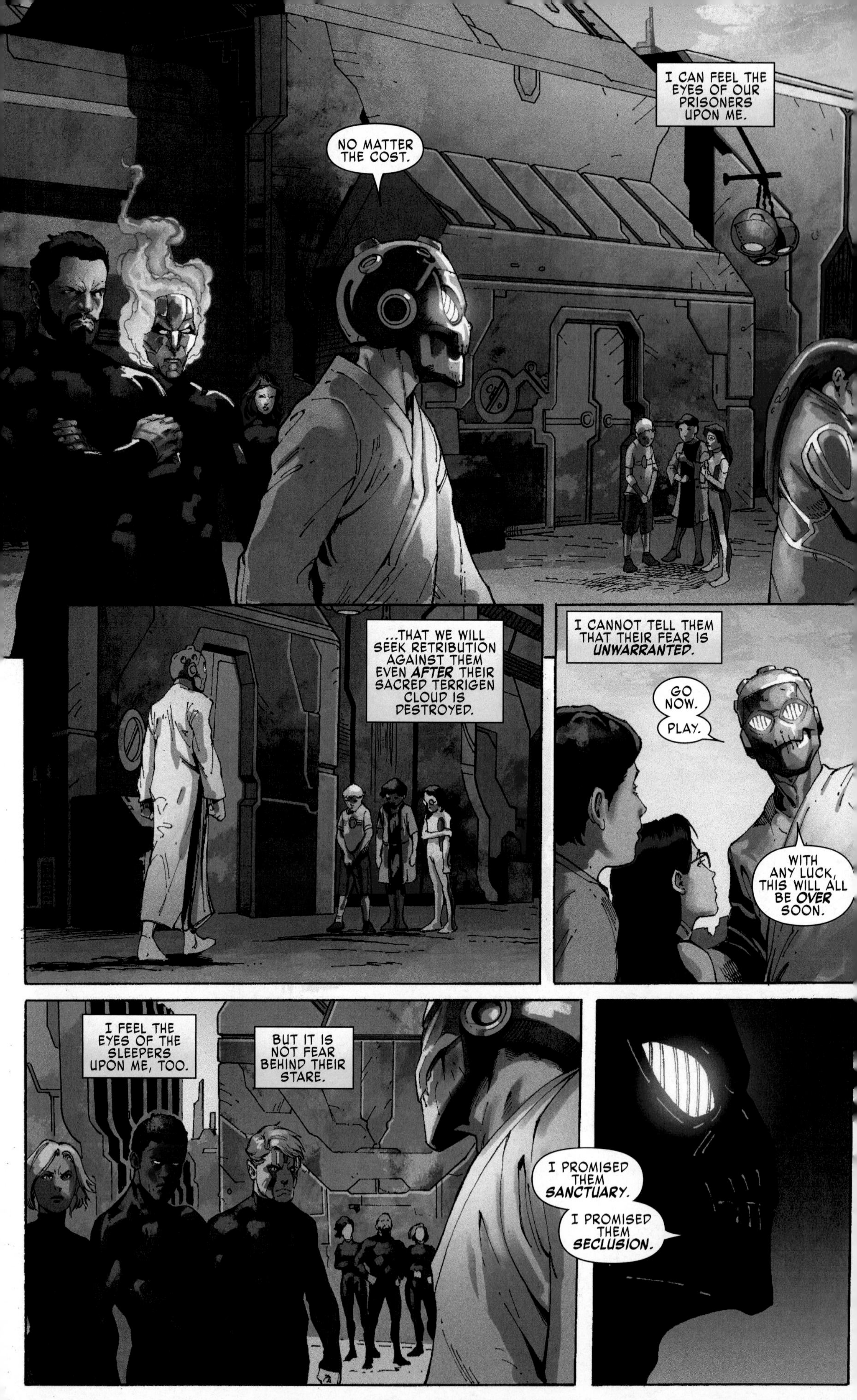

I CAN FEEL THE EYES OF OUR PRISONERS UPON ME.
NO MATTER THE COST.
...THAT WE WILL SEEK RETRIBUTION AGAINST THEM EVEN AFTER THEIR SACRED TERRIGEN CLOUD IS DESTROYED.
I CANNOT TELL THEM THAT THEIR FEAR IS UNWARRANTED.
GO NOW.
PLAY.
WITH ANY LUCK, THIS WILL ALL BE OVER SOON.
I FEEL THE EYES OF THE SLEEPERS UPON ME, TOO.
BUT IT IS NOT FEAR BEHIND THEIR STARE.
I PROMISED THEM SANCTUARY.
I PROMISED THEM SECLUSION.

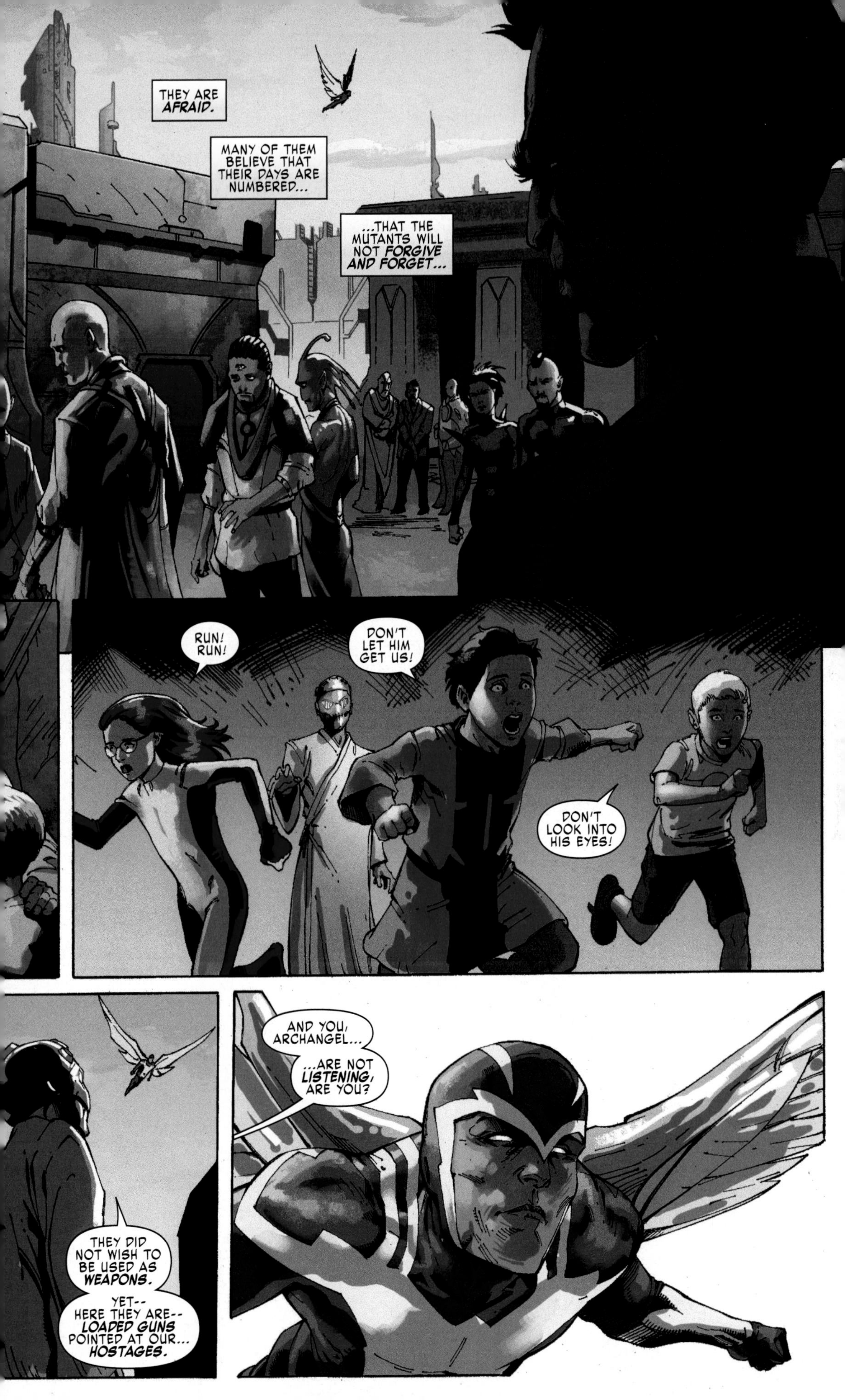
THEY ARE AFRAID.
MANY OF THEM BELIEVE THAT THEIR DAYS ARE NUMBERED...
...THAT THE MUTANTS WILL NOT FORGIVE AND FORGET...
RUN! RUN!
DON'T LET HIM GET US!
DON'T LOOK INTO HIS EYES!
THEY DID NOT WISH TO BE USED AS WEAPONS.
YET-- HERE THEY ARE-- LOADED GUNS POINTED AT OUR... HOSTAGES.
AND YOU, ARCHANGEL...
...ARE NOT LISTENING, ARE YOU?

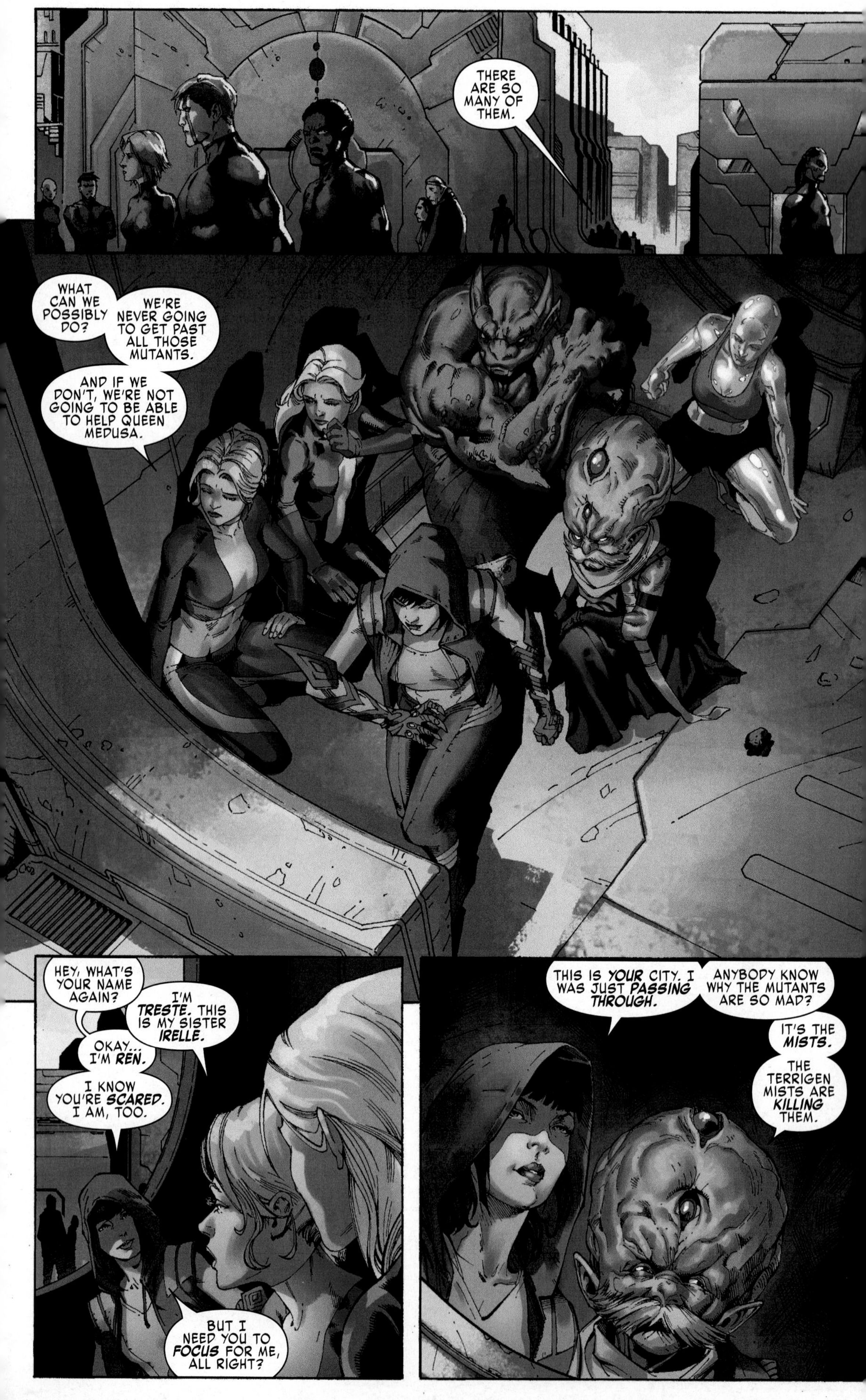
THERE ARE SO MANY OF THEM.
WHAT CAN WE POSSIBLY DO?
WE'RE NEVER GOING TO GET PAST ALL THOSE MUTANTS.
AND IF WE DON'T, WE'RE NOT GOING TO BE ABLE TO HELP QUEEN MEDUSA.
HEY, WHAT'S YOUR NAME AGAIN?
I'M TRESTE. THIS IS MY SISTER IRELLE.
OKAY... I'M REN.
I KNOW YOU'RE SCARED. I AM, TOO.
BUT I NEED YOU TO FOCUS FOR ME, ALL RIGHT?
THIS IS YOUR CITY. I WAS JUST PASSING THROUGH.
ANYBODY KNOW WHY THE MUTANTS ARE SO MAD?
IT'S THE MISTS.
THE TERRIGEN MISTS ARE KILLING THEM.

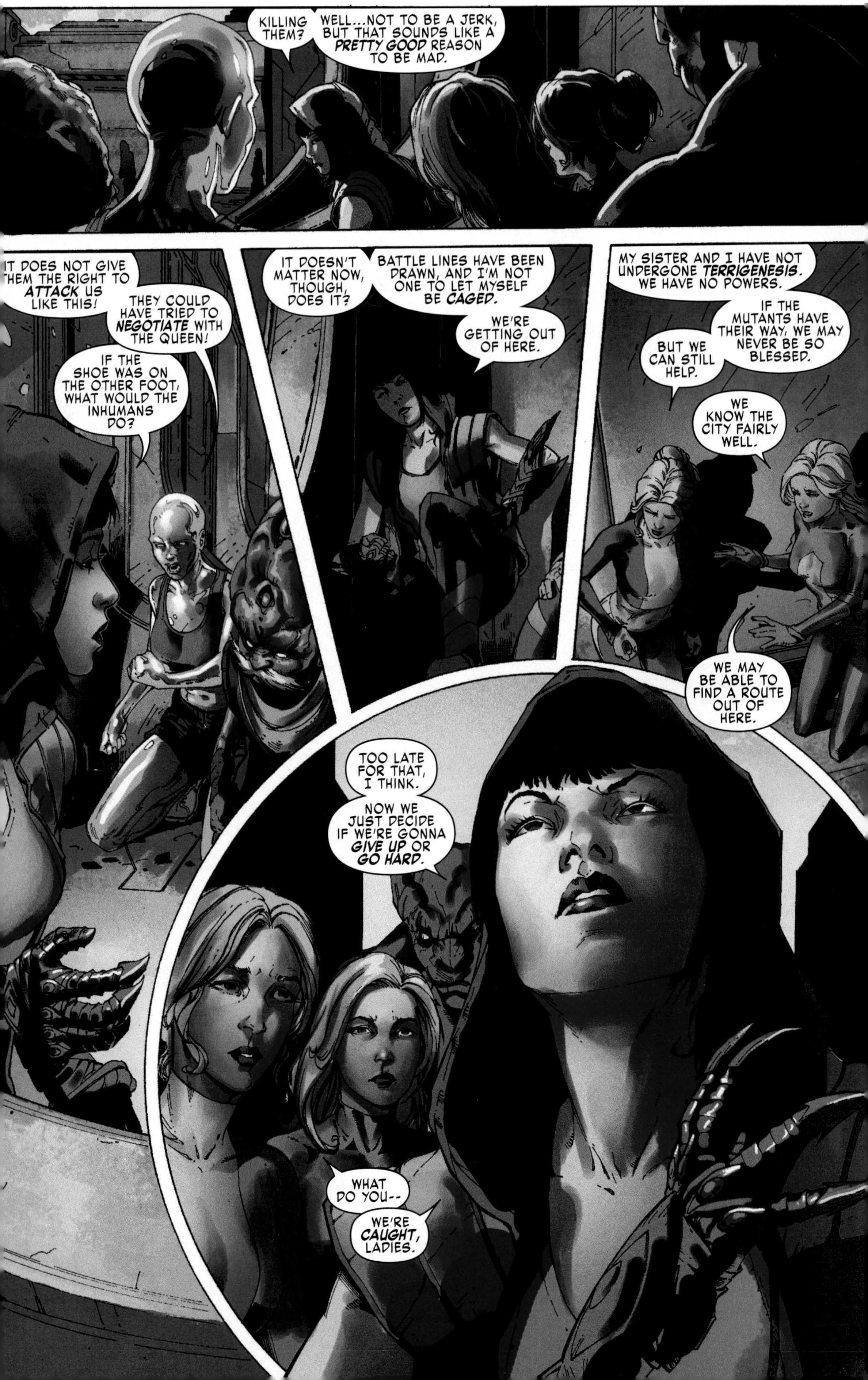
KILLING THEM?
WELL...NOT TO BE A JERK, BUT THAT SOUNDS LIKE A PRETTY GOOD REASON TO BE MAD.
IT DOES NOT GIVE THEM THE RIGHT TO ATTACK US LIKE THIS!
THEY COULD HAVE TRIED TO NEGOTIATE WITH THE QUEEN!
IF THE SHOE WAS ON THE OTHER FOOT, WHAT WOULD THE INHUMANS DO?
IT DOESN'T MATTER NOW, THOUGH, DOES IT?
BATTLE LINES HAVE BEEN DRAWN, AND I'M NOT ONE TO LET MYSELF BE CAGED.
WE'RE GETTING OUT OF HERE.
MY SISTER AND I HAVE NOT UNDERGONE TERRIGENESIS. WE HAVE NO POWERS.
IF THE MUTANTS HAVE THEIR WAY, WE MAY NEVER BE SO BLESSED.
BUT WE CAN STILL HELP.
WE KNOW THE CITY FAIRLY WELL.
WE MAY BE ABLE TO FIND A ROUTE OUT OF HERE.
TOO LATE FOR THAT, I THINK.
NOW WE JUST DECIDE IF WE'RE GONNA GIVE UP OR GO HARD.
WHAT DO YOU--
WE'RE CAUGHT, LADIES.

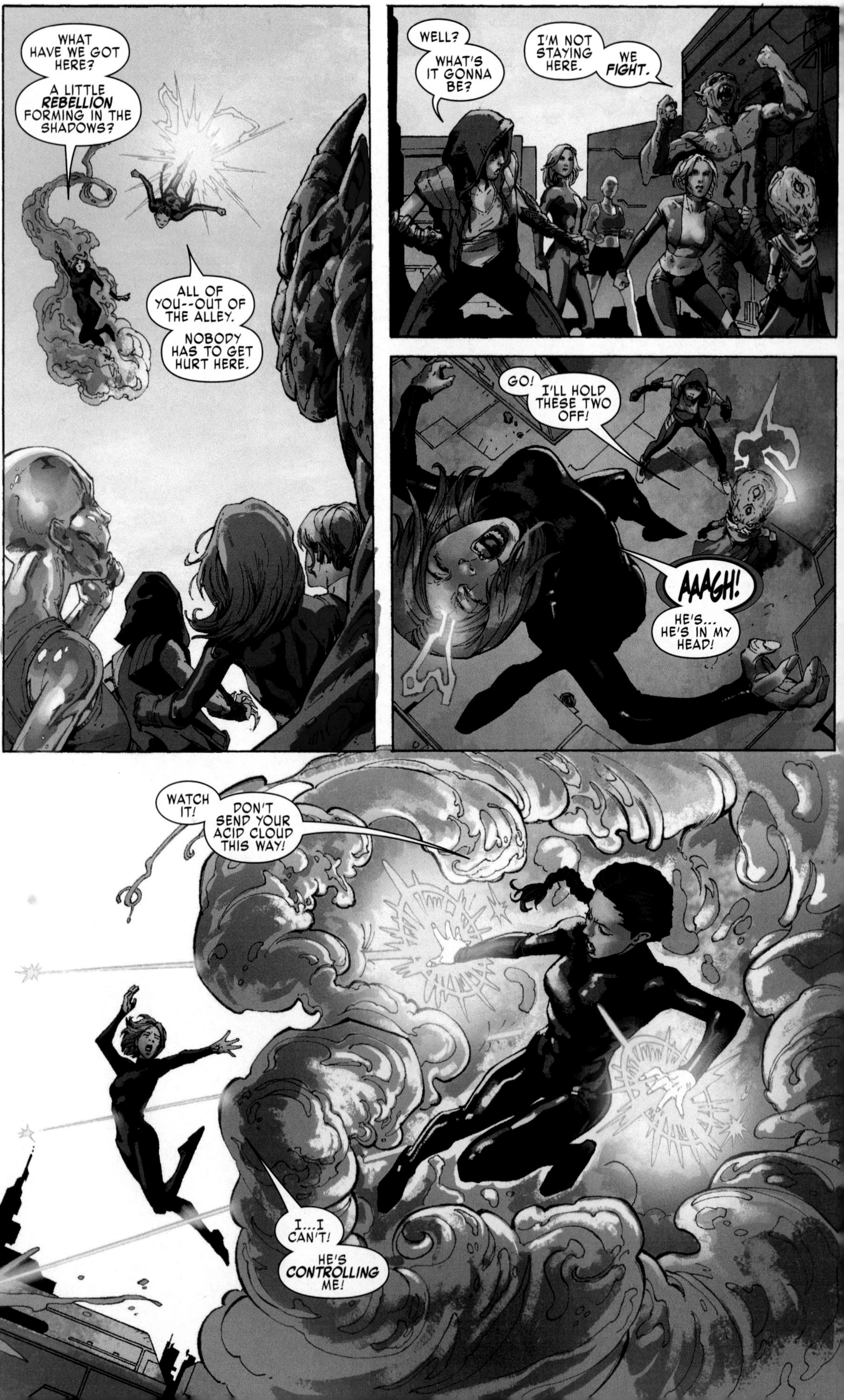

WHAT HAVE WE GOT HERE?
A LITTLE REBELLION FORMING IN THE SHADOWS?
ALL OF YOU--OUT OF THE ALLEY.
NOBODY HAS TO GET HURT HERE.
WELL?
WHAT'S IT GONNA BE?
I'M NOT STAYING HERE.
WE FIGHT.
GO!
I'LL HOLD THESE TWO OFF!
AAAGH!
HE'S... HE'S IN MY HEAD!
WATCH IT!
DON'T SEND YOUR ACID CLOUD THIS WAY!
I...I CAN'T!
HE'S CONTROLLING ME!

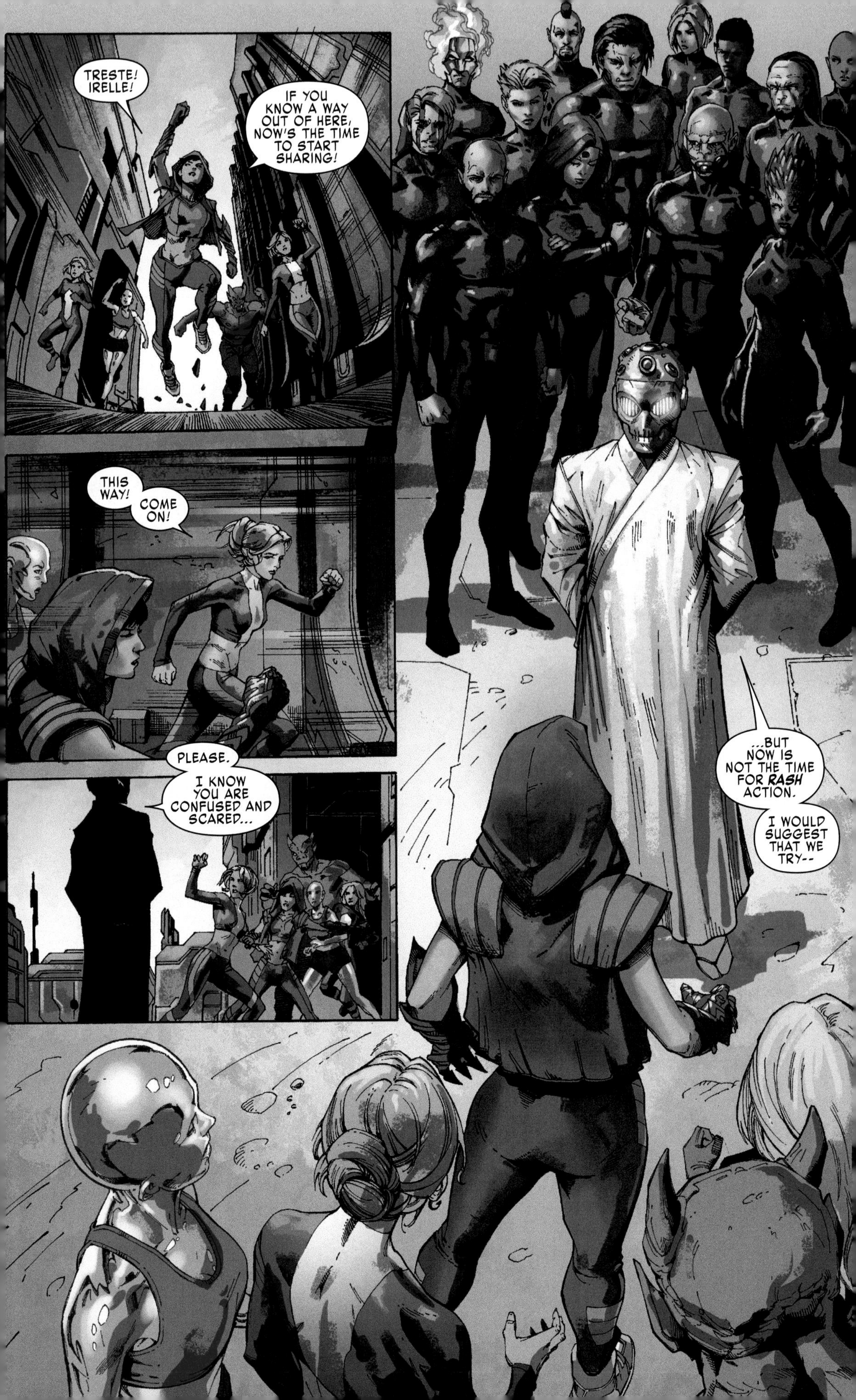

TRESTE! IRELLE!
IF YOU KNOW A WAY OUT OF HERE, NOW'S THE TIME TO START SHARING!
THIS WAY!
COME ON!
PLEASE.
I KNOW YOU ARE CONFUSED AND SCARED...
...BUT NOW IS NOT THE TIME FOR RASH ACTION.
I WOULD SUGGEST THAT WE TRY--

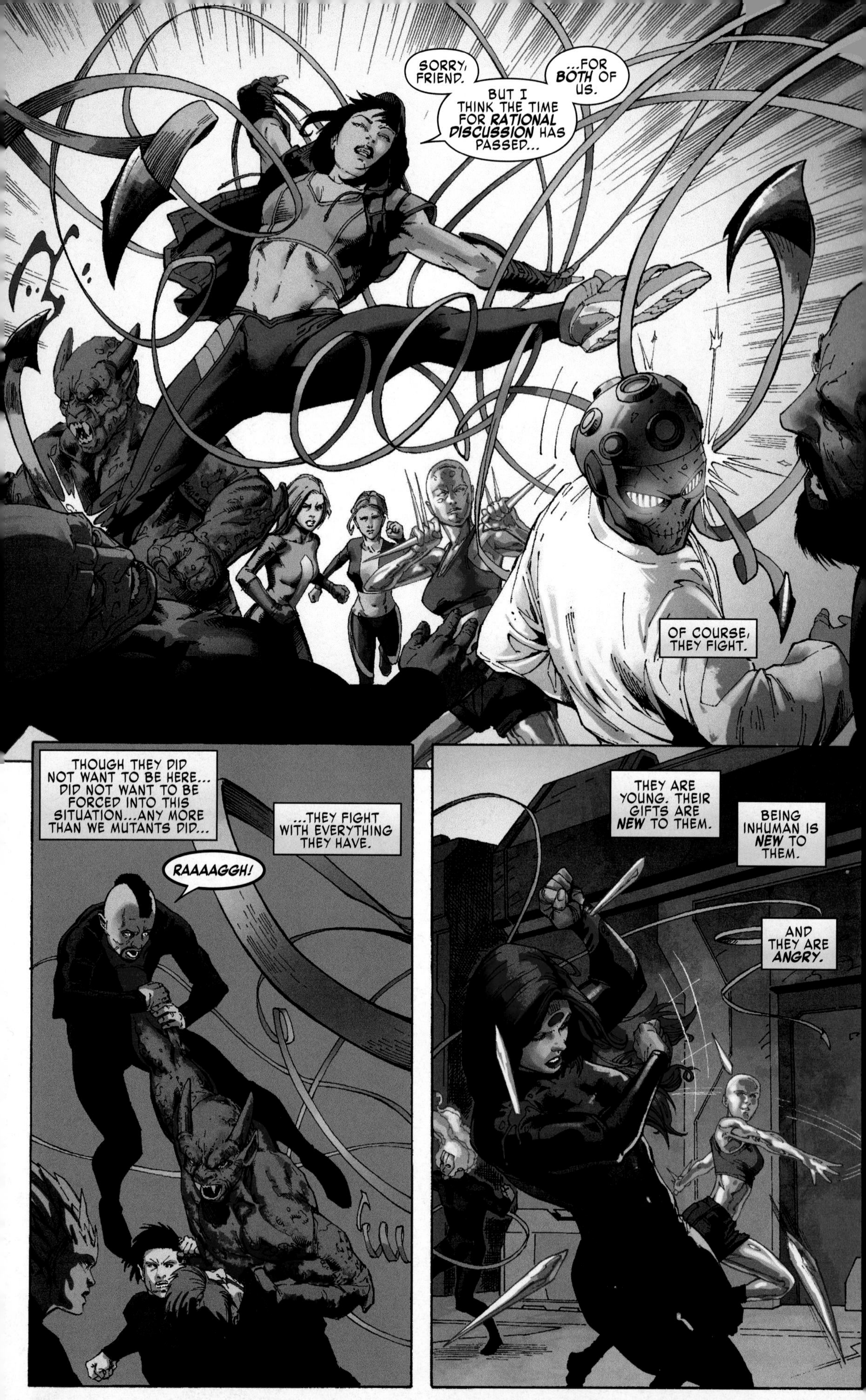
SORRY, FRIEND.
BUT I THINK THE TIME FOR RATIONAL DISCUSSION HAS PASSED...
...FOR BOTH OF US.
OF COURSE, THEY FIGHT.
THOUGH THEY DID NOT WANT TO BE HERE... DID NOT WANT TO BE FORCED INTO THIS SITUATION...ANY MORE THAN WE MUTANTS DID...
...THEY FIGHT WITH EVERYTHING THEY HAVE.
RAAAAGGH!
THEY ARE YOUNG. THEIR GIFTS ARE NEW TO THEM.
BEING INHUMAN IS NEW TO THEM.
AND THEY ARE ANGRY.

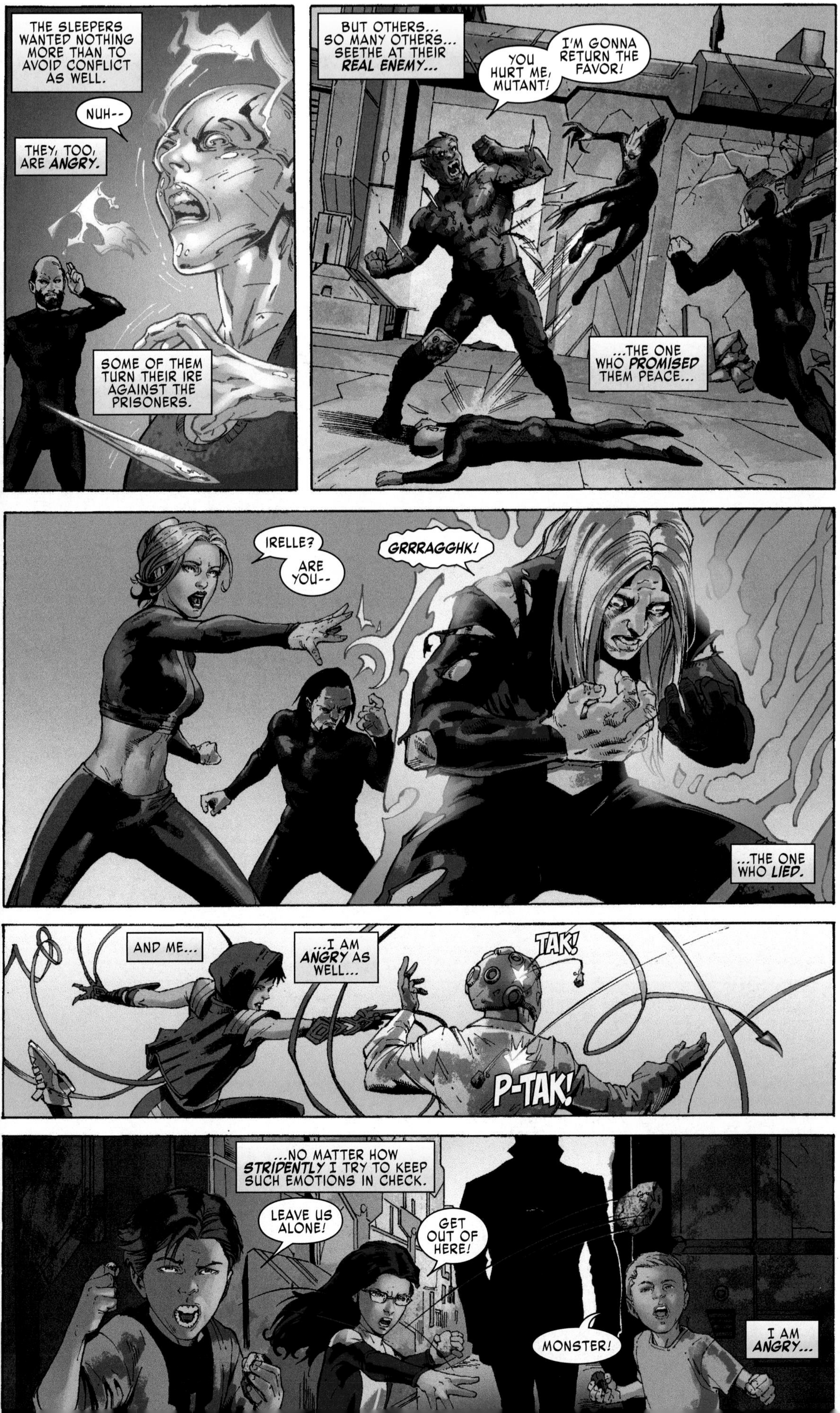
THE SLEEPERS WANTED NOTHING MORE THAN TO AVOID CONFLICT AS WELL.
NUH--
THEY, TOO, ARE ANGRY.
SOME OF THEM TURN THEIR IRE AGAINST THE PRISONERS.
BUT OTHERS... SO MANY OTHERS... SEETHE AT THEIR REAL ENEMY...
YOU HURT ME, MUTANT!
I'M GONNA RETURN THE FAVOR!
...THE ONE WHO PROMISED THEM PEACE...
IRELLE? ARE YOU--
GRRRAGGHK!
...THE ONE WHO LIED.
AND ME...
...I AM ANGRY AS WELL...
TAK!
P-TAK!
...NO MATTER HOW STRIDENTLY I TRY TO KEEP SUCH EMOTIONS IN CHECK.
LEAVE US ALONE!
GET OUT OF HERE!
MONSTER!
I AM ANGRY...

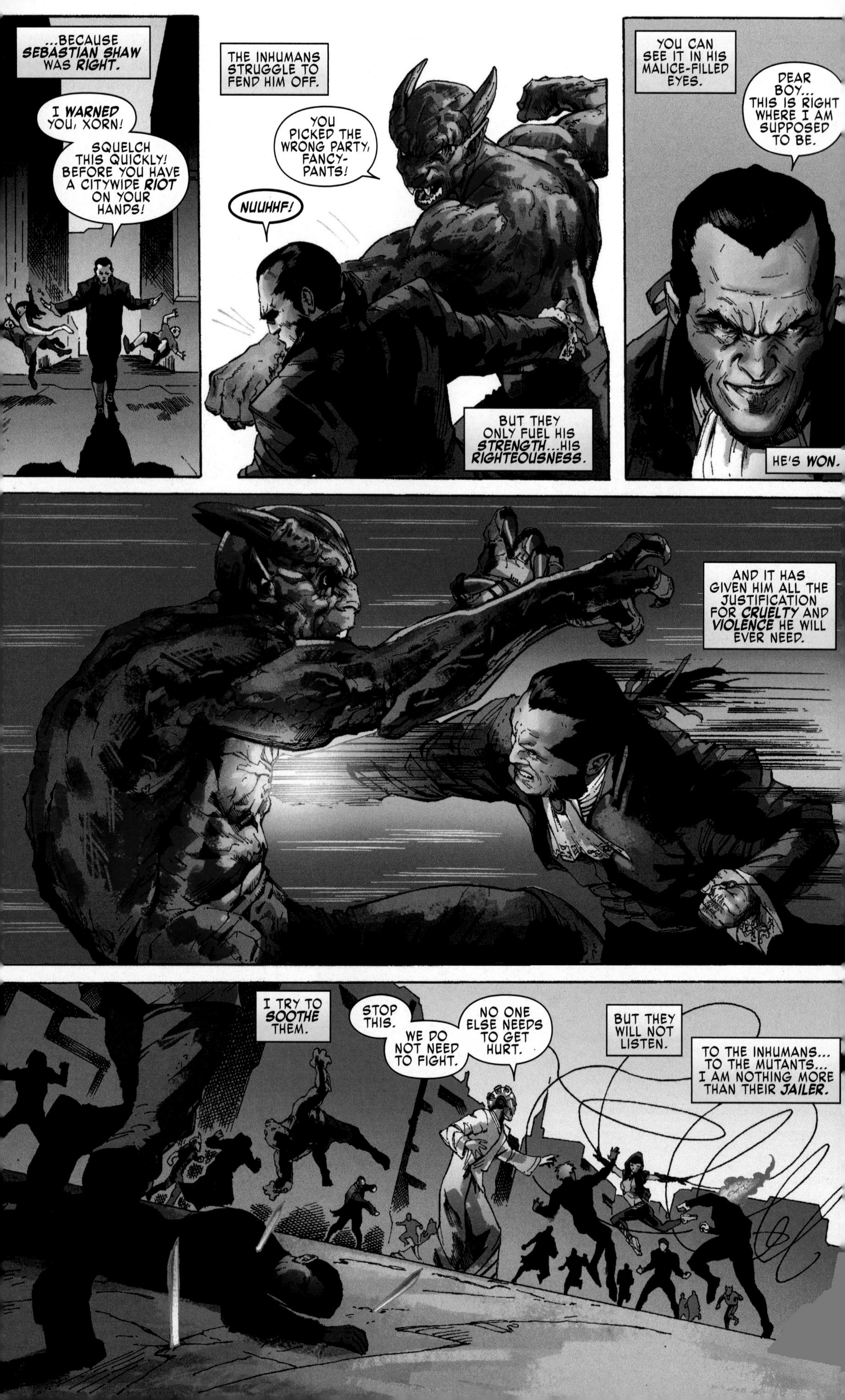
...BECAUSE SEBASTIAN SHAW WAS RIGHT.
I WARNED YOU, XORN!
SQUELCH THIS QUICKLY! BEFORE YOU HAVE A CITYWIDE RIOT ON YOUR HANDS!
THE INHUMANS STRUGGLE TO FEND HIM OFF.
YOU PICKED THE WRONG PARTY, FANCY-PANTS!
NUUHHF!
BUT THEY ONLY FUEL HIS STRENGTH...HIS RIGHTEOUSNESS.
YOU CAN SEE IT IN HIS MALICE-FILLED EYES.
DEAR BOY... THIS IS RIGHT WHERE I AM SUPPOSED TO BE.
HE'S WON.
AND IT HAS GIVEN HIM ALL THE JUSTIFICATION FOR CRUELTY AND VIOLENCE HE WILL EVER NEED.
I TRY TO SOOTHE THEM.
STOP THIS.
WE DO NOT NEED TO FIGHT.
NO ONE ELSE NEEDS TO GET HURT.
BUT THEY WILL NOT LISTEN.
TO THE INHUMANS... TO THE MUTANTS... I AM NOTHING MORE THAN THEIR JAILER.

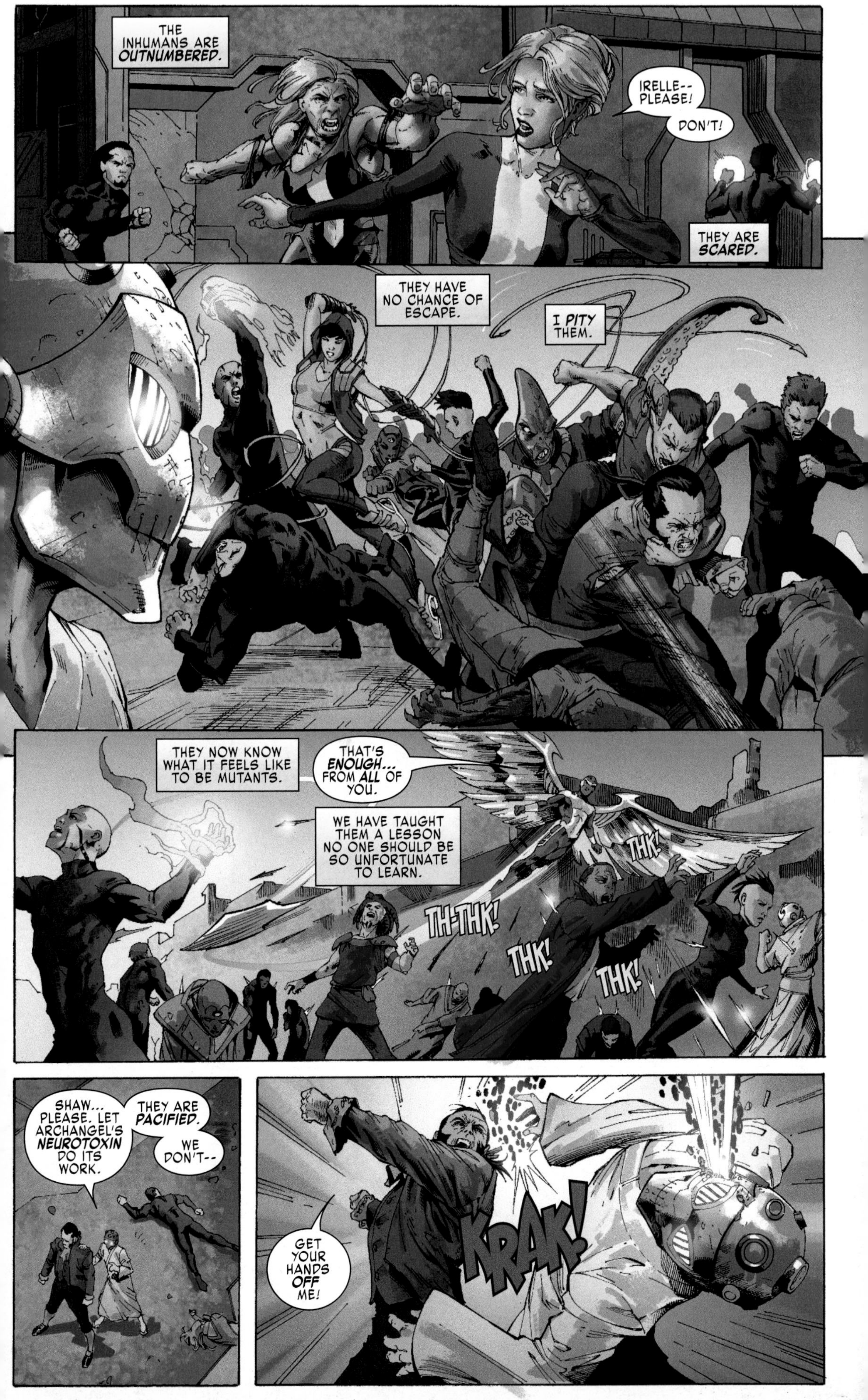
THE INHUMANS ARE OUTNUMBERED.
IRELLE-- PLEASE!
DON'T!
THEY ARE SCARED.
THEY HAVE NO CHANCE OF ESCAPE.
I PITY THEM.
THEY NOW KNOW WHAT IT FEELS LIKE TO BE MUTANTS.
THAT'S ENOUGH... FROM ALL OF YOU.
WE HAVE TAUGHT THEM A LESSON NO ONE SHOULD BE SO UNFORTUNATE TO LEARN.
THK!
TH-THK!
THK!
THK!
SHAW... PLEASE. LET ARCHANGEL'S NEUROTOXIN DO ITS WORK.
THEY ARE PACIFIED.
WE DON'T--
GET YOUR HANDS OFF ME!
KRAK!

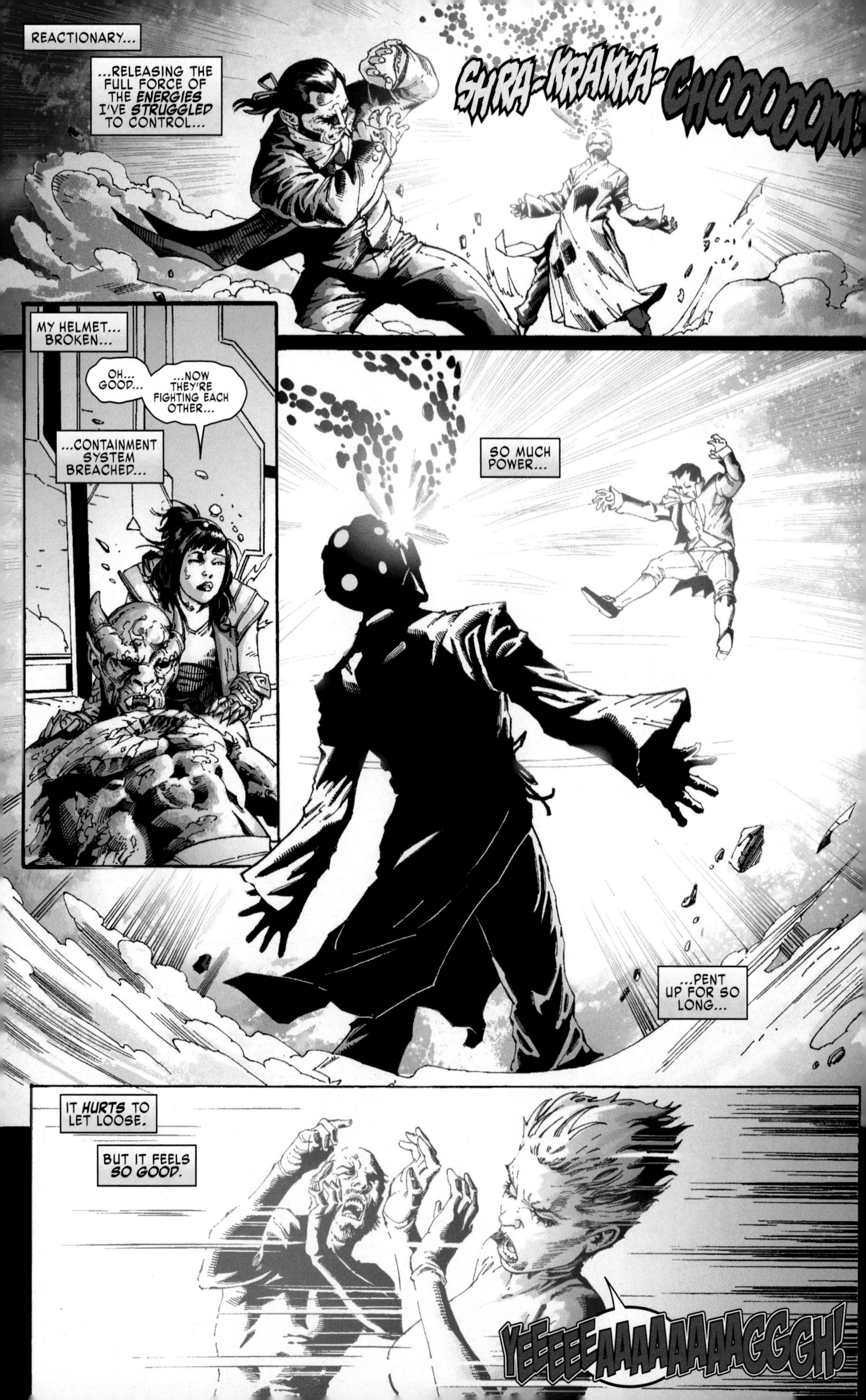
REACTIONARY...
...RELEASING THE FULL FORCE OF THE ENERGIES I'VE STRUGGLED TO CONTROL...
SHRA-KRAKKA-CHOOOOOM!
MY HELMET... BROKEN...
OH... GOOD...
...NOW THEY'RE FIGHTING EACH OTHER...
...CONTAINMENT SYSTEM BREACHED...
SO MUCH POWER...
...PENT UP FOR SO LONG...
IT HURTS TO LET LOOSE.
BUT IT FEELS SO GOOD.
YEEEEEAAAAAAAAGGGH!

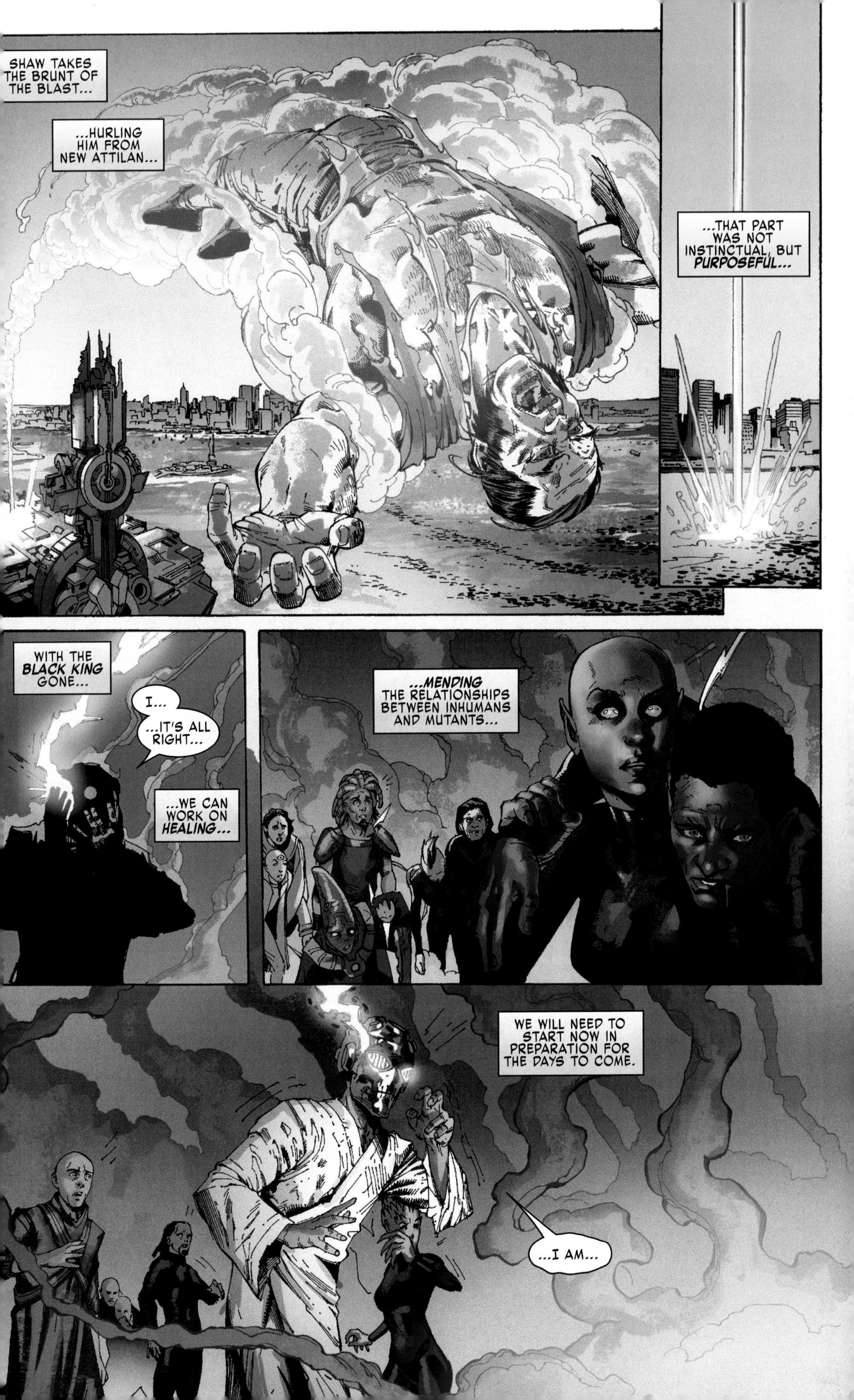
SHAW TAKES THE BRUNT OF THE BLAST...
...HURLING HIM FROM NEW ATTILAN...
...THAT PART WAS NOT INSTINCTUAL, BUT PURPOSEFUL...
WITH THE BLACK KING GONE...
I...
...IT'S ALL RIGHT...
...WE CAN WORK ON HEALING...
...MENDING THE RELATIONSHIPS BETWEEN INHUMANS AND MUTANTS...
WE WILL NEED TO START NOW IN PREPARATION FOR THE DAYS TO COME.
...I AM...

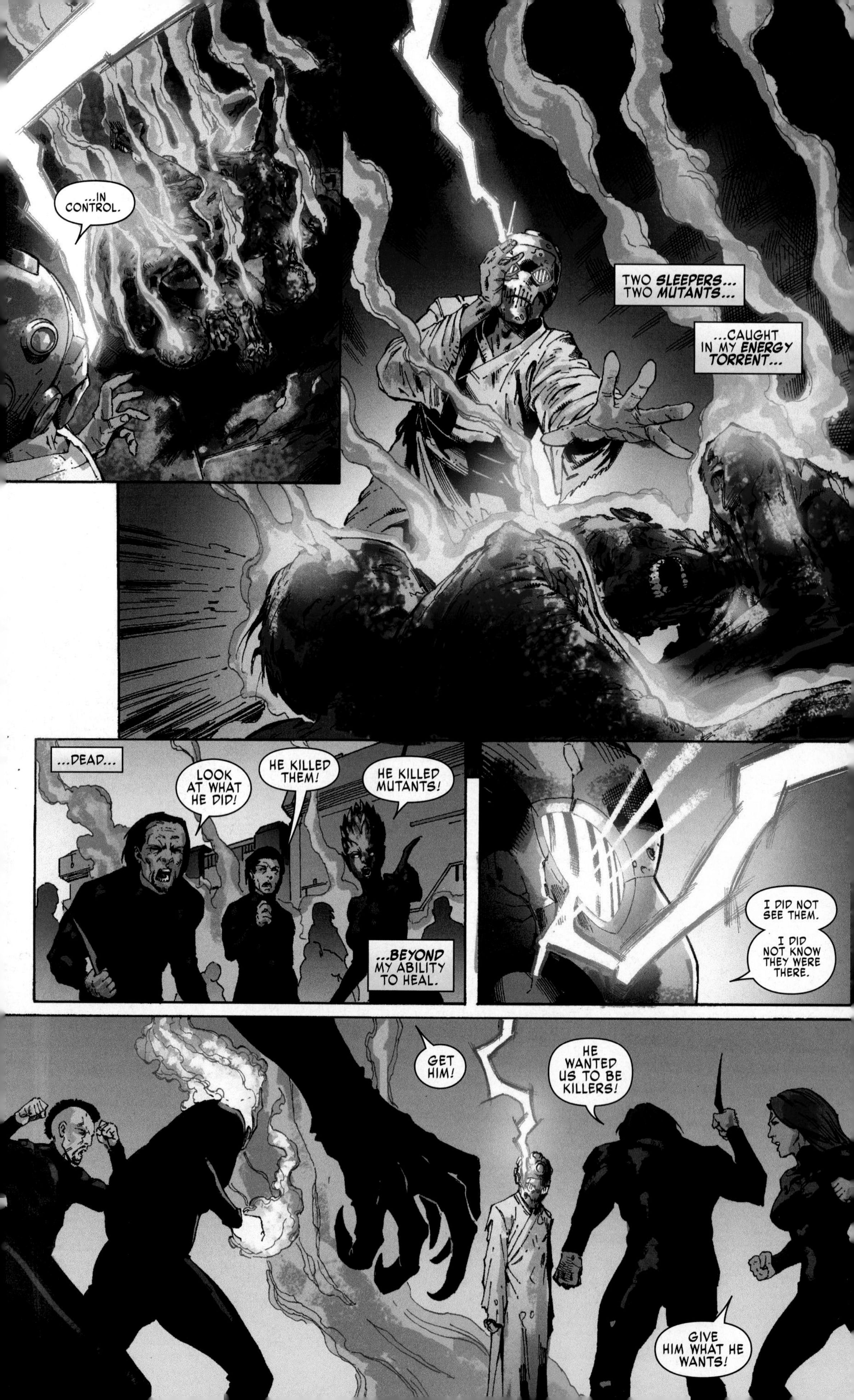
...IN CONTROL.
TWO SLEEPERS... TWO MUTANTS...
...CAUGHT IN MY ENERGY TORRENT...
...DEAD...
LOOK AT WHAT HE DID!
HE KILLED THEM!
HE KILLED MUTANTS!
...BEYOND MY ABILITY TO HEAL.
I DID NOT SEE THEM.
I DID NOT KNOW THEY WERE THERE.
GET HIM!
HE WANTED US TO BE KILLERS!
GIVE HIM WHAT HE WANTS!

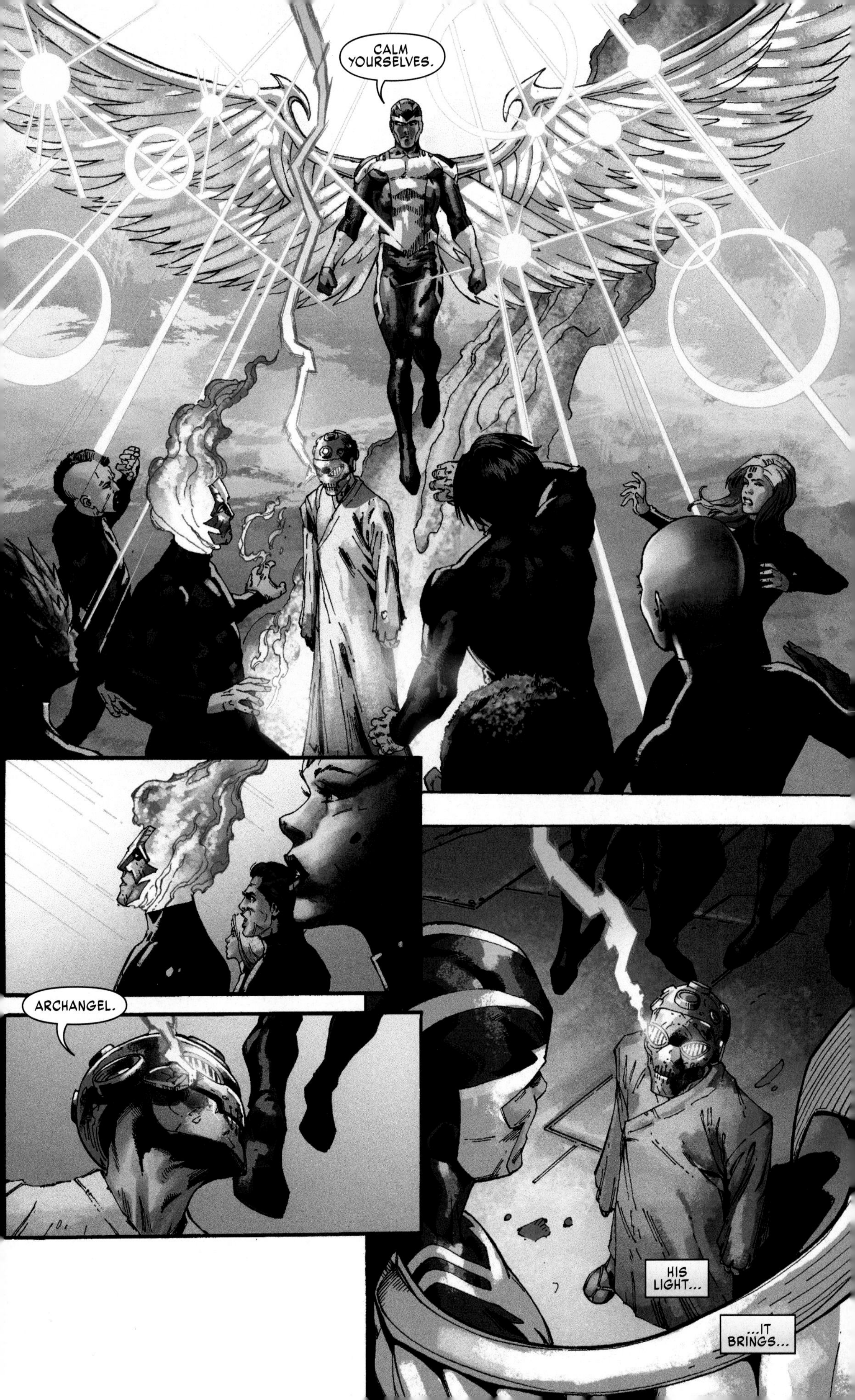

CALM YOURSELVES.
ARCHANGEL.
HIS LIGHT...
...IT BRINGS...

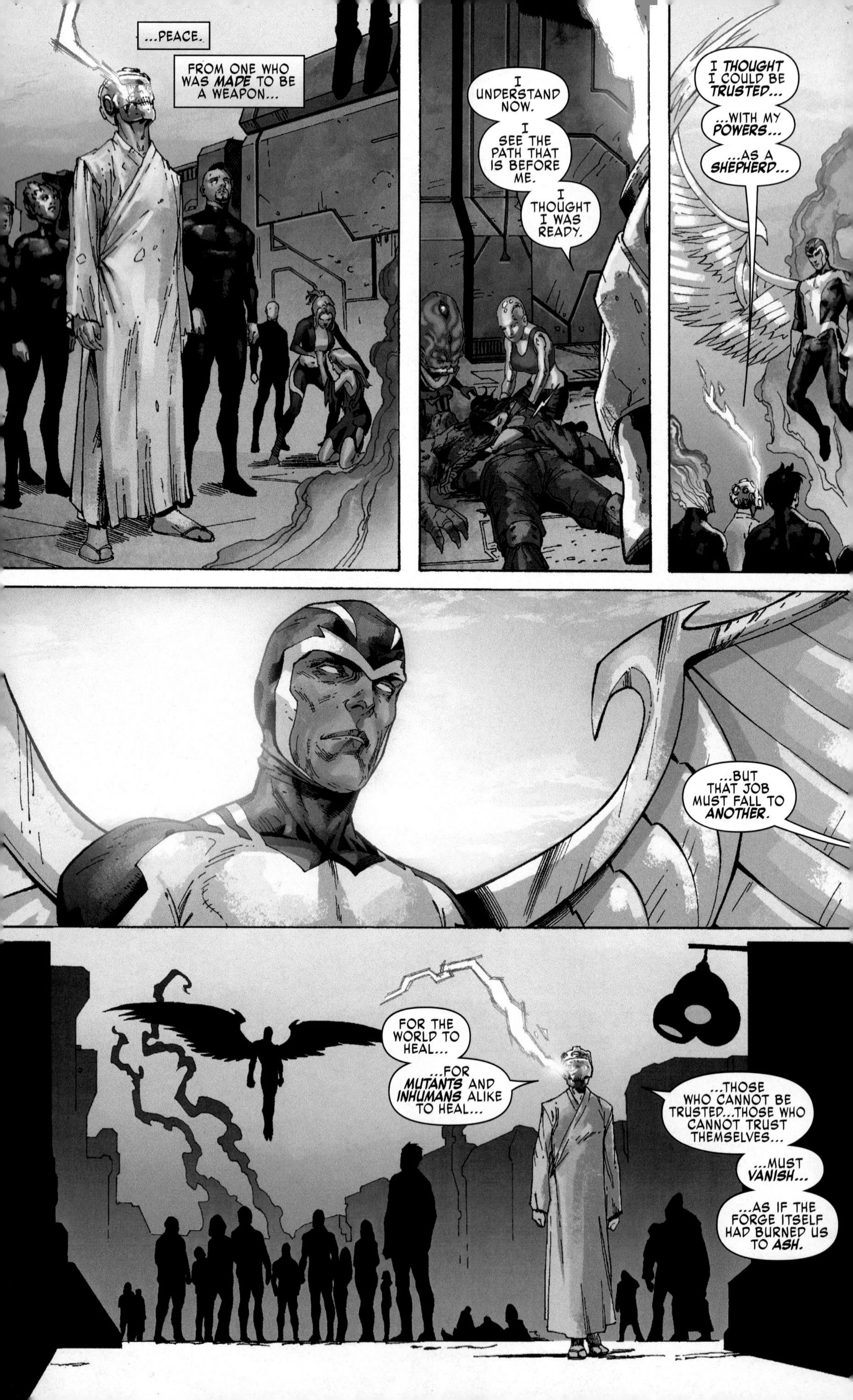
...PEACE.
FROM ONE WHO WAS MADE TO BE A WEAPON...
I UNDERSTAND NOW.
I SEE THE PATH THAT IS BEFORE ME.
I THOUGHT I WAS READY.
I THOUGHT I COULD BE TRUSTED...
...WITH MY POWERS...
...AS A SHEPHERD...
...BUT THAT JOB MUST FALL TO ANOTHER.
FOR THE WORLD TO HEAL...
...FOR MUTANTS AND INHUMANS ALIKE TO HEAL...
...THOSE WHO CANNOT BE TRUSTED...THOSE WHO CANNOT TRUST THEMSELVES...
...MUST VANISH...
...AS IF THE FORGE ITSELF HAD BURNED US TO ASH.

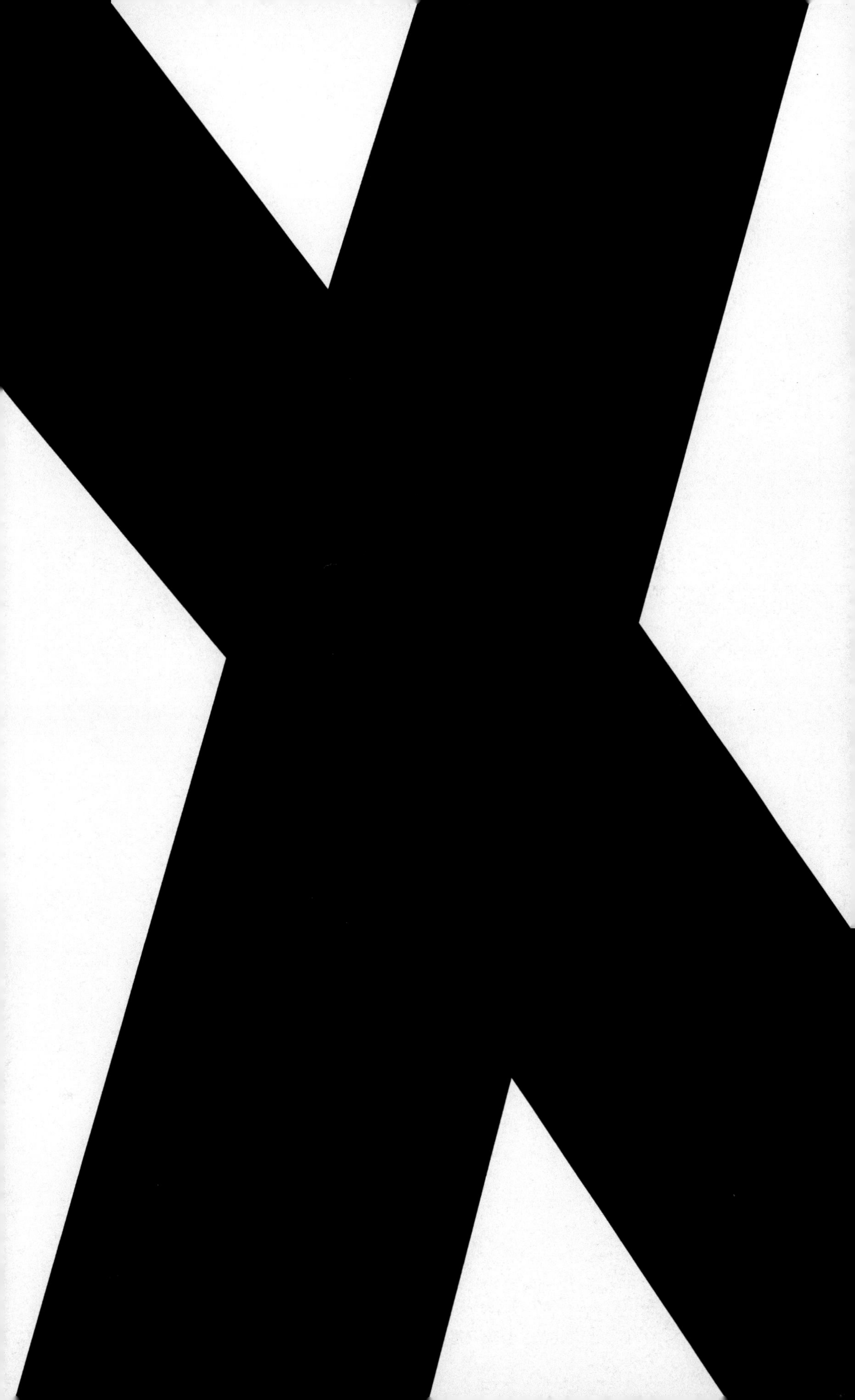

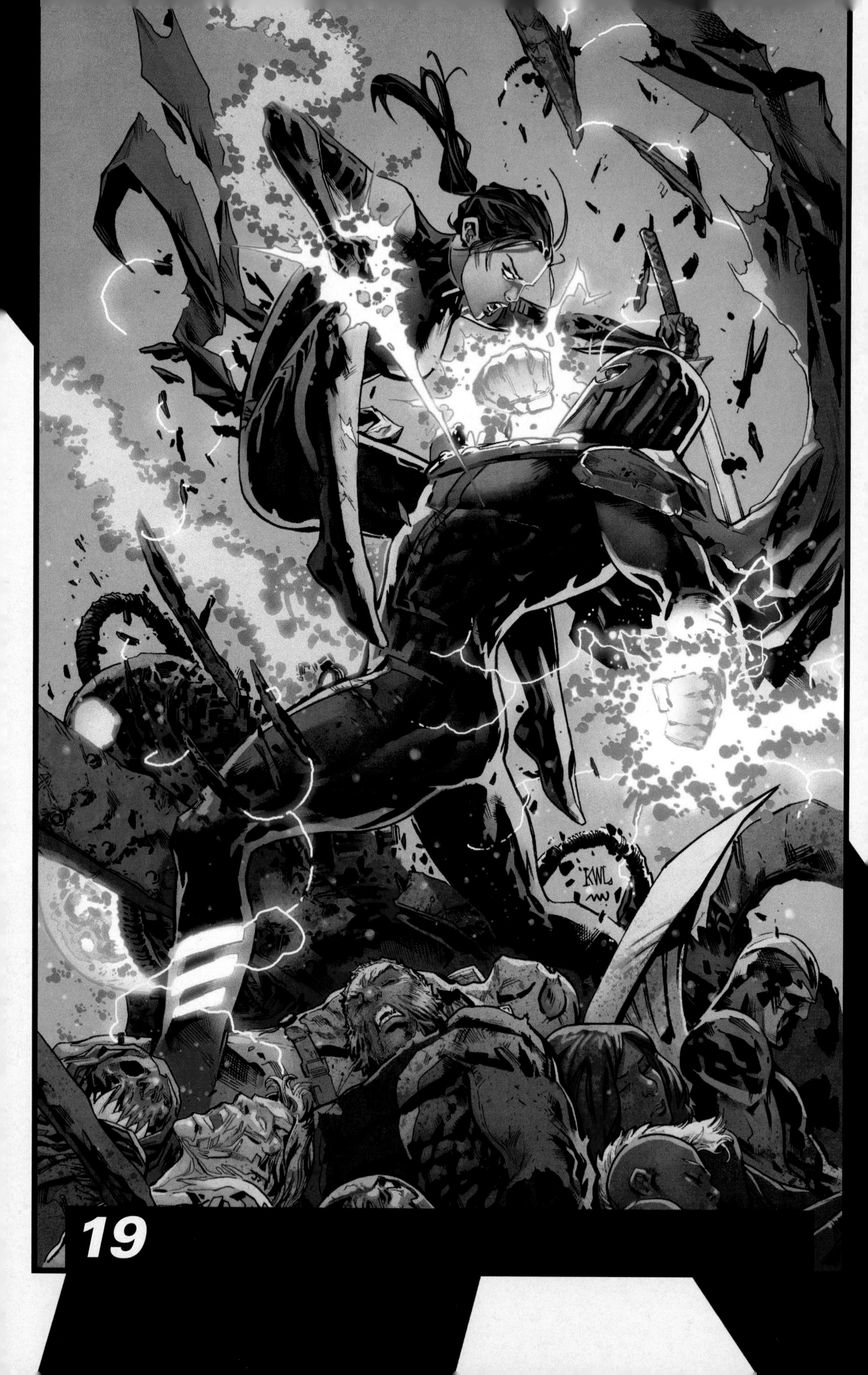

19

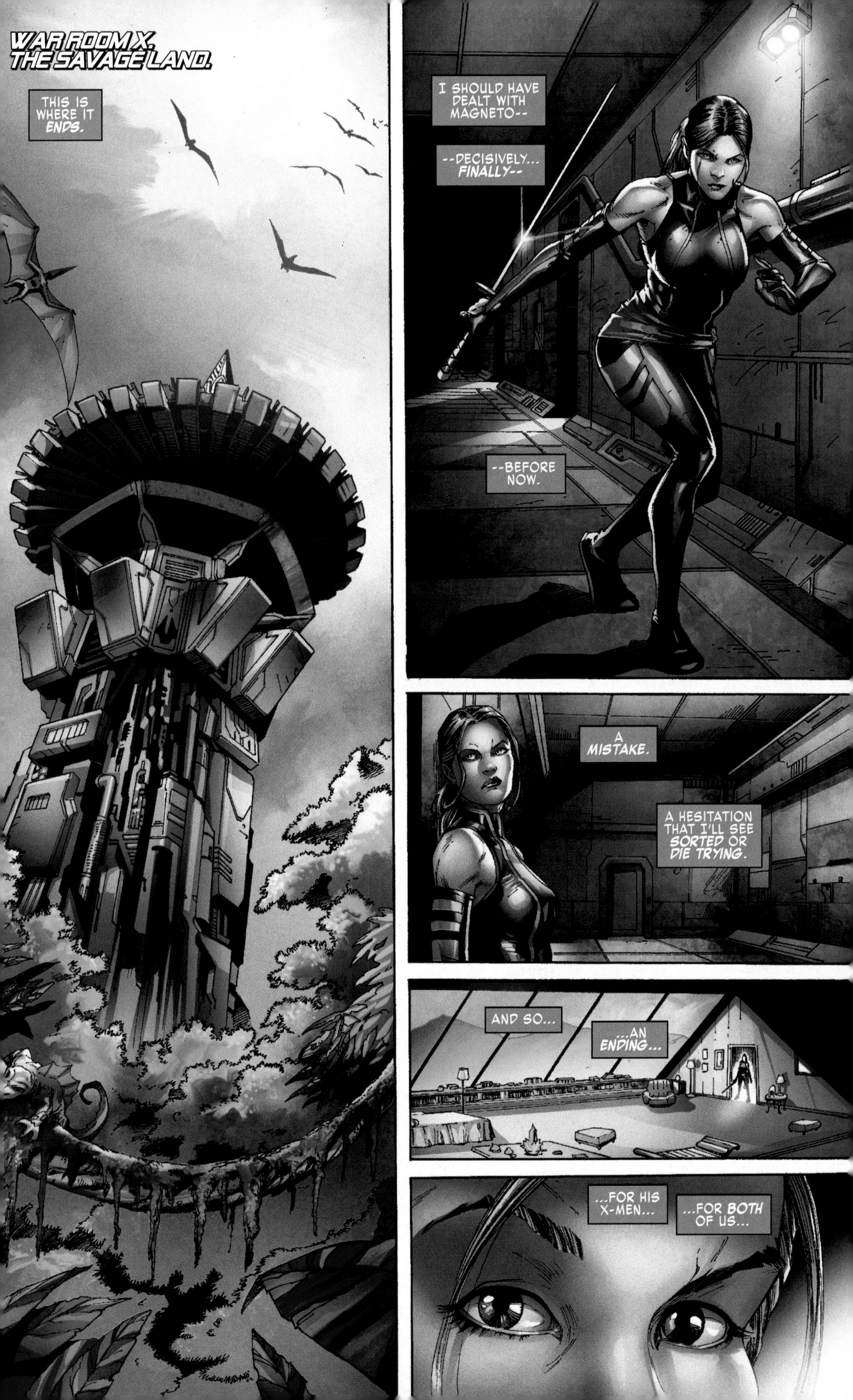
WAR ROOM X.
THE SAVAGE LAND.
THIS IS WHERE IT ENDS.
I SHOULD HAVE DEALT WITH MAGNETO--
--DECISIVELY... FINALLY--
--BEFORE NOW.
A MISTAKE.
A HESITATION THAT I'LL SEE SORTED OR DIE TRYING.
AND SO...
...AN ENDING...
...FOR HIS X-MEN...
...FOR BOTH OF US...

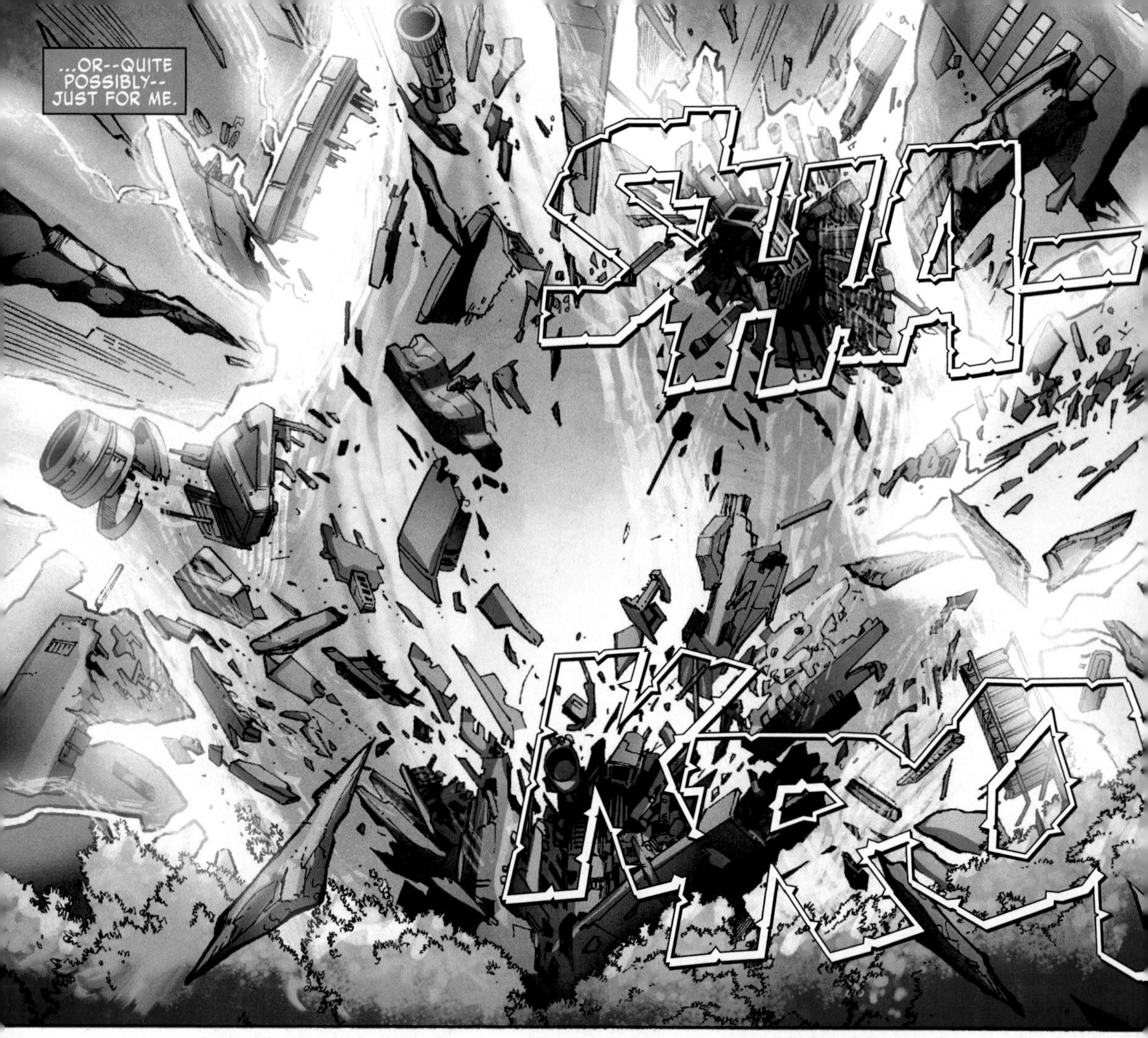
...OR--QUITE POSSIBLY-- JUST FOR ME.

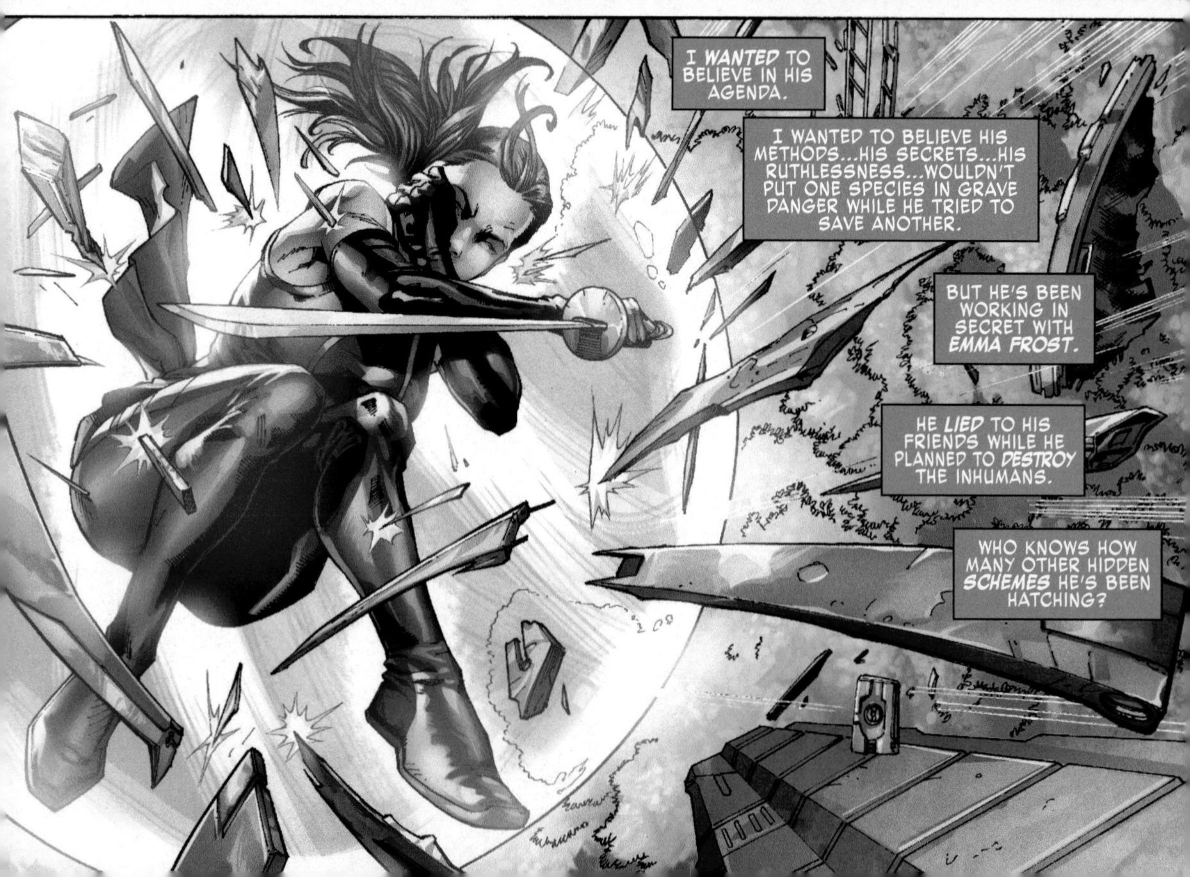
I *WANTED* TO BELIEVE IN HIS AGENDA.
I WANTED TO BELIEVE HIS METHODS...HIS SECRETS...HIS RUTHLESSNESS...WOULDN'T PUT ONE SPECIES IN GRAVE DANGER WHILE HE TRIED TO SAVE ANOTHER.
BUT HE'S BEEN WORKING IN SECRET WITH *EMMA FROST*.
HE *LIED* TO HIS FRIENDS WHILE HE PLANNED TO *DESTROY* THE INHUMANS.
WHO KNOWS HOW MANY OTHER HIDDEN *SCHEMES* HE'S BEEN HATCHING?

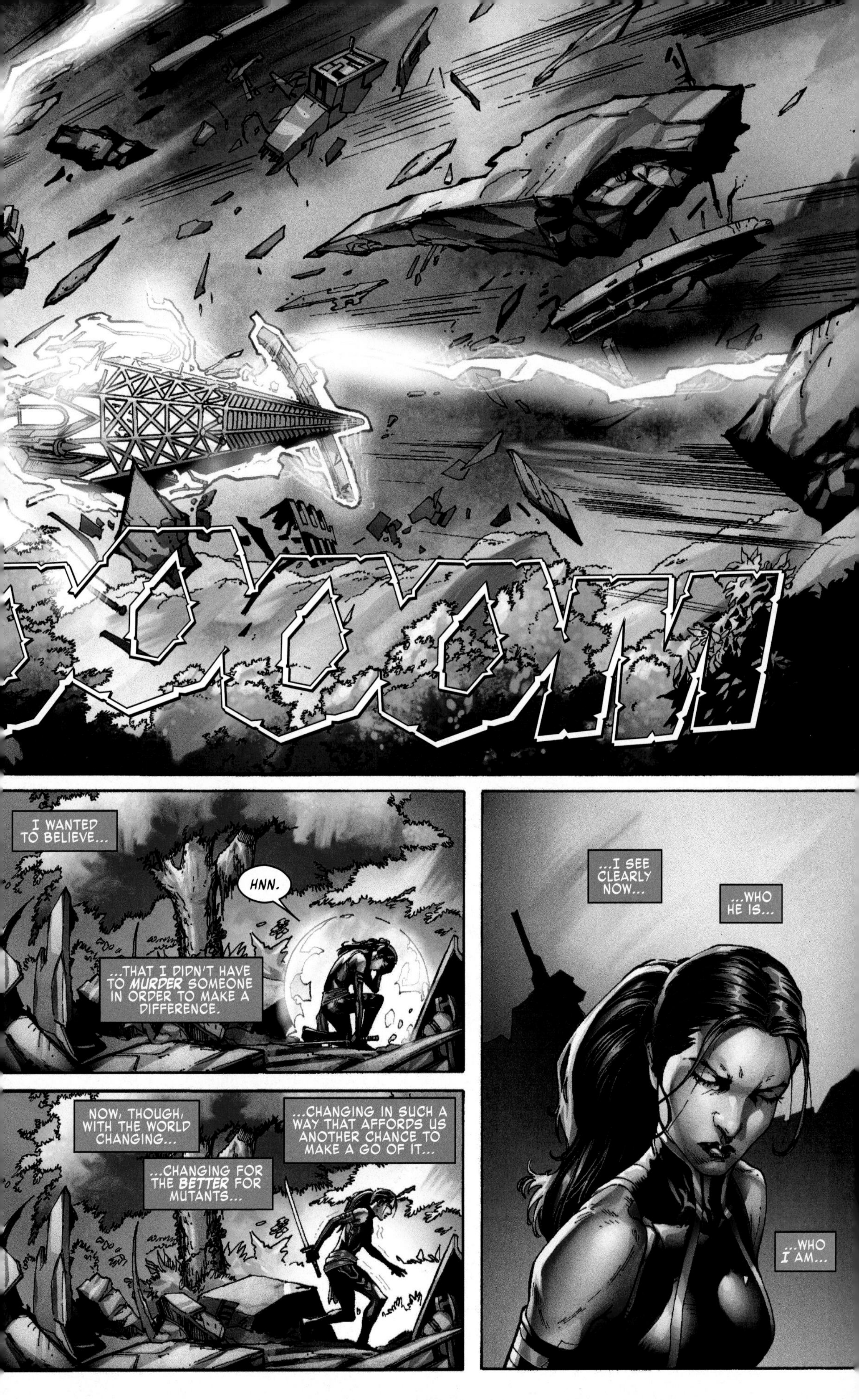
KOOOM
I WANTED TO BELIEVE...
HNN.
...THAT I DIDN'T HAVE TO MURDER SOMEONE IN ORDER TO MAKE A DIFFERENCE.
NOW, THOUGH, WITH THE WORLD CHANGING...
...CHANGING FOR THE BETTER FOR MUTANTS...
...CHANGING IN SUCH A WAY THAT AFFORDS US ANOTHER CHANCE TO MAKE A GO OF IT...
...I SEE CLEARLY NOW...
...WHO HE IS...
...WHO I AM...

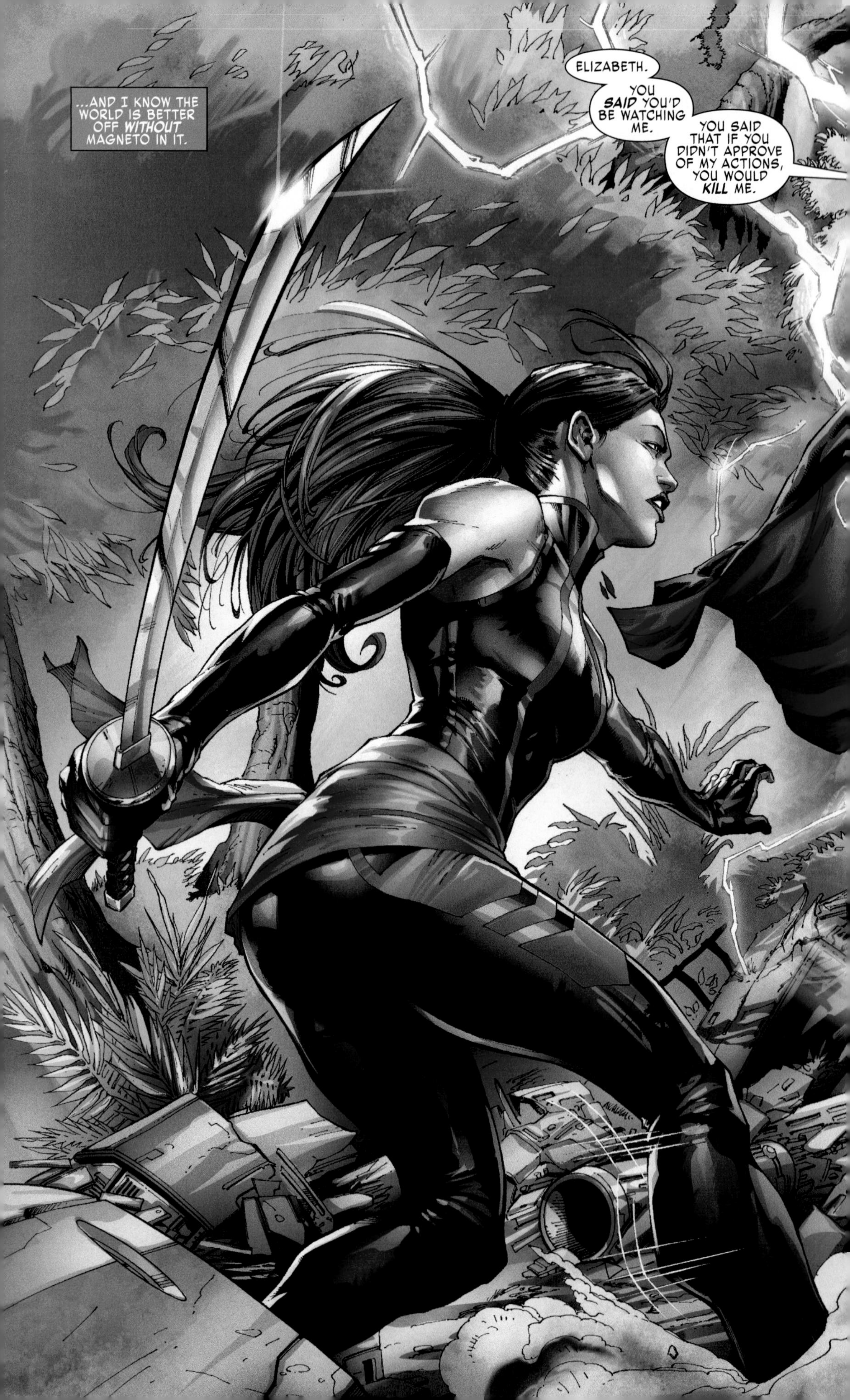
...AND I KNOW THE WORLD IS BETTER OFF WITHOUT MAGNETO IN IT.
ELIZABETH.
YOU SAID YOU'D BE WATCHING ME.
YOU SAID THAT IF YOU DIDN'T APPROVE OF MY ACTIONS, YOU WOULD KILL ME.

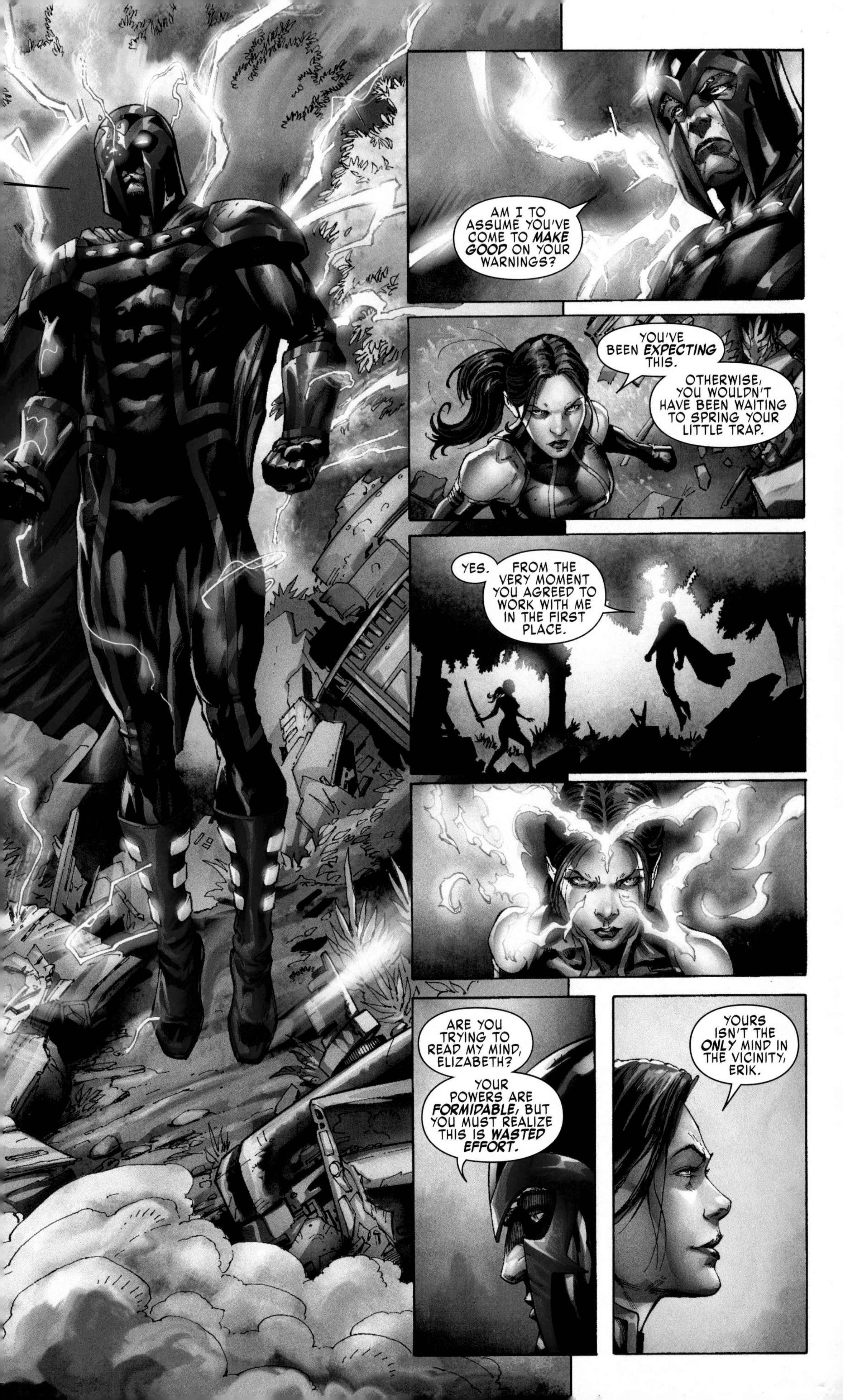
AM I TO ASSUME YOU'VE COME TO MAKE GOOD ON YOUR WARNINGS?
YOU'VE BEEN EXPECTING THIS.
OTHERWISE, YOU WOULDN'T HAVE BEEN WAITING TO SPRING YOUR LITTLE TRAP.
YES.
FROM THE VERY MOMENT YOU AGREED TO WORK WITH ME IN THE FIRST PLACE.
ARE YOU TRYING TO READ MY MIND, ELIZABETH?
YOUR POWERS ARE FORMIDABLE, BUT YOU MUST REALIZE THIS IS WASTED EFFORT.
YOURS ISN'T THE ONLY MIND IN THE VICINITY, ERIK.

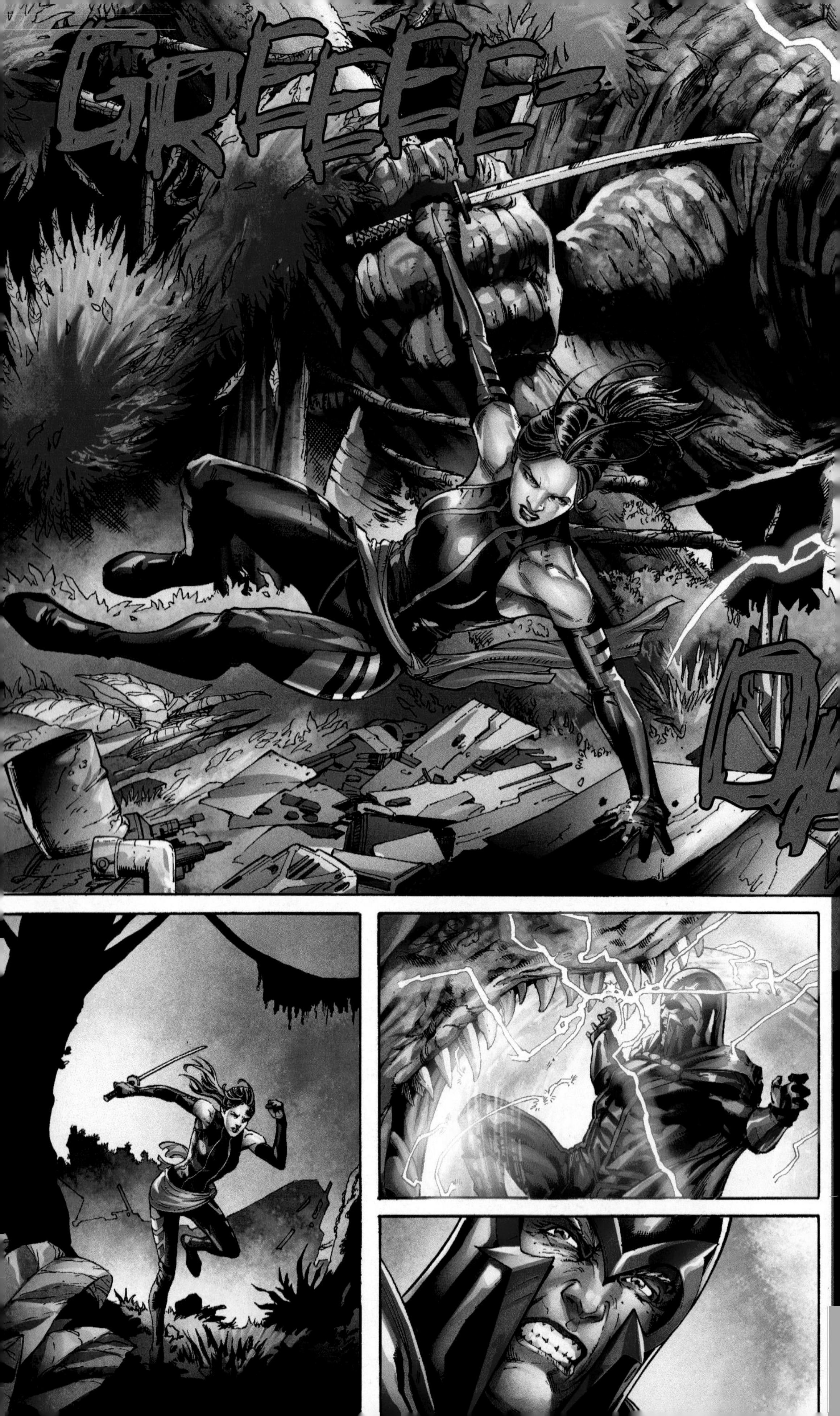
GREEEE-

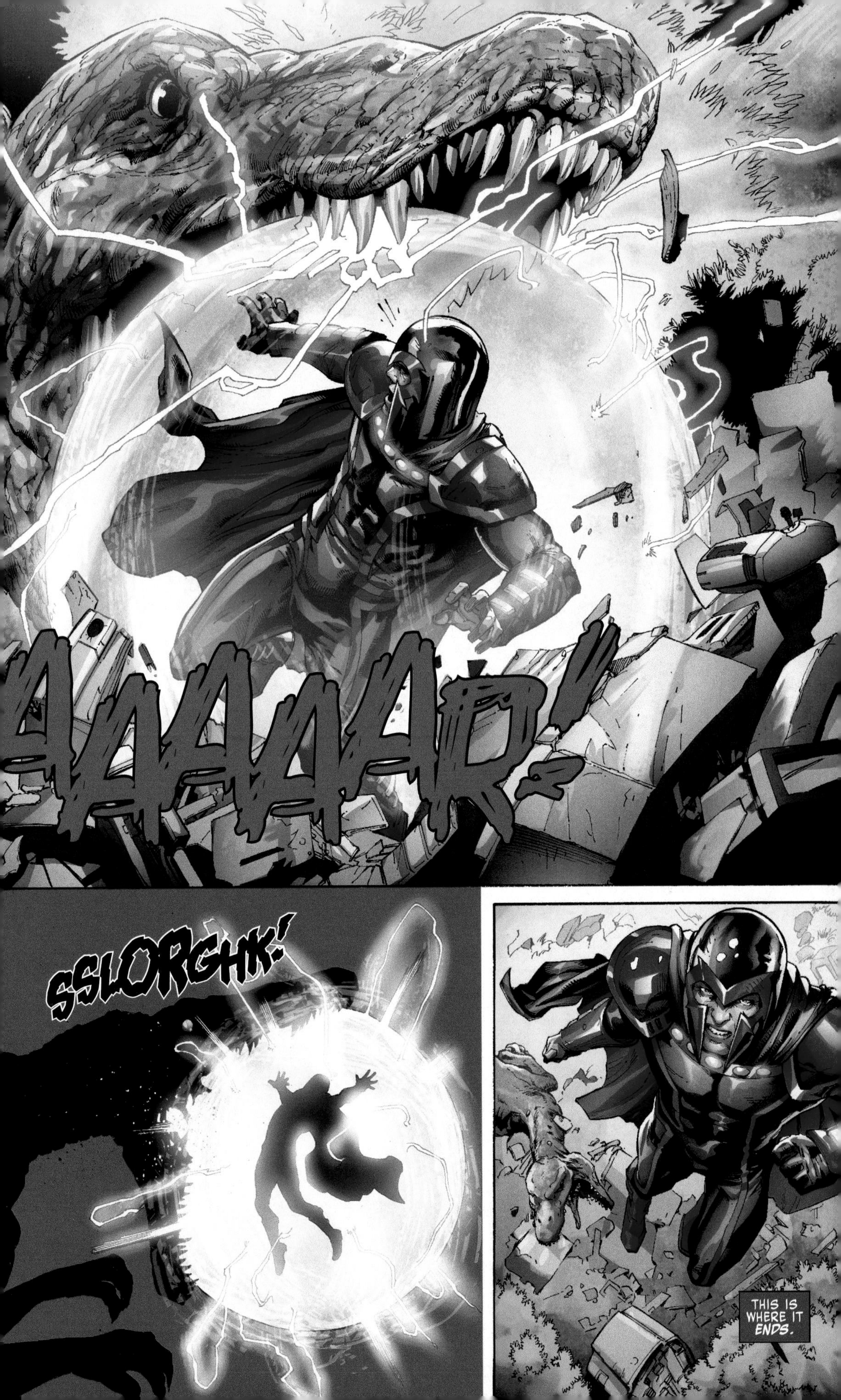
AAAAAAR!
SSLORGHK!
THIS IS WHERE IT ENDS.

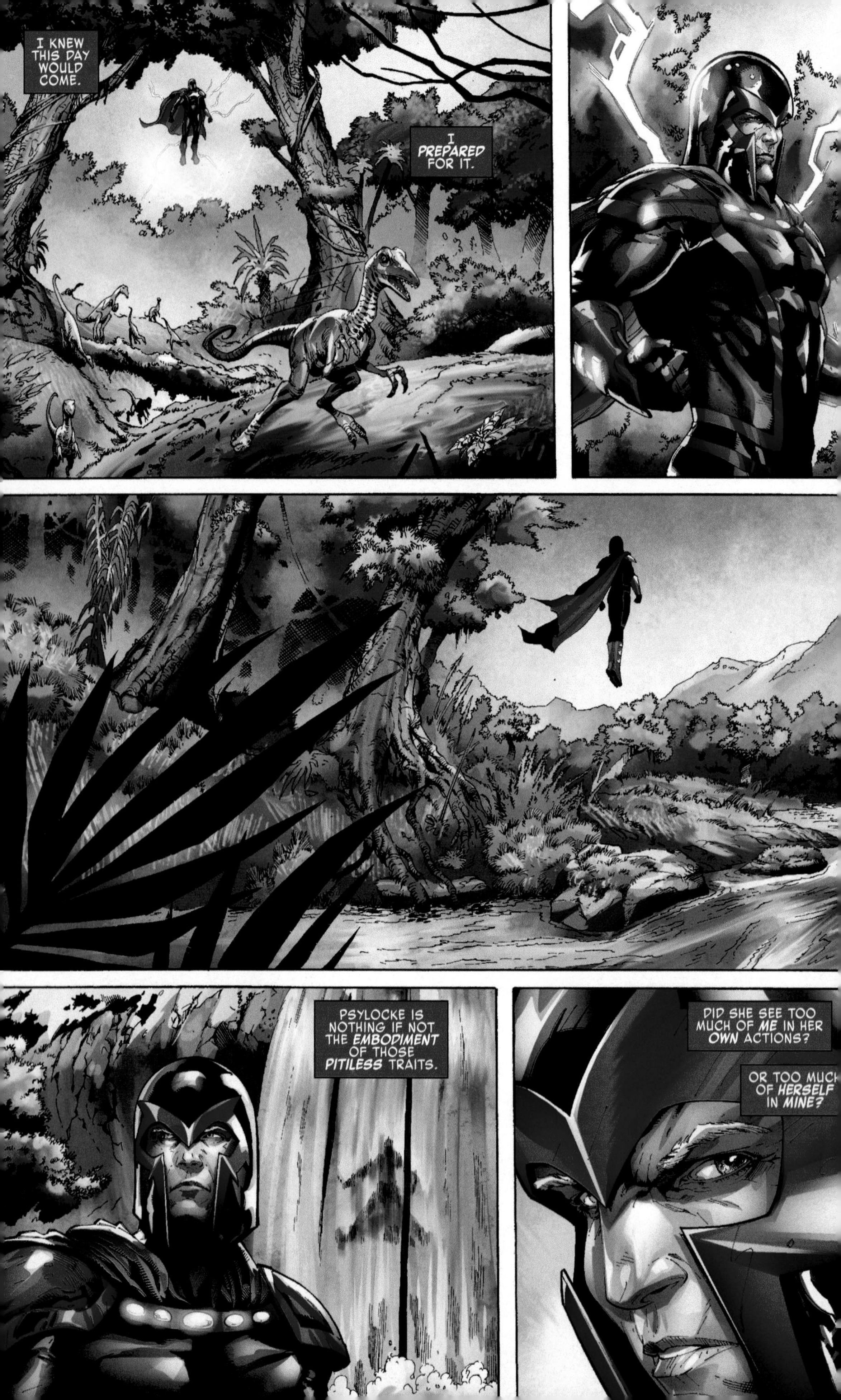
I KNEW THIS DAY WOULD COME.
I PREPARED FOR IT.
PSYLOCKE IS NOTHING IF NOT THE EMBODIMENT OF THOSE PITILESS TRAITS.
DID SHE SEE TOO MUCH OF ME IN HER OWN ACTIONS?
OR TOO MUCH OF HERSELF IN MINE?

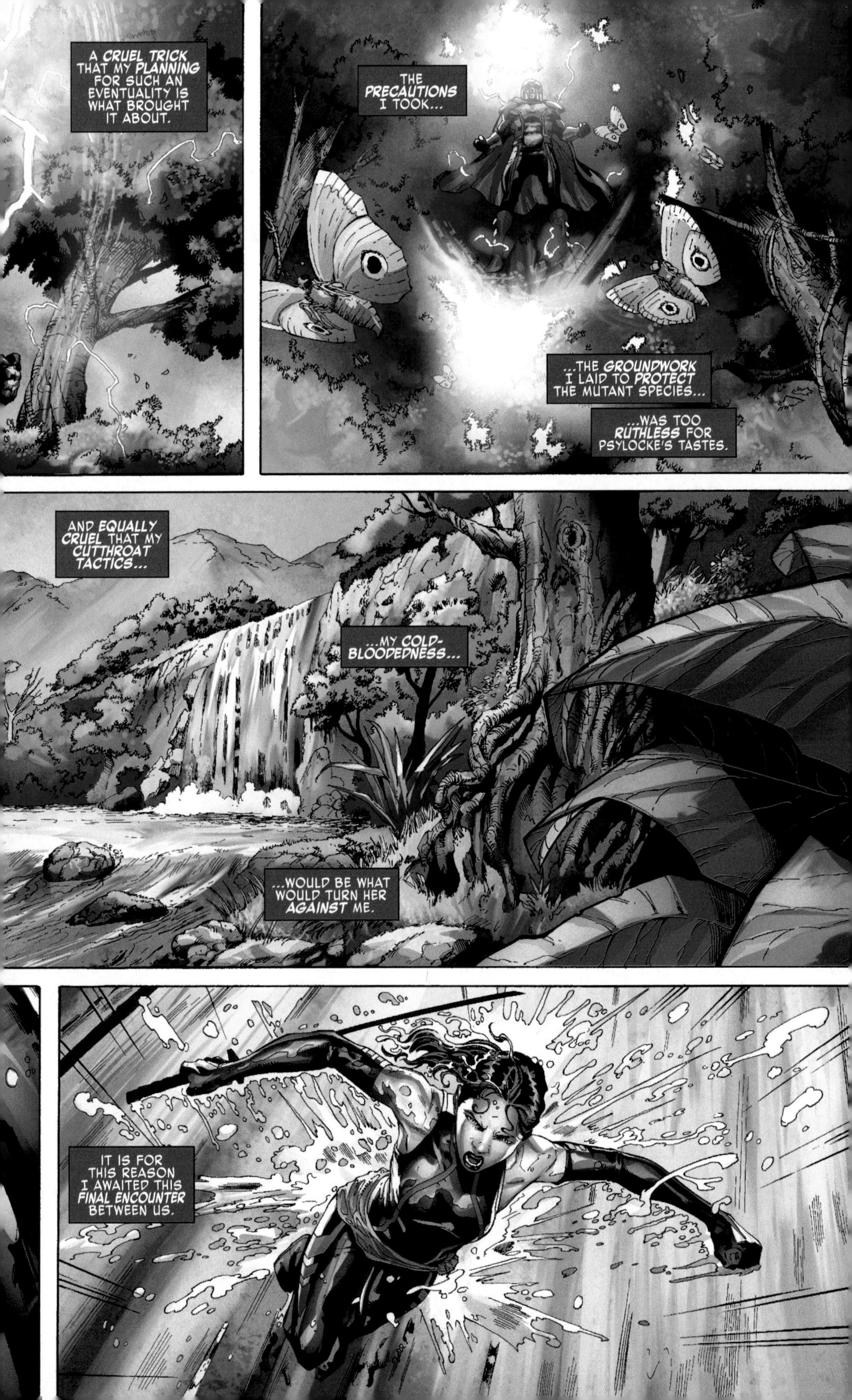
A CRUEL TRICK THAT MY PLANNING FOR SUCH AN EVENTUALITY IS WHAT BROUGHT IT ABOUT.
THE PRECAUTIONS I TOOK...
...THE GROUNDWORK I LAID TO PROTECT THE MUTANT SPECIES...
...WAS TOO RUTHLESS FOR PSYLOCKE'S TASTES.
AND EQUALLY CRUEL THAT MY CUTTHROAT TACTICS...
...MY COLD-BLOODEDNESS...
...WOULD BE WHAT WOULD TURN HER AGAINST ME.
IT IS FOR THIS REASON I AWAITED THIS FINAL ENCOUNTER BETWEEN US.

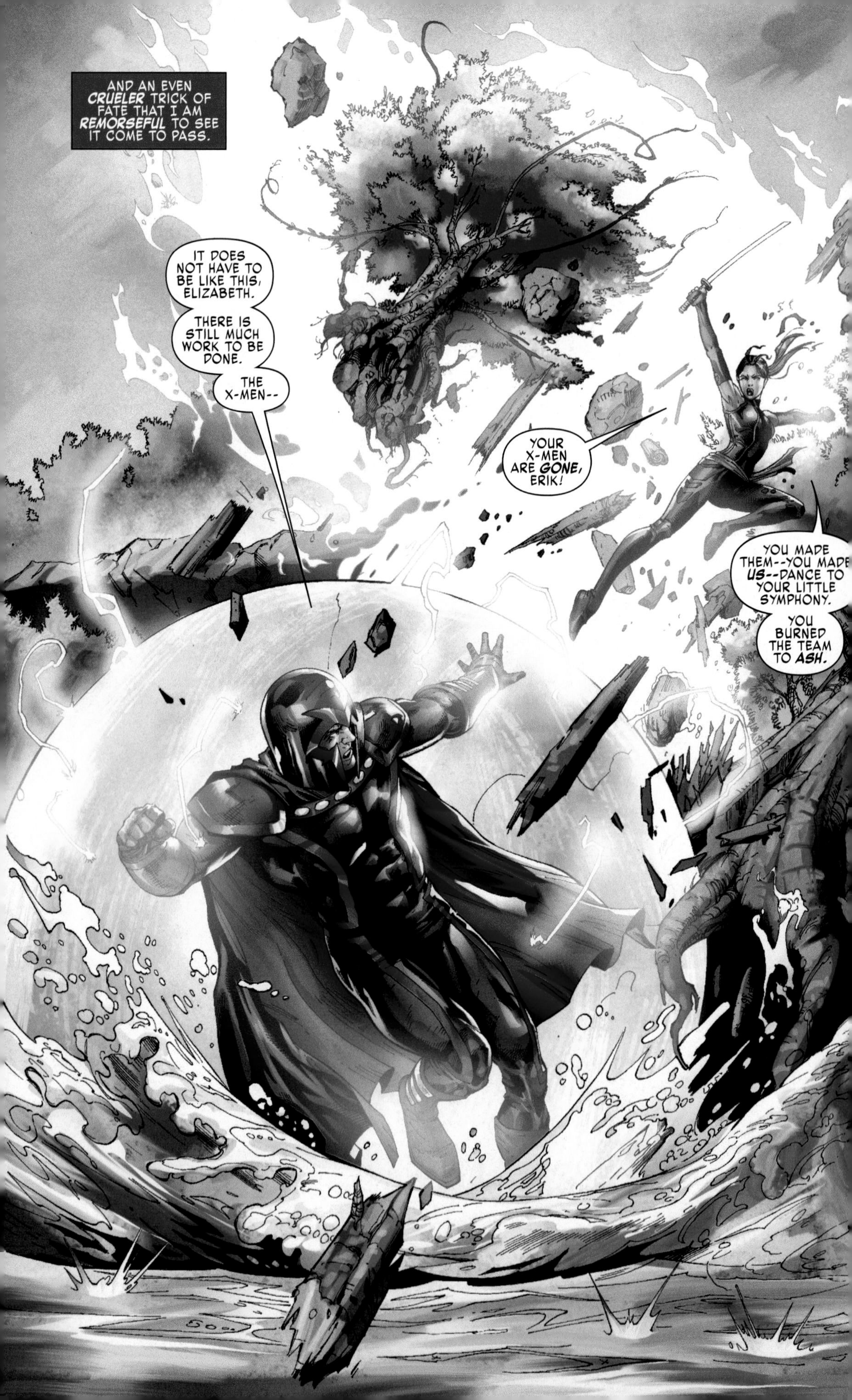
AND AN EVEN CRUELER TRICK OF FATE THAT I AM REMORSEFUL TO SEE IT COME TO PASS.
IT DOES NOT HAVE TO BE LIKE THIS, ELIZABETH.
THERE IS STILL MUCH WORK TO BE DONE.
THE X-MEN--
YOUR X-MEN ARE GONE, ERIK!
YOU MADE THEM--YOU MADE US--DANCE TO YOUR LITTLE SYMPHONY.
YOU BURNED THE TEAM TO ASH.

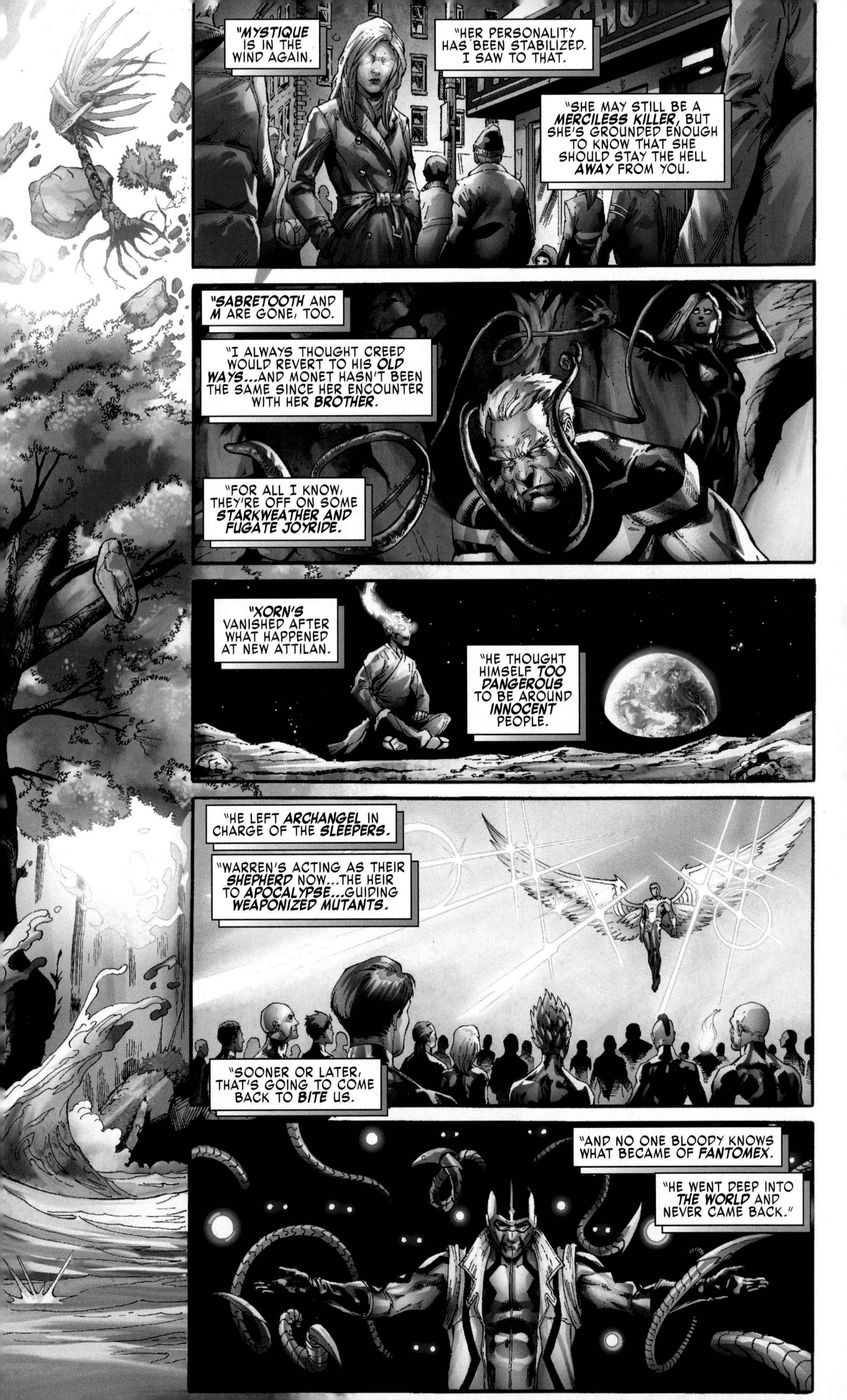

"MYSTIQUE IS IN THE WIND AGAIN.
"HER PERSONALITY HAS BEEN STABILIZED. I SAW TO THAT.
"SHE MAY STILL BE A MERCILESS KILLER, BUT SHE'S GROUNDED ENOUGH TO KNOW THAT SHE SHOULD STAY THE HELL AWAY FROM YOU.
"SABRETOOTH AND M ARE GONE, TOO.
"I ALWAYS THOUGHT CREED WOULD REVERT TO HIS OLD WAYS...AND MONET HASN'T BEEN THE SAME SINCE HER ENCOUNTER WITH HER BROTHER.
"FOR ALL I KNOW, THEY'RE OFF ON SOME STARKWEATHER AND FUGATE JOYRIDE.
"XORN'S VANISHED AFTER WHAT HAPPENED AT NEW ATTILAN.
"HE THOUGHT HIMSELF TOO DANGEROUS TO BE AROUND INNOCENT PEOPLE.
"HE LEFT ARCHANGEL IN CHARGE OF THE SLEEPERS.
"WARREN'S ACTING AS THEIR SHEPHERD NOW...THE HEIR TO APOCALYPSE...GUIDING WEAPONIZED MUTANTS.
"SOONER OR LATER, THAT'S GOING TO COME BACK TO BITE US.
"AND NO ONE BLOODY KNOWS WHAT BECAME OF FANTOMEX.
"HE WENT DEEP INTO THE WORLD AND NEVER CAME BACK."

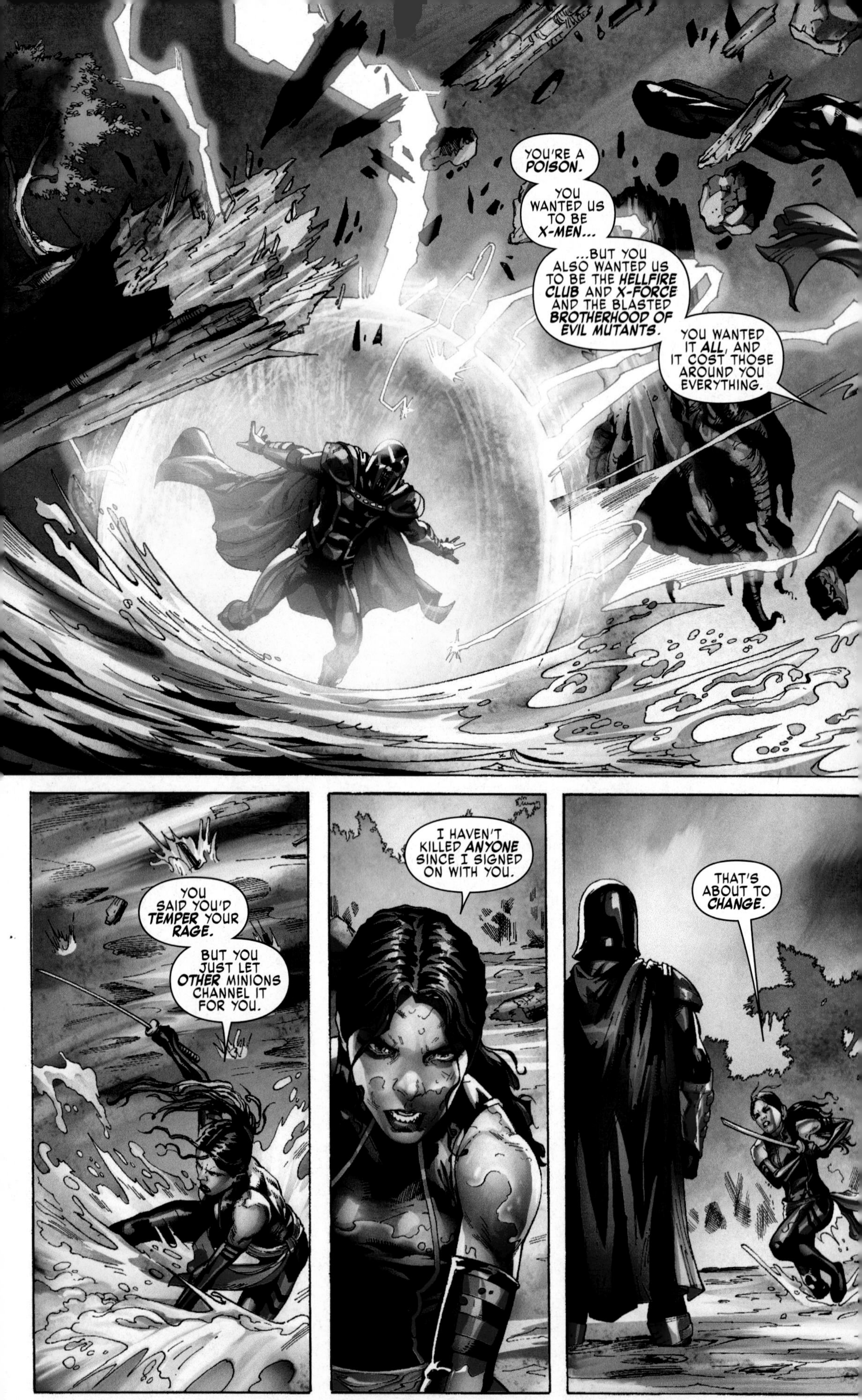
YOU'RE A POISON.
YOU WANTED US TO BE X-MEN...
...BUT YOU ALSO WANTED US TO BE THE HELLFIRE CLUB AND X-FORCE AND THE BLASTED BROTHERHOOD OF EVIL MUTANTS.
YOU WANTED IT ALL, AND IT COST THOSE AROUND YOU EVERYTHING.
YOU SAID YOU'D TEMPER YOUR RAGE.
BUT YOU JUST LET OTHER MINIONS CHANNEL IT FOR YOU.
I HAVEN'T KILLED ANYONE SINCE I SIGNED ON WITH YOU.
THAT'S ABOUT TO CHANGE.

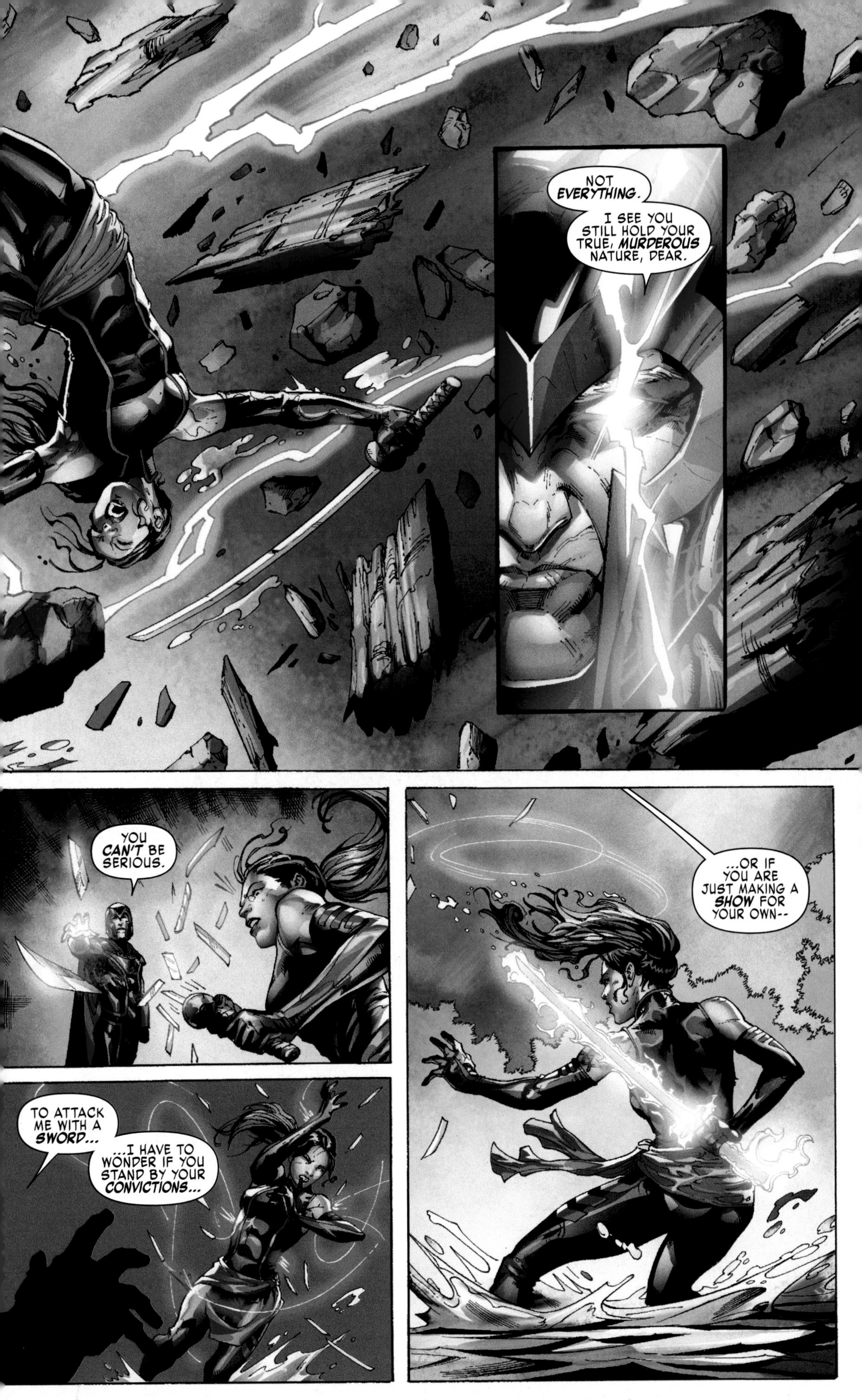
NOT EVERYTHING.
I SEE YOU STILL HOLD YOUR TRUE, MURDEROUS NATURE, DEAR.
YOU CAN'T BE SERIOUS.
TO ATTACK ME WITH A SWORD...
...I HAVE TO WONDER IF YOU STAND BY YOUR CONVICTIONS...
...OR IF YOU ARE JUST MAKING A SHOW FOR YOUR OWN--

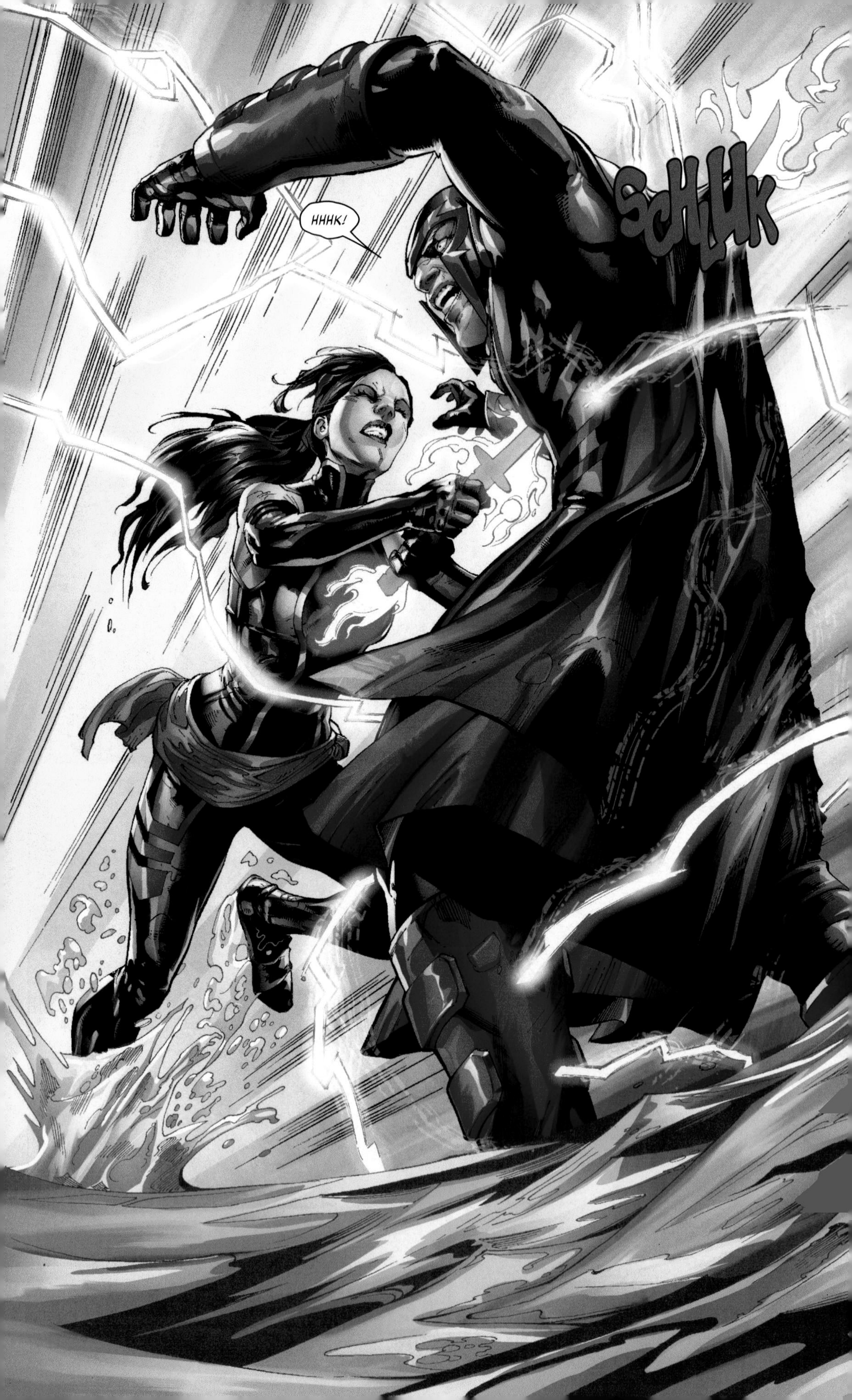
HHHK!
SCHLUK

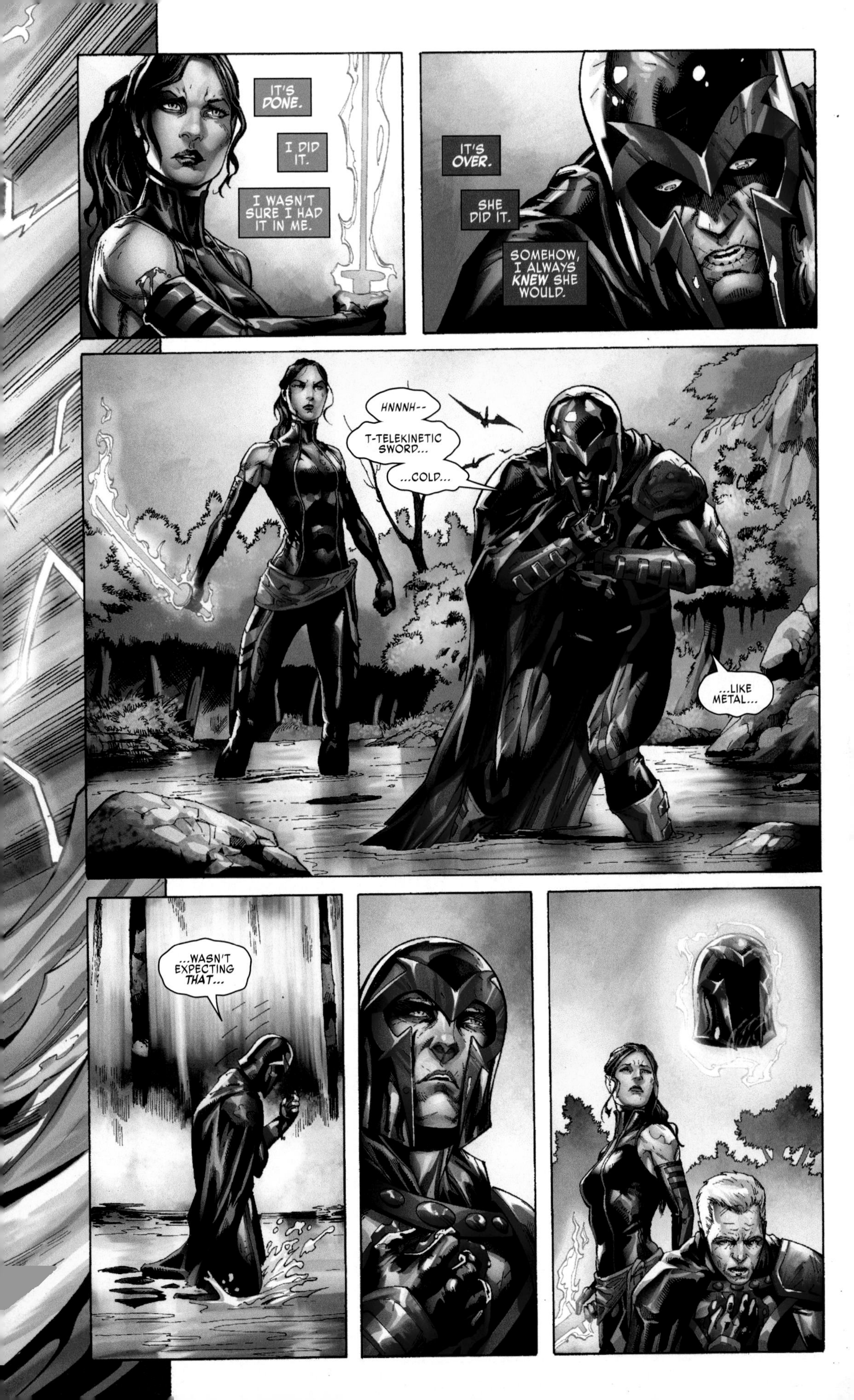
IT'S DONE.
I DID IT.
I WASN'T SURE I HAD IT IN ME.
IT'S OVER.
SHE DID IT.
SOMEHOW, I ALWAYS KNEW SHE WOULD.
HNNNH--
T-TELEKINETIC SWORD...
...COLD...
...LIKE METAL...
...WASN'T EXPECTING THAT...

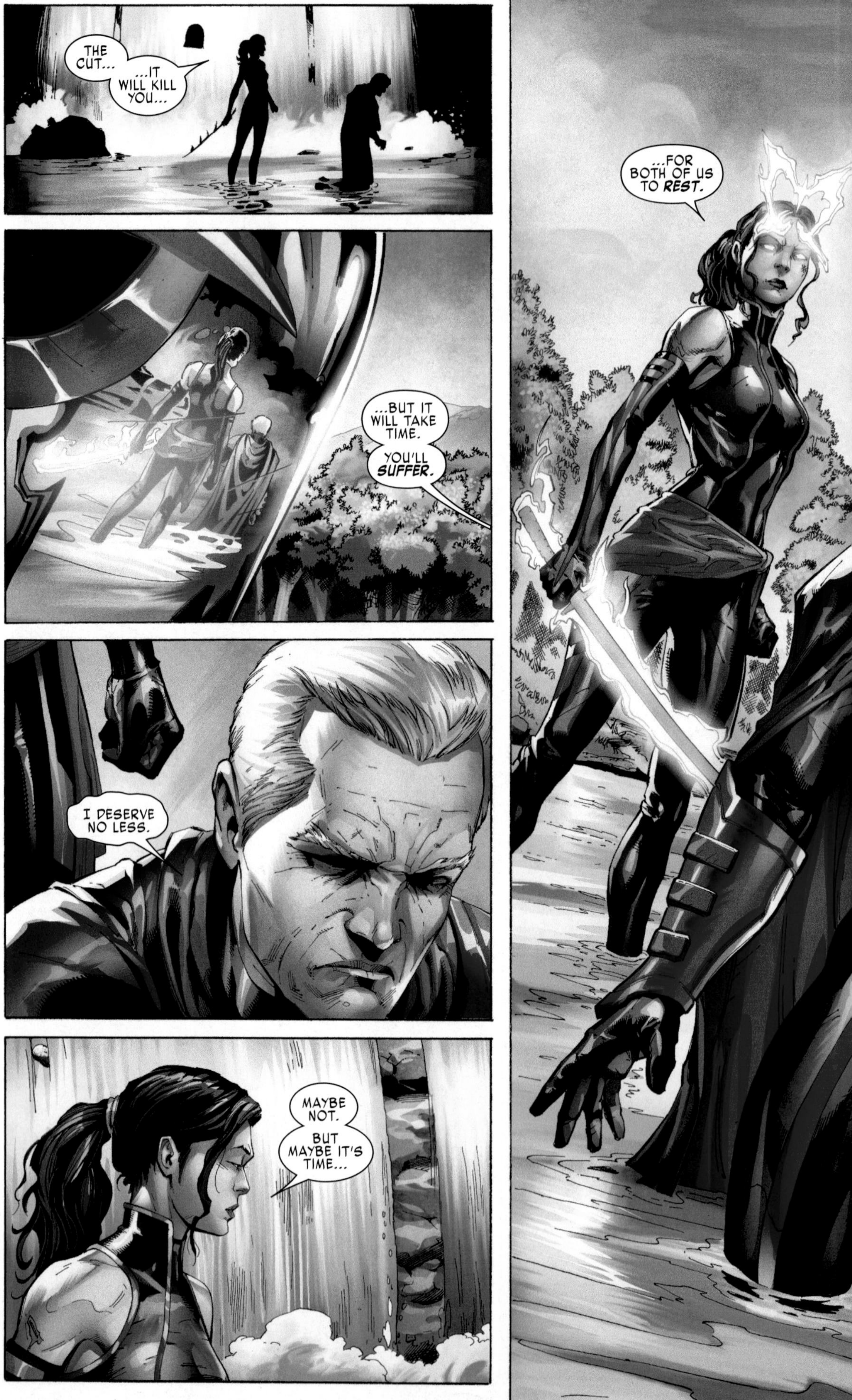
THE CUT...
...IT WILL KILL YOU...
...BUT IT WILL TAKE TIME.
YOU'LL SUFFER.
I DESERVE NO LESS.
MAYBE NOT.
BUT MAYBE IT'S TIME...
...FOR BOTH OF US TO REST.

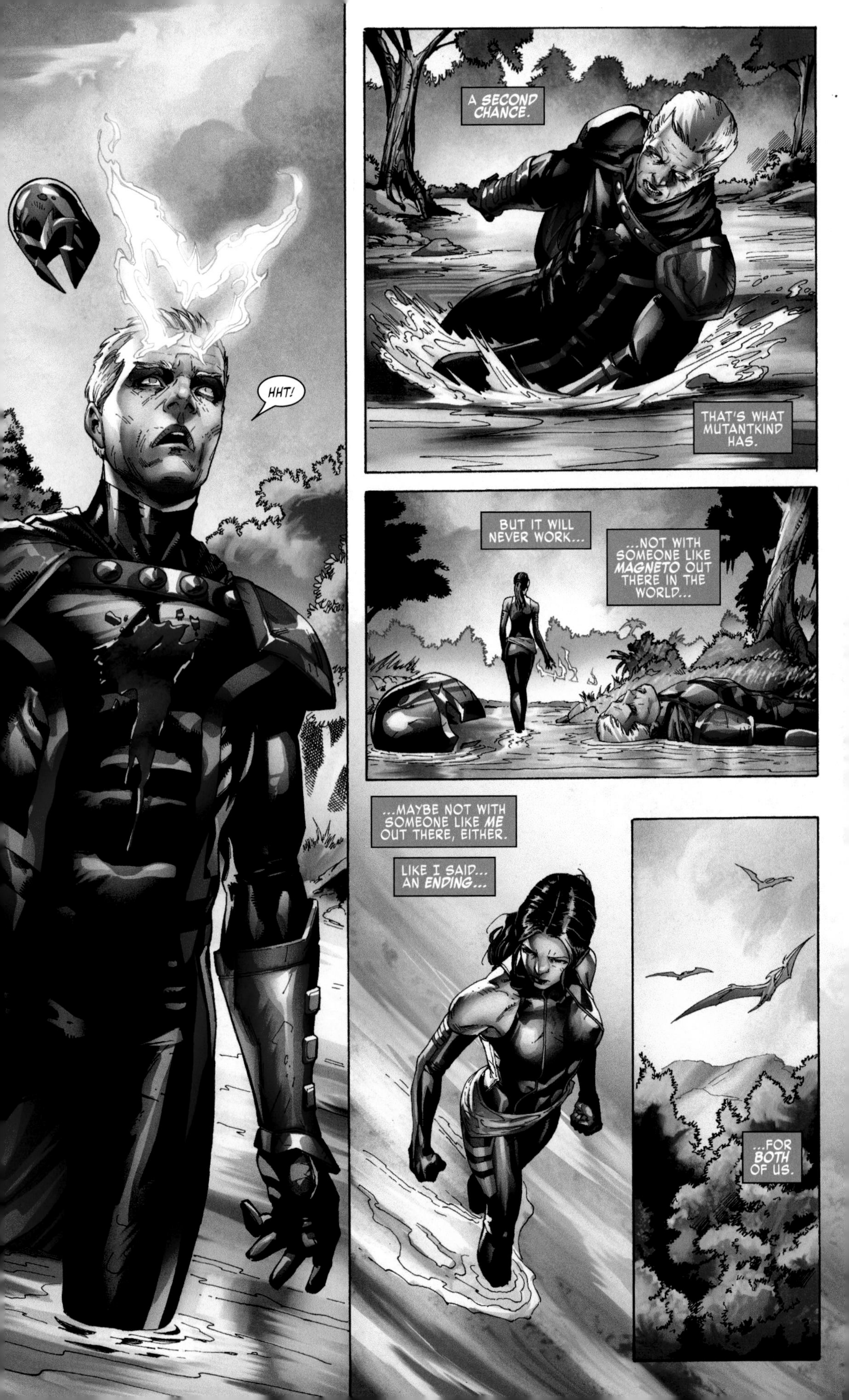
HHT!
A SECOND CHANCE.
THAT'S WHAT MUTANTKIND HAS.
BUT IT WILL NEVER WORK...
...NOT WITH SOMEONE LIKE MAGNETO OUT THERE IN THE WORLD...
...MAYBE NOT WITH SOMEONE LIKE ME OUT THERE, EITHER.
LIKE I SAID... AN ENDING...
...FOR BOTH OF US.

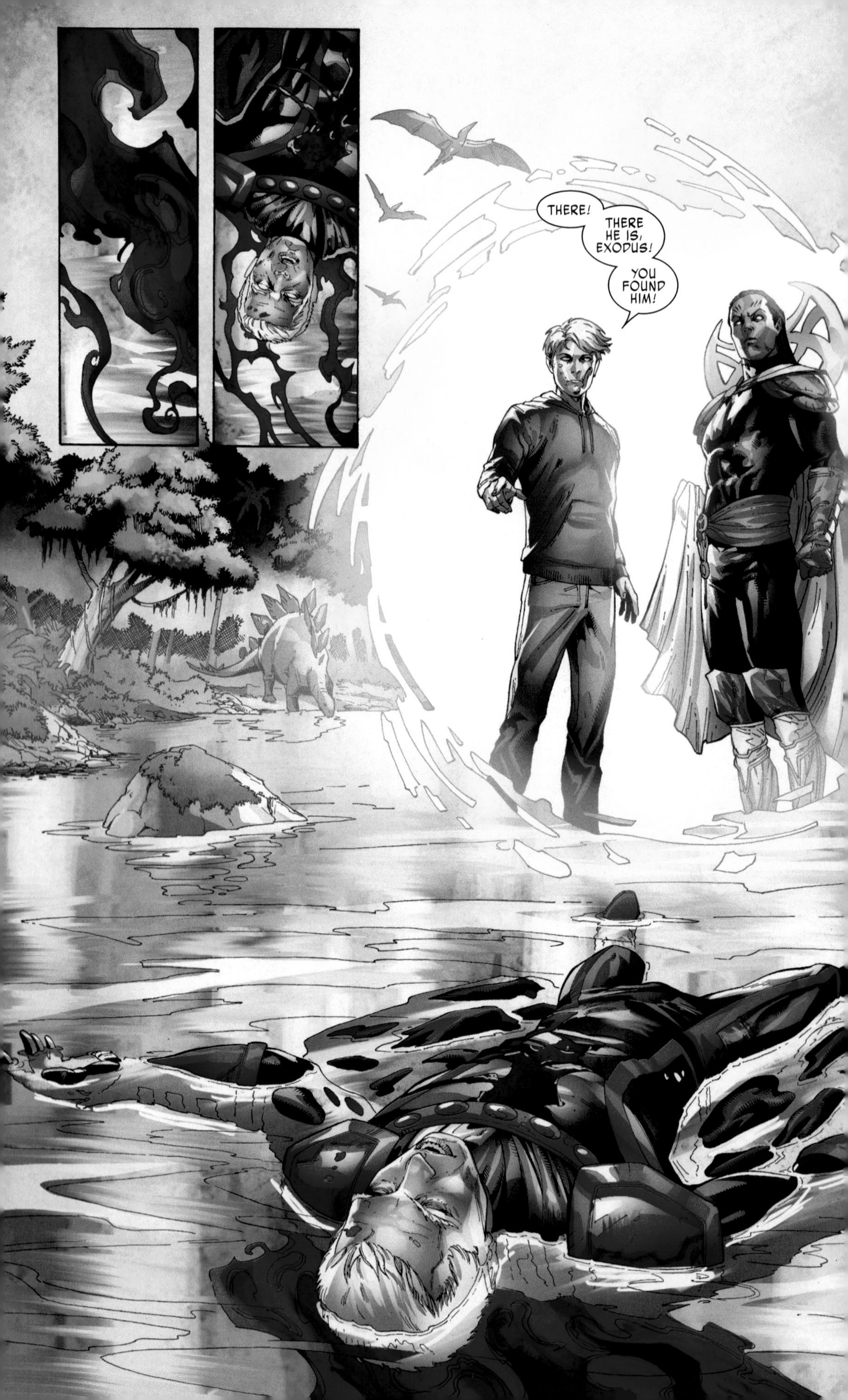
THERE!
THERE HE IS, EXODUS!
YOU FOUND HIM!

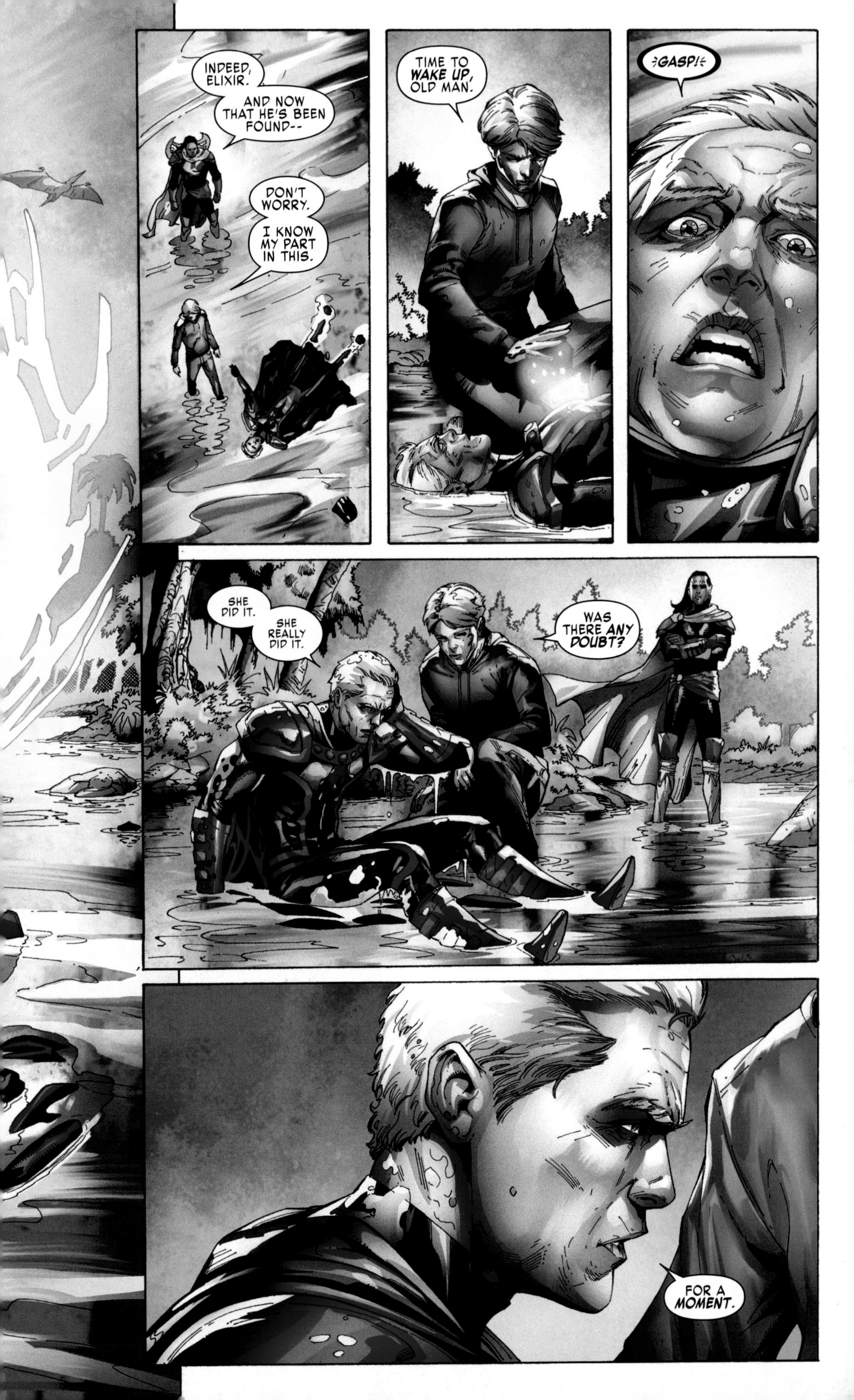
INDEED, ELIXIR.
AND NOW THAT HE'S BEEN FOUND--
DON'T WORRY.
I KNOW MY PART IN THIS.
TIME TO WAKE UP, OLD MAN.
GASP!
SHE DID IT.
SHE REALLY DID IT.
WAS THERE ANY DOUBT?
FOR A MOMENT.

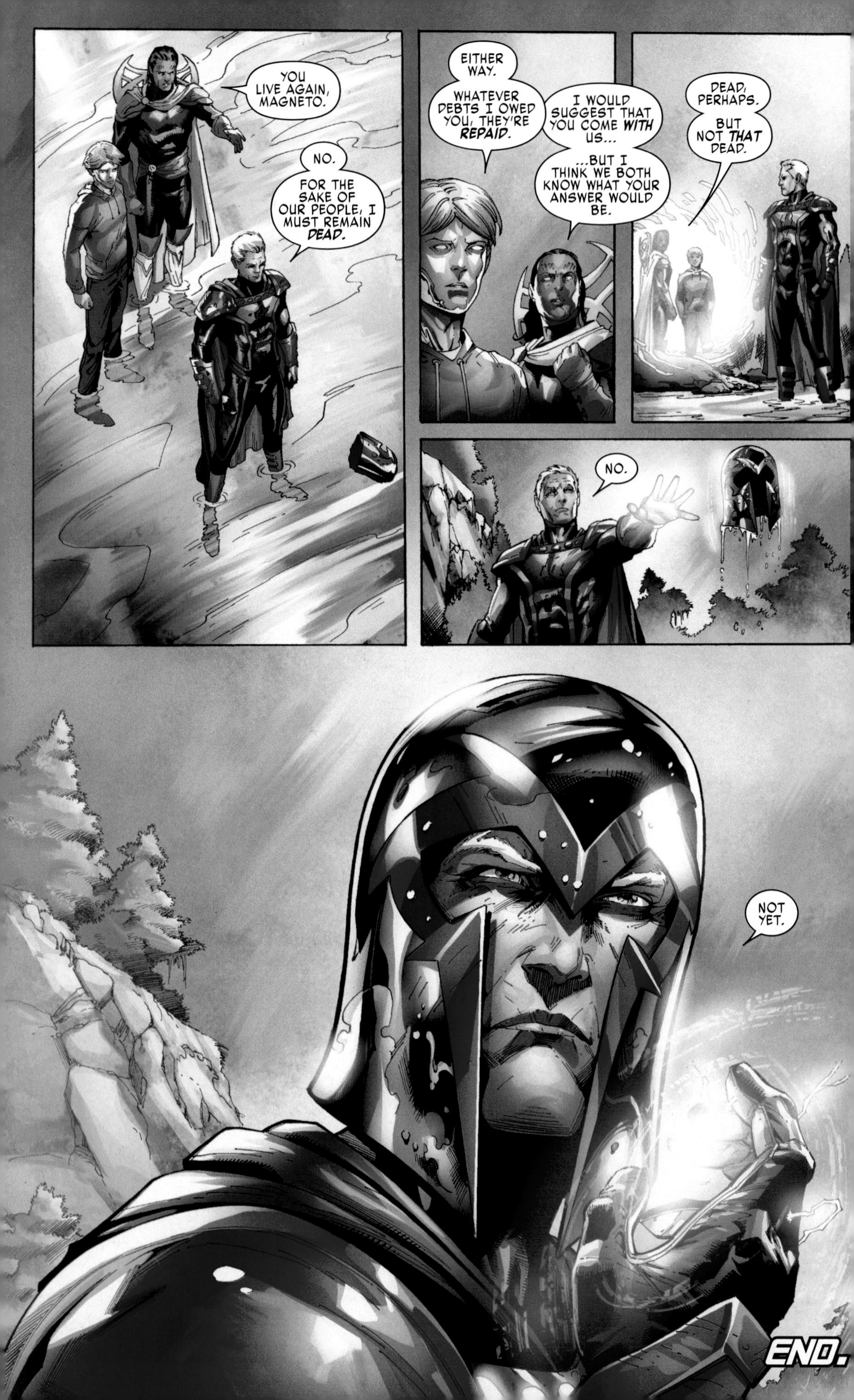
YOU LIVE AGAIN, MAGNETO.
NO.
FOR THE SAKE OF OUR PEOPLE, I MUST REMAIN DEAD.
EITHER WAY.
WHATEVER DEBTS I OWED YOU, THEY'RE REPAID.
I WOULD SUGGEST THAT YOU COME WITH US...
...BUT I THINK WE BOTH KNOW WHAT YOUR ANSWER WOULD BE.
DEAD, PERHAPS.
BUT NOT THAT DEAD.
NO.
NOT YET.
END.

ANNUAL 1

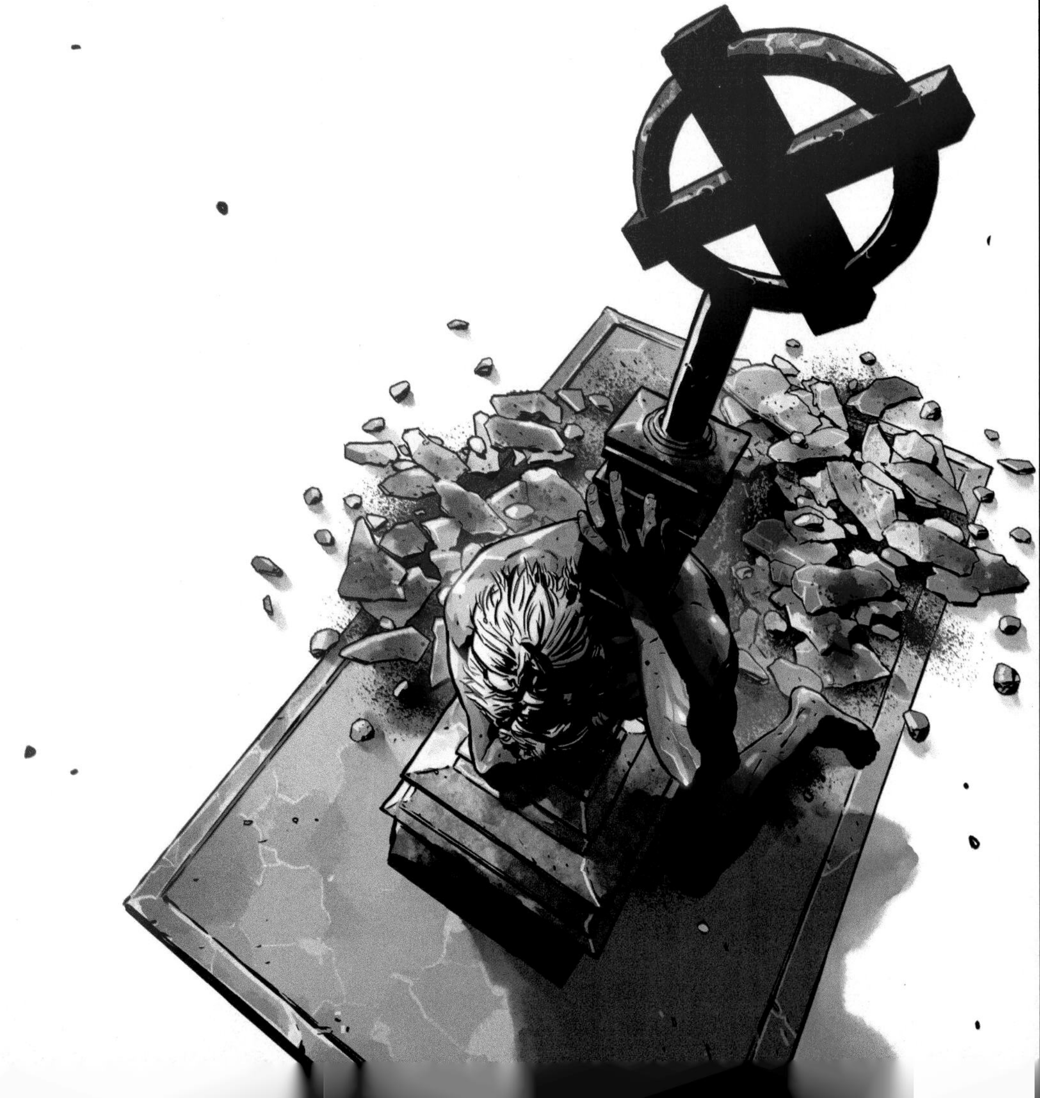

TERRIGEN MISTS CIRCLE THE GLOBE, WHITTLING DOWN MUTANTKIND'S NUMBERS AND SUPPRESSING ANY NEW MUTANT MANIFESTATIONS. BELIEVING BIGGER THREATS REQUIRE MORE THREATENING X-MEN, MAGNETO IS JOINED BY A TEAM OF THE MOST RUTHLESS MUTANTS ALIVE TO STEM THE THREAT OF EXTINCTION...

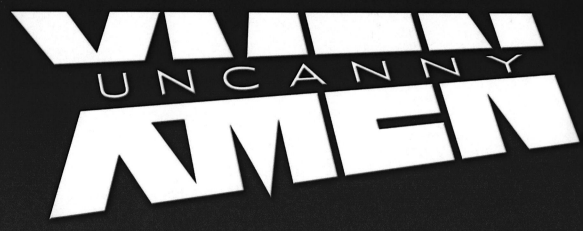

UNCANNY X-MEN

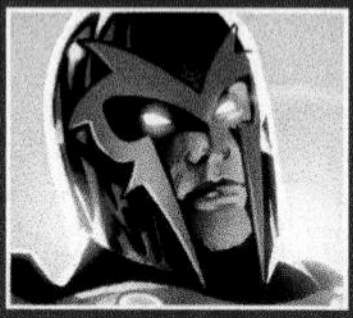

MAGNETO

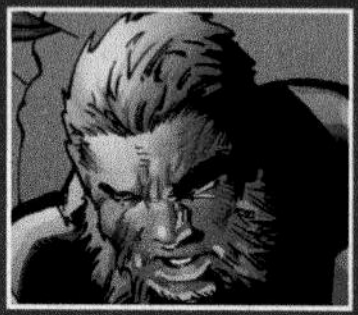

SABRETOOTH

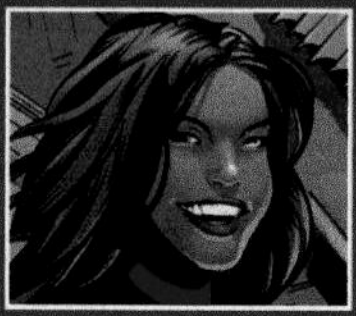

M

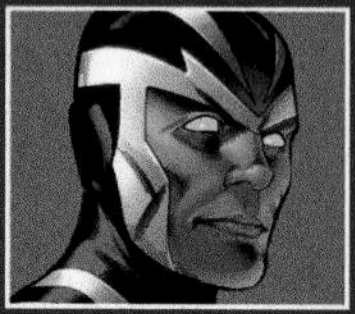

ARCHANGEL

WHILE INVESTIGATING A SERIES OF KILLINGS INVOLVING MUTANT HEALERS, THE X-MEN DISCOVER THAT THE DARK RIDERS ARE RESPONSIBLE — HUNTING DOWN ANY MUTANTS WHO MIGHT BE ABLE TO KEEP OTHERS FROM SUCCUMBING TO THE TERRIGEN MISTS. THOUGH THE X-MEN TRIED TO PROTECT POWERFUL MUTANT HEALER JOSHUA FOLEY, A.K.A. ELIXIR, FROM THIS SAVAGE CRUSADE, HE WAS BRUTALLY MURDERED.

PSYLOCKE RECENTLY LEFT THE TEAM AFTER VOICING DISSATISFACTION AT MAGNETO'S ABILITY TO LEAD.

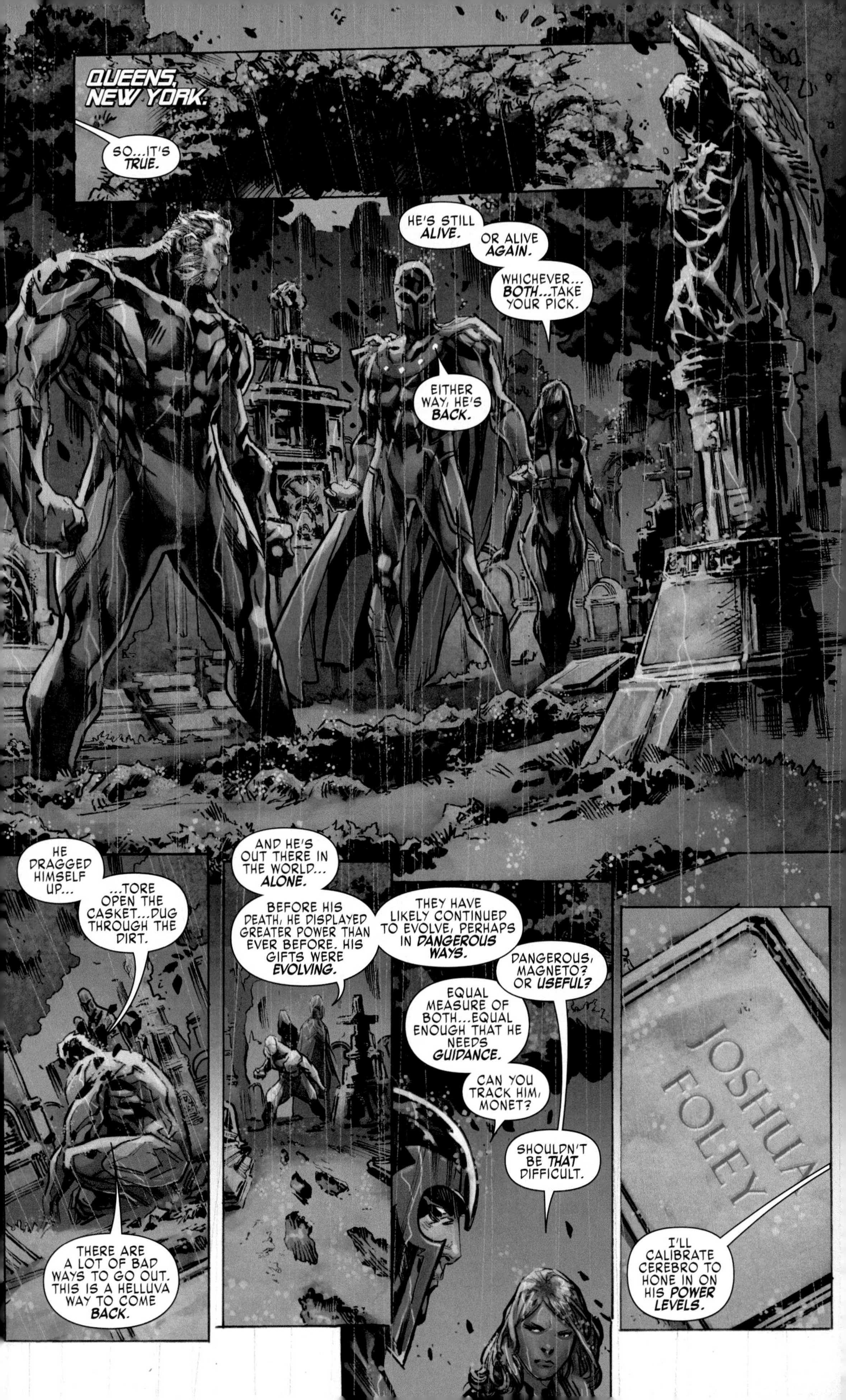
QUEENS, NEW YORK.
SO...IT'S TRUE.
HE'S STILL ALIVE.
OR ALIVE AGAIN.
WHICHEVER... BOTH...TAKE YOUR PICK.
EITHER WAY, HE'S BACK.
HE DRAGGED HIMSELF UP...
...TORE OPEN THE CASKET...DUG THROUGH THE DIRT.
THERE ARE A LOT OF BAD WAYS TO GO OUT. THIS IS A HELLUVA WAY TO COME BACK.
AND HE'S OUT THERE IN THE WORLD... ALONE.
BEFORE HIS DEATH, HE DISPLAYED GREATER POWER THAN EVER BEFORE. HIS GIFTS WERE EVOLVING.
THEY HAVE LIKELY CONTINUED TO EVOLVE, PERHAPS IN DANGEROUS WAYS.
DANGEROUS, MAGNETO? OR USEFUL?
EQUAL MEASURE OF BOTH...EQUAL ENOUGH THAT HE NEEDS GUIDANCE.
CAN YOU TRACK HIM, MONET?
SHOULDN'T BE THAT DIFFICULT.
JOSHUA FOLEY
I'LL CALIBRATE CEREBRO TO HONE IN ON HIS POWER LEVELS.

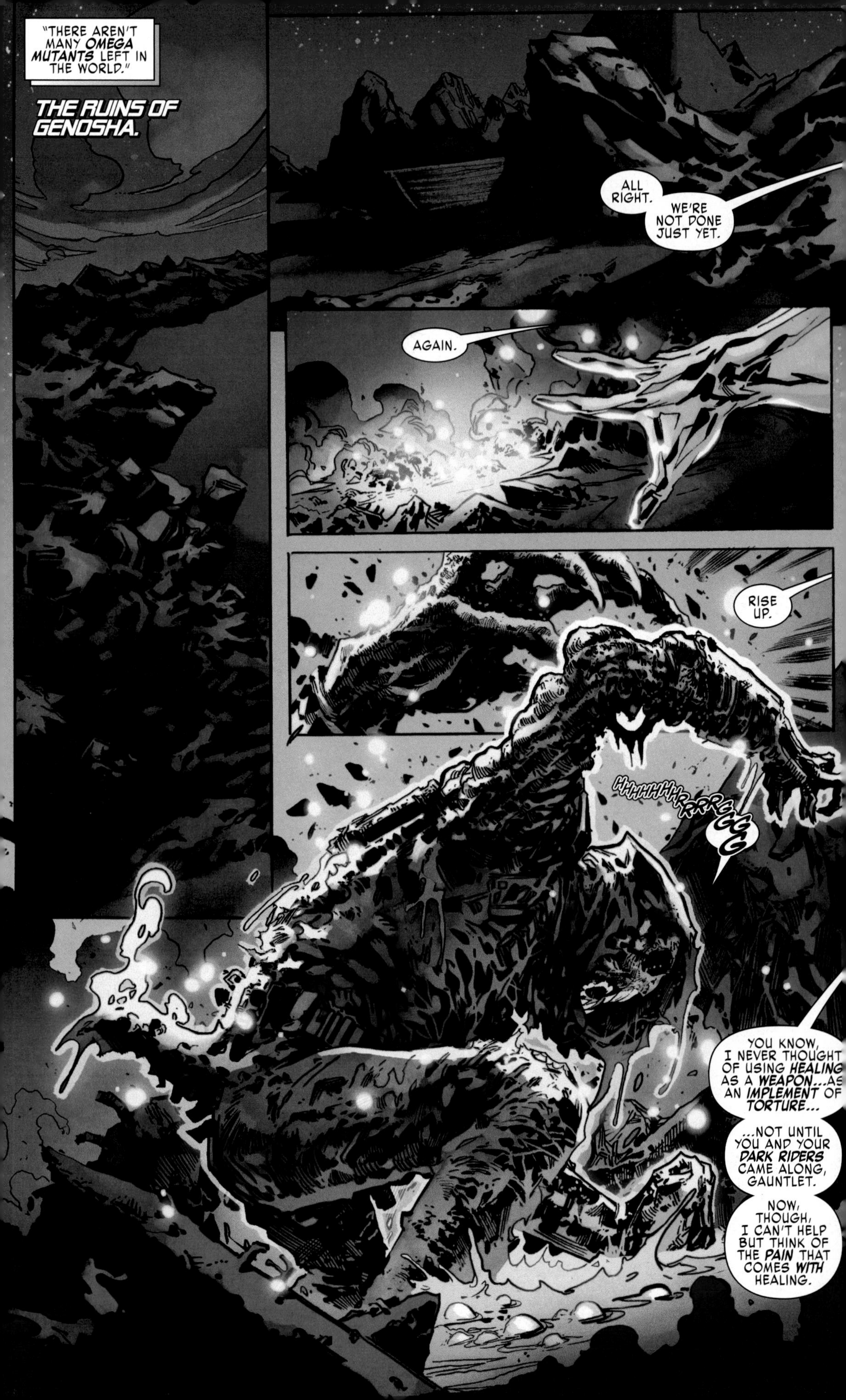

"THERE AREN'T MANY OMEGA MUTANTS LEFT IN THE WORLD."
THE RUINS OF GENOSHA.
ALL RIGHT.
WE'RE NOT DONE JUST YET.
AGAIN.
RISE UP.
HHHHHHHRRRRGGGG
YOU KNOW, I NEVER THOUGHT OF USING HEALING AS A WEAPON...AS AN IMPLEMENT OF TORTURE...
...NOT UNTIL YOU AND YOUR DARK RIDERS CAME ALONG, GAUNTLET.
NOW, THOUGH, I CAN'T HELP BUT THINK OF THE PAIN THAT COMES WITH HEALING.

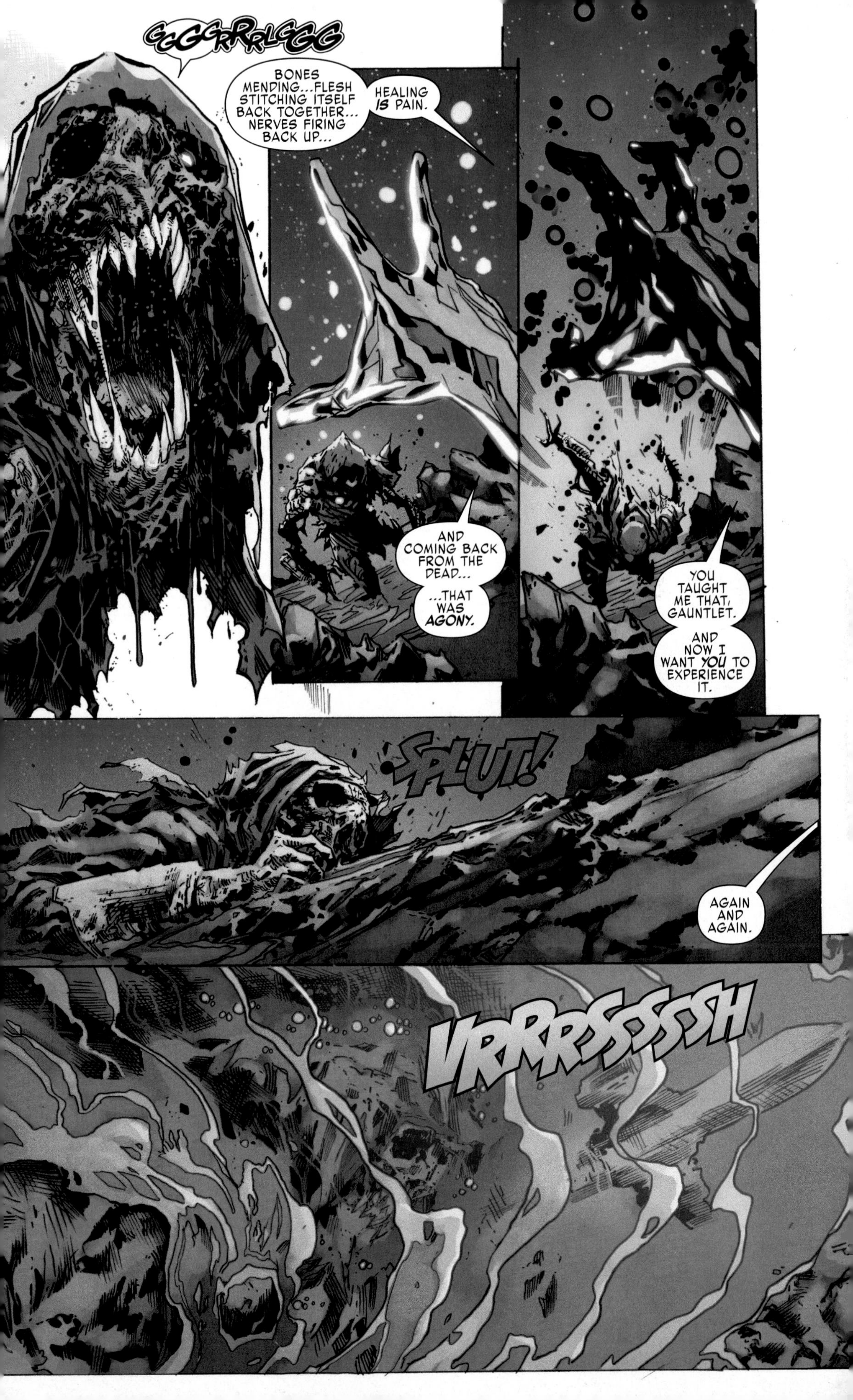
GGGGRRRLGGG
BONES MENDING...FLESH STITCHING ITSELF BACK TOGETHER... NERVES FIRING BACK UP...
HEALING IS PAIN.
AND COMING BACK FROM THE DEAD...
...THAT WAS AGONY.
YOU TAUGHT ME THAT, GAUNTLET.
AND NOW I WANT YOU TO EXPERIENCE IT.
SPLUT!
AGAIN AND AGAIN.
VRRRSSSSSH

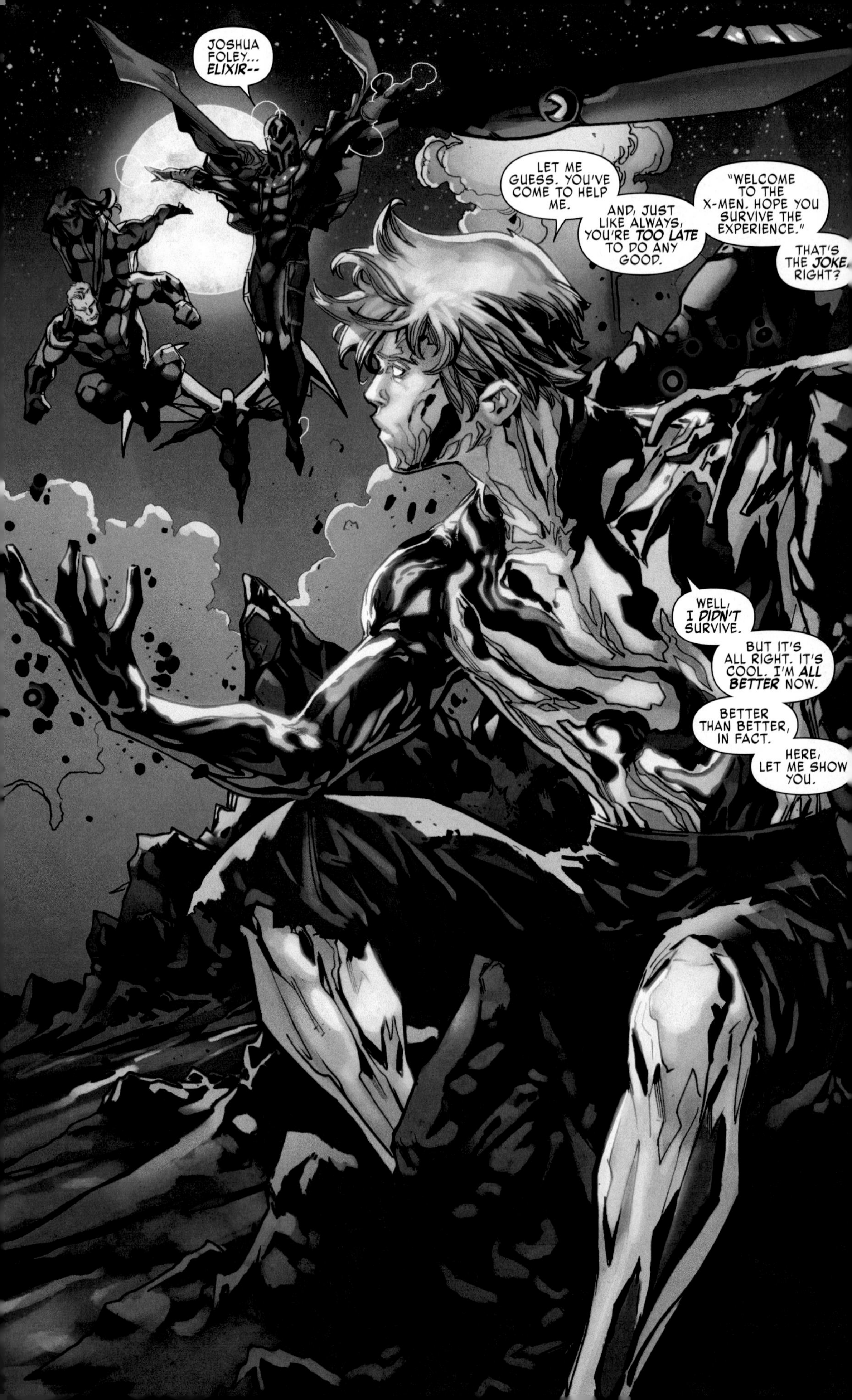
JOSHUA FOLEY... ELIXIR--
LET ME GUESS. YOU'VE COME TO HELP ME.
AND, JUST LIKE ALWAYS, YOU'RE TOO LATE TO DO ANY GOOD.
"WELCOME TO THE X-MEN. HOPE YOU SURVIVE THE EXPERIENCE."
THAT'S THE JOKE, RIGHT?
WELL, I DIDN'T SURVIVE.
BUT IT'S ALL RIGHT. IT'S COOL. I'M ALL BETTER NOW.
BETTER THAN BETTER, IN FACT.
HERE, LET ME SHOW YOU.

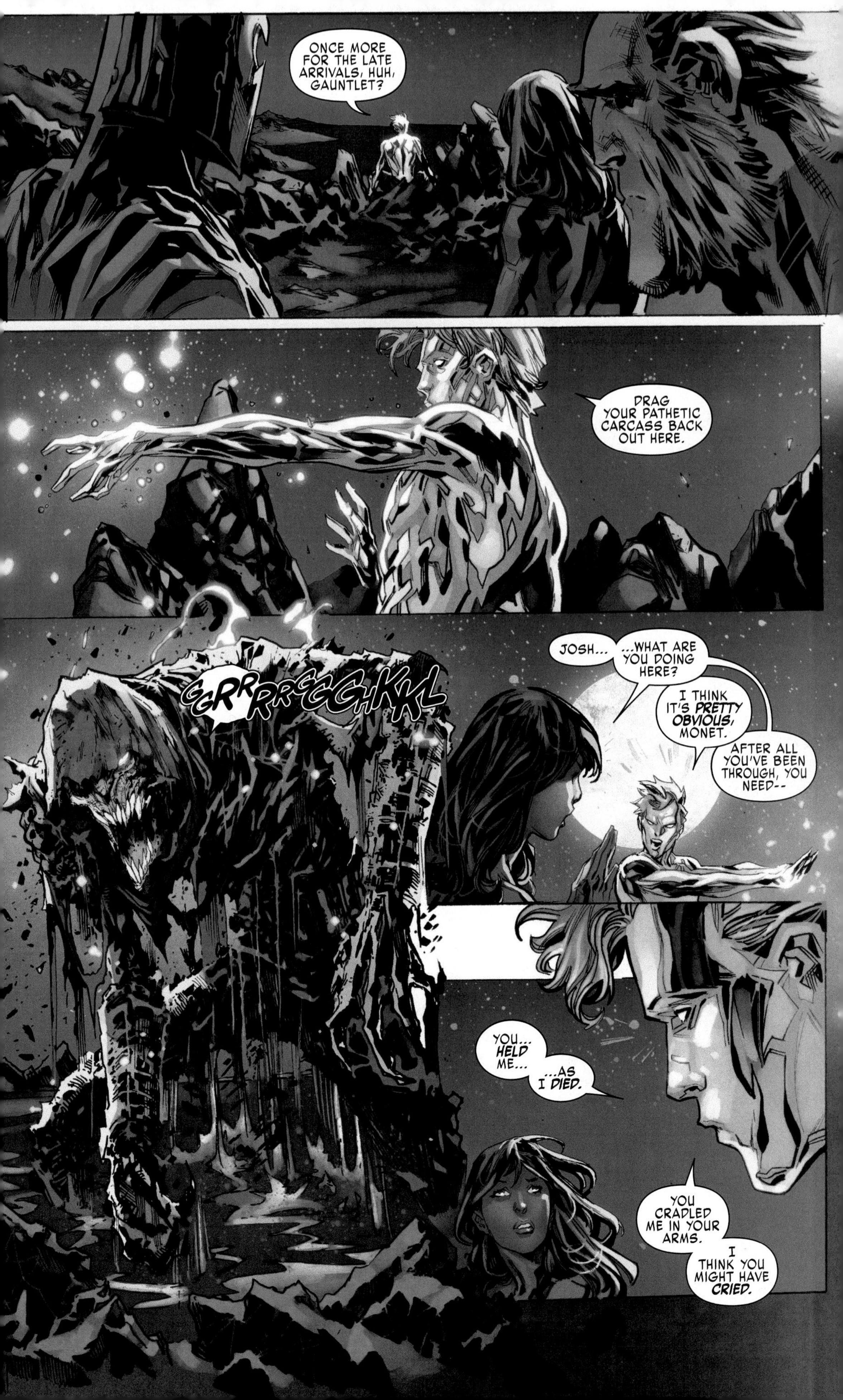
ONCE MORE FOR THE LATE ARRIVALS, HUH, GAUNTLET?
DRAG YOUR PATHETIC CARCASS BACK OUT HERE.
GGRRRRRGGGHKKL
JOSH...
...WHAT ARE YOU DOING HERE?
I THINK IT'S PRETTY OBVIOUS, MONET.
AFTER ALL YOU'VE BEEN THROUGH, YOU NEED--
YOU... HELD ME...
...AS I DIED.
YOU CRADLED ME IN YOUR ARMS.
I THINK YOU MIGHT HAVE CRIED.

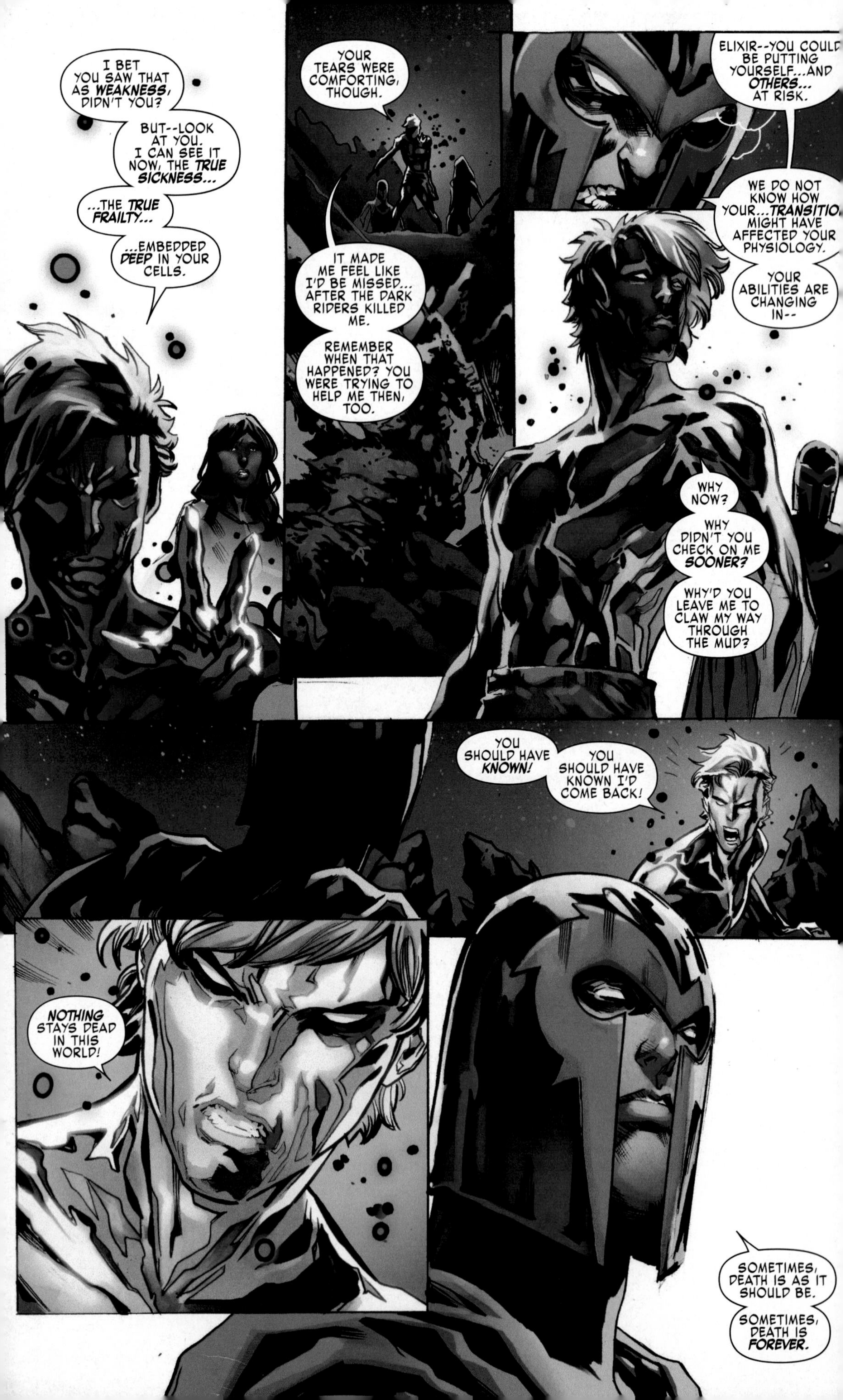

I BET YOU SAW THAT AS WEAKNESS, DIDN'T YOU?
BUT--LOOK AT YOU. I CAN SEE IT NOW, THE TRUE SICKNESS...
...THE TRUE FRAILTY...
...EMBEDDED DEEP IN YOUR CELLS.
YOUR TEARS WERE COMFORTING, THOUGH.
IT MADE ME FEEL LIKE I'D BE MISSED... AFTER THE DARK RIDERS KILLED ME.
REMEMBER WHEN THAT HAPPENED? YOU WERE TRYING TO HELP ME THEN, TOO.
ELIXIR--YOU COULD BE PUTTING YOURSELF...AND OTHERS... AT RISK.
WE DO NOT KNOW HOW YOUR...TRANSITION MIGHT HAVE AFFECTED YOUR PHYSIOLOGY.
YOUR ABILITIES ARE CHANGING IN--
WHY NOW?
WHY DIDN'T YOU CHECK ON ME SOONER?
WHY'D YOU LEAVE ME TO CLAW MY WAY THROUGH THE MUD?
YOU SHOULD HAVE KNOWN!
YOU SHOULD HAVE KNOWN I'D COME BACK!
NOTHING STAYS DEAD IN THIS WORLD!
SOMETIMES, DEATH IS AS IT SHOULD BE.
SOMETIMES, DEATH IS FOREVER.

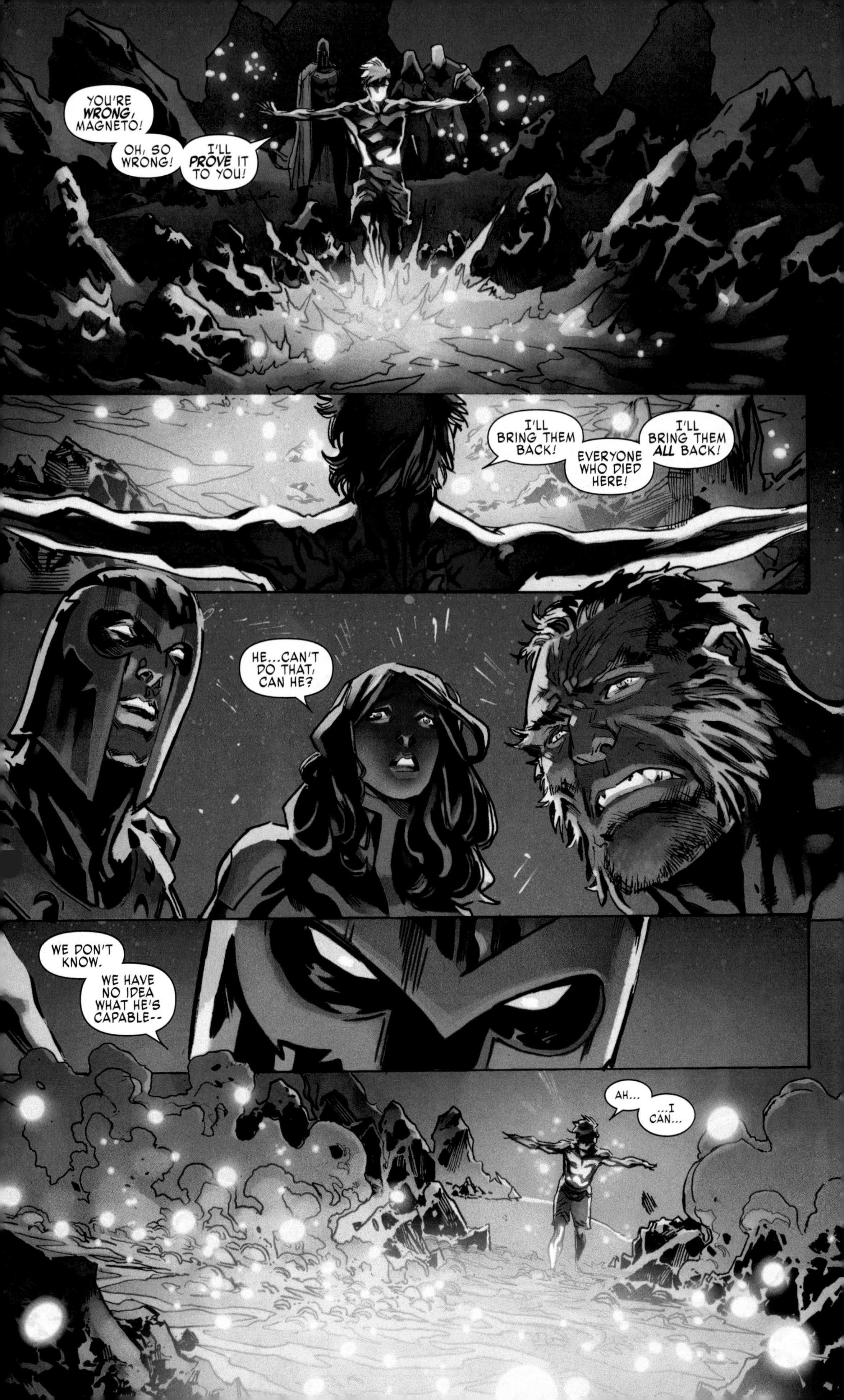
YOU'RE WRONG, MAGNETO!
OH, SO WRONG!
I'LL PROVE IT TO YOU!
I'LL BRING THEM BACK!
EVERYONE WHO DIED HERE!
I'LL BRING THEM ALL BACK!
HE...CAN'T DO THAT, CAN HE?
WE DON'T KNOW.
WE HAVE NO IDEA WHAT HE'S CAPABLE--
AH...
...I CAN...

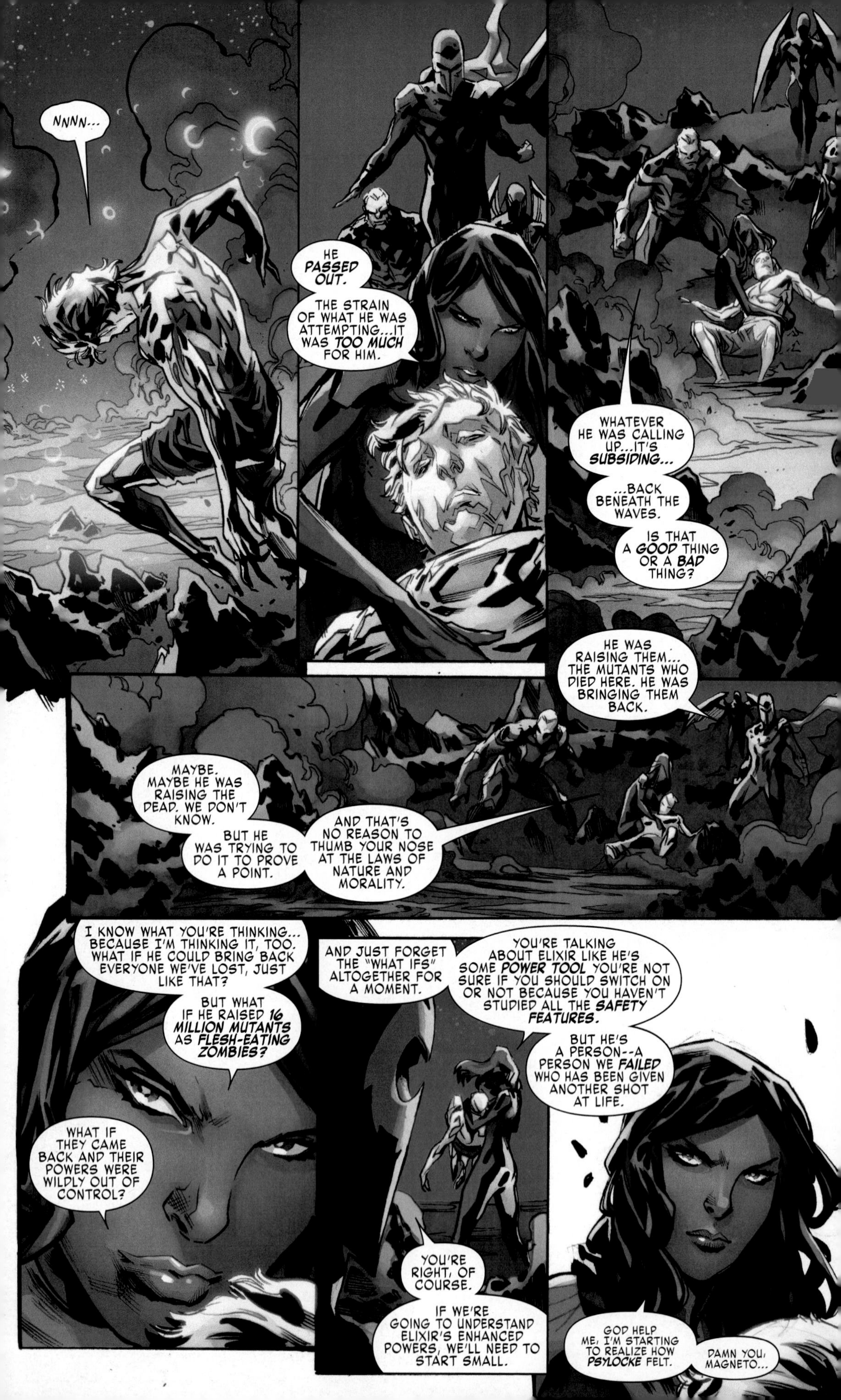
NNNN...
HE PASSED OUT.
THE STRAIN OF WHAT HE WAS ATTEMPTING...IT WAS TOO MUCH FOR HIM.
WHATEVER HE WAS CALLING UP...IT'S SUBSIDING...
...BACK BENEATH THE WAVES.
IS THAT A GOOD THING OR A BAD THING?
HE WAS RAISING THEM... THE MUTANTS WHO DIED HERE. HE WAS BRINGING THEM BACK.
MAYBE. MAYBE HE WAS RAISING THE DEAD. WE DON'T KNOW.
BUT HE WAS TRYING TO DO IT TO PROVE A POINT.
AND THAT'S NO REASON TO THUMB YOUR NOSE AT THE LAWS OF NATURE AND MORALITY.
I KNOW WHAT YOU'RE THINKING... BECAUSE I'M THINKING IT, TOO. WHAT IF HE COULD BRING BACK EVERYONE WE'VE LOST, JUST LIKE THAT?
BUT WHAT IF HE RAISED 16 MILLION MUTANTS AS FLESH-EATING ZOMBIES?
WHAT IF THEY CAME BACK AND THEIR POWERS WERE WILDLY OUT OF CONTROL?
AND JUST FORGET THE "WHAT IFS" ALTOGETHER FOR A MOMENT.
YOU'RE TALKING ABOUT ELIXIR LIKE HE'S SOME POWER TOOL YOU'RE NOT SURE IF YOU SHOULD SWITCH ON OR NOT BECAUSE YOU HAVEN'T STUDIED ALL THE SAFETY FEATURES.
BUT HE'S A PERSON--A PERSON WE FAILED WHO HAS BEEN GIVEN ANOTHER SHOT AT LIFE.
YOU'RE RIGHT, OF COURSE.
IF WE'RE GOING TO UNDERSTAND ELIXIR'S ENHANCED POWERS, WE'LL NEED TO START SMALL.
GOD HELP ME, I'M STARTING TO REALIZE HOW PSYLOCKE FELT.
DAMN YOU, MAGNETO...

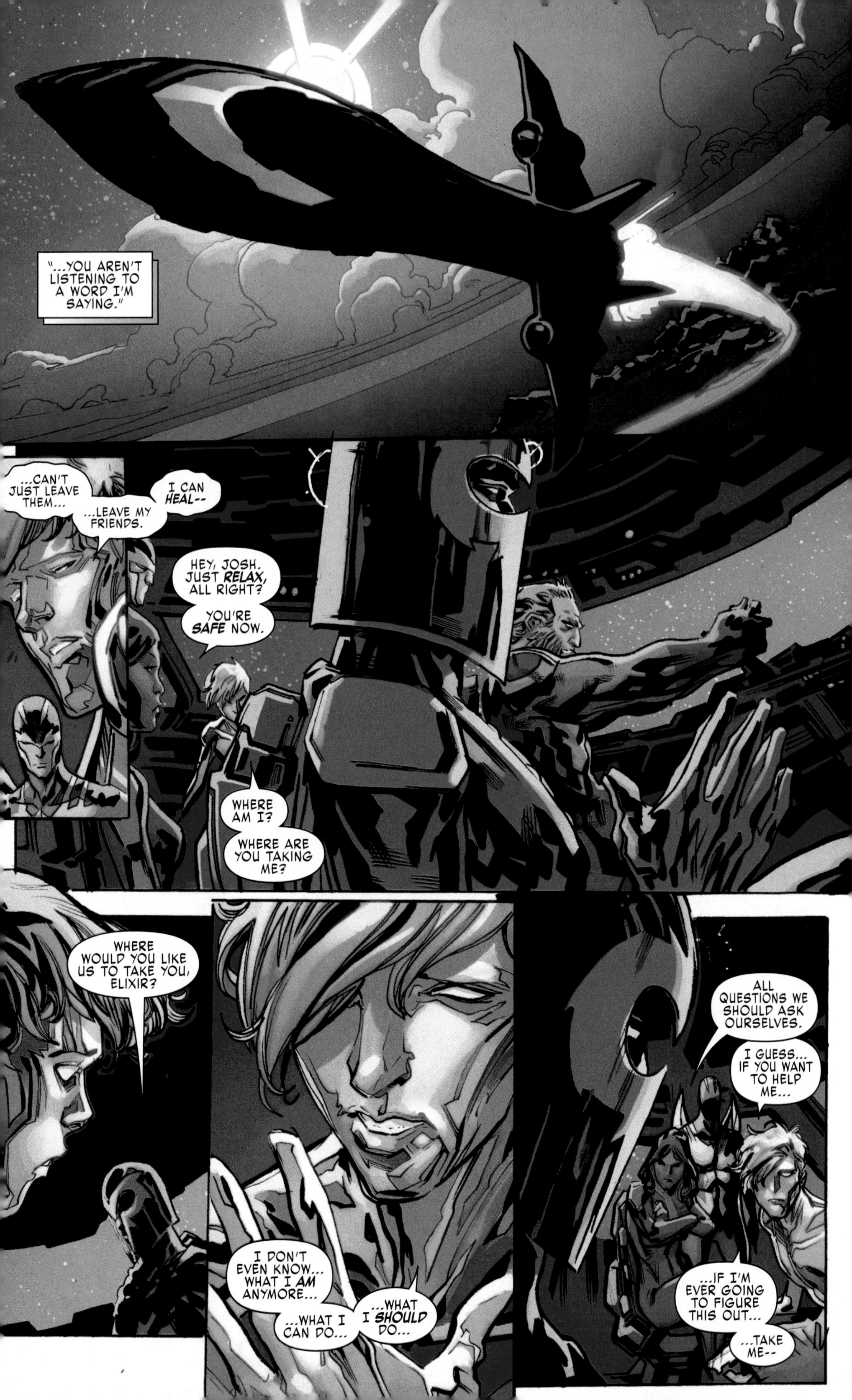
"...YOU AREN'T LISTENING TO A WORD I'M SAYING."
...CAN'T JUST LEAVE THEM...
...LEAVE MY FRIENDS.
I CAN HEAL--
HEY, JOSH. JUST RELAX, ALL RIGHT?
YOU'RE SAFE NOW.
WHERE AM I?
WHERE ARE YOU TAKING ME?
WHERE WOULD YOU LIKE US TO TAKE YOU, ELIXIR?
I DON'T EVEN KNOW... WHAT I AM ANYMORE...
...WHAT I CAN DO...
...WHAT I SHOULD DO...
ALL QUESTIONS WE SHOULD ASK OURSELVES.
I GUESS... IF YOU WANT TO HELP ME...
...IF I'M EVER GOING TO FIGURE THIS OUT...
...TAKE ME--

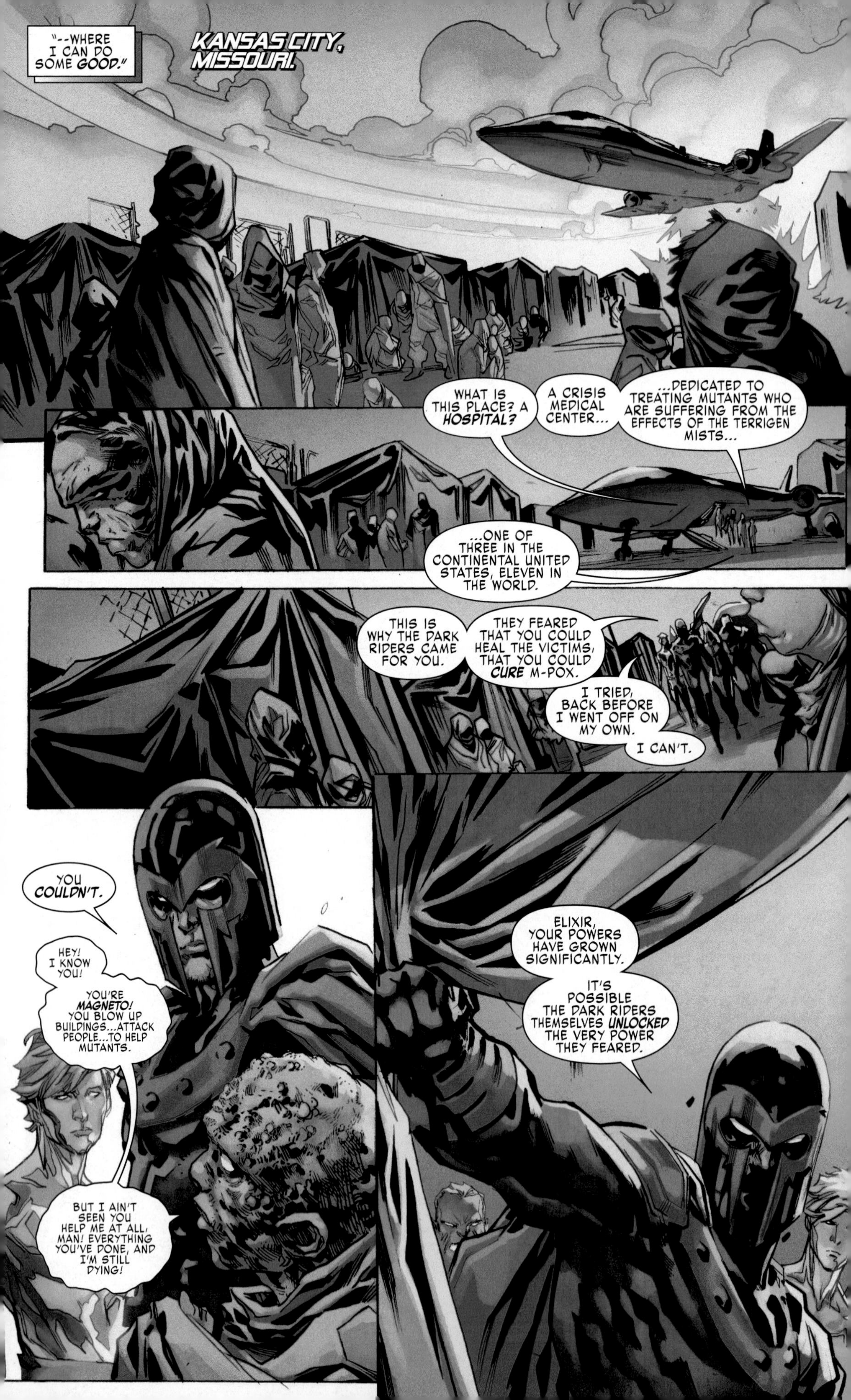
"--WHERE I CAN DO SOME GOOD."
KANSAS CITY, MISSOURI.
WHAT IS THIS PLACE? A HOSPITAL?
A CRISIS MEDICAL CENTER...
...DEDICATED TO TREATING MUTANTS WHO ARE SUFFERING FROM THE EFFECTS OF THE TERRIGEN MISTS...
...ONE OF THREE IN THE CONTINENTAL UNITED STATES, ELEVEN IN THE WORLD.
THIS IS WHY THE DARK RIDERS CAME FOR YOU.
THEY FEARED THAT YOU COULD HEAL THE VICTIMS, THAT YOU COULD CURE M-POX.
I TRIED, BACK BEFORE I WENT OFF ON MY OWN.
I CAN'T.
YOU COULDN'T.
HEY! I KNOW YOU!
YOU'RE MAGNETO! YOU BLOW UP BUILDINGS...ATTACK PEOPLE...TO HELP MUTANTS.
BUT I AIN'T SEEN YOU HELP ME AT ALL, MAN! EVERYTHING YOU'VE DONE, AND I'M STILL DYING!
ELIXIR, YOUR POWERS HAVE GROWN SIGNIFICANTLY.
IT'S POSSIBLE THE DARK RIDERS THEMSELVES UNLOCKED THE VERY POWER THEY FEARED.

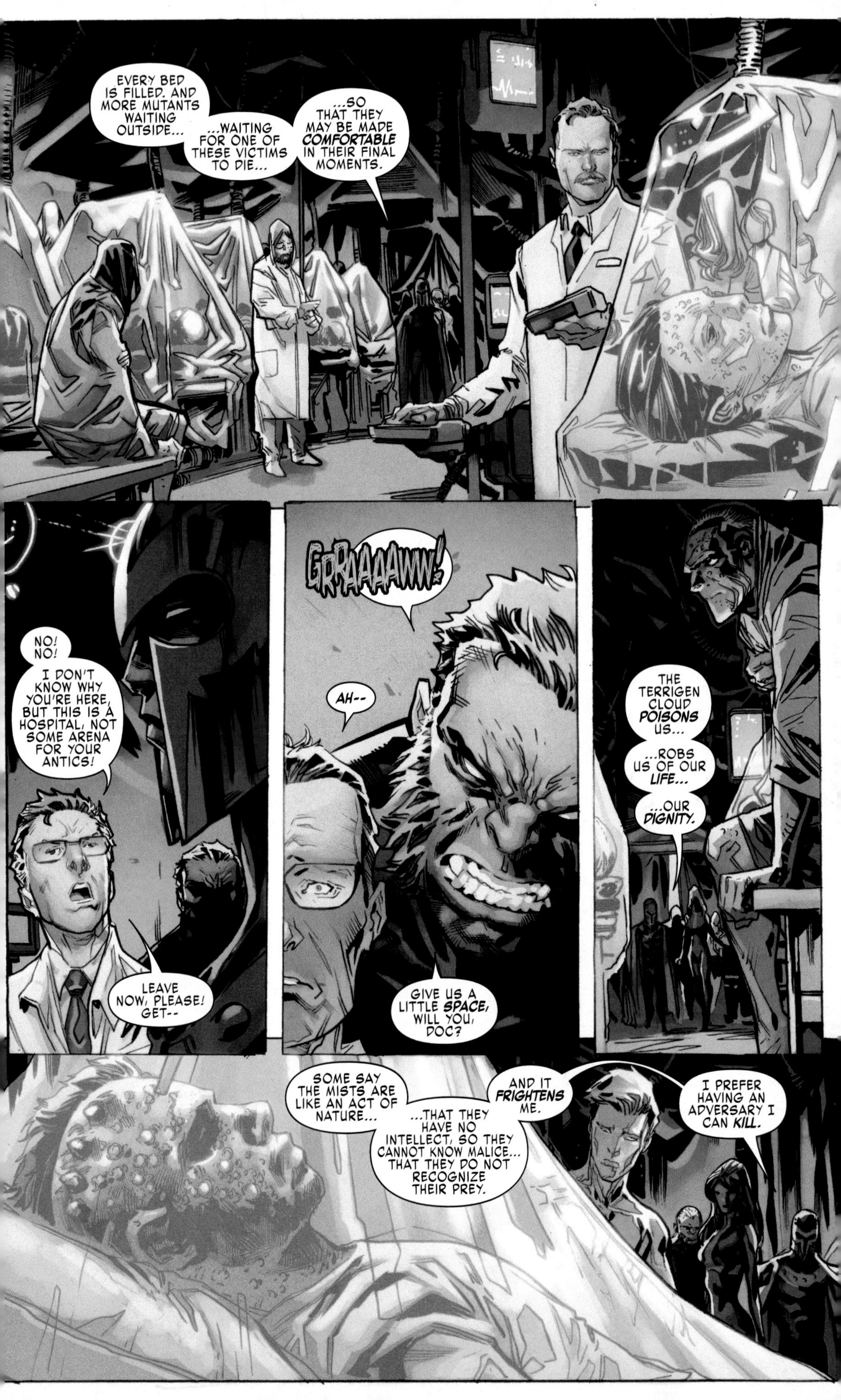
EVERY BED IS FILLED. AND MORE MUTANTS WAITING OUTSIDE...
...WAITING FOR ONE OF THESE VICTIMS TO DIE...
...SO THAT THEY MAY BE MADE COMFORTABLE IN THEIR FINAL MOMENTS.
NO! NO!
I DON'T KNOW WHY YOU'RE HERE, BUT THIS IS A HOSPITAL, NOT SOME ARENA FOR YOUR ANTICS!
LEAVE NOW, PLEASE! GET--
GRRAAAAWN!
AH--
GIVE US A LITTLE SPACE, WILL YOU, DOC?
THE TERRIGEN CLOUD POISONS US...
...ROBS US OF OUR LIFE...
...OUR DIGNITY.
SOME SAY THE MISTS ARE LIKE AN ACT OF NATURE...
...THAT THEY HAVE NO INTELLECT, SO THEY CANNOT KNOW MALICE... THAT THEY DO NOT RECOGNIZE THEIR PREY.
AND IT FRIGHTENS ME.
I PREFER HAVING AN ADVERSARY I CAN KILL.

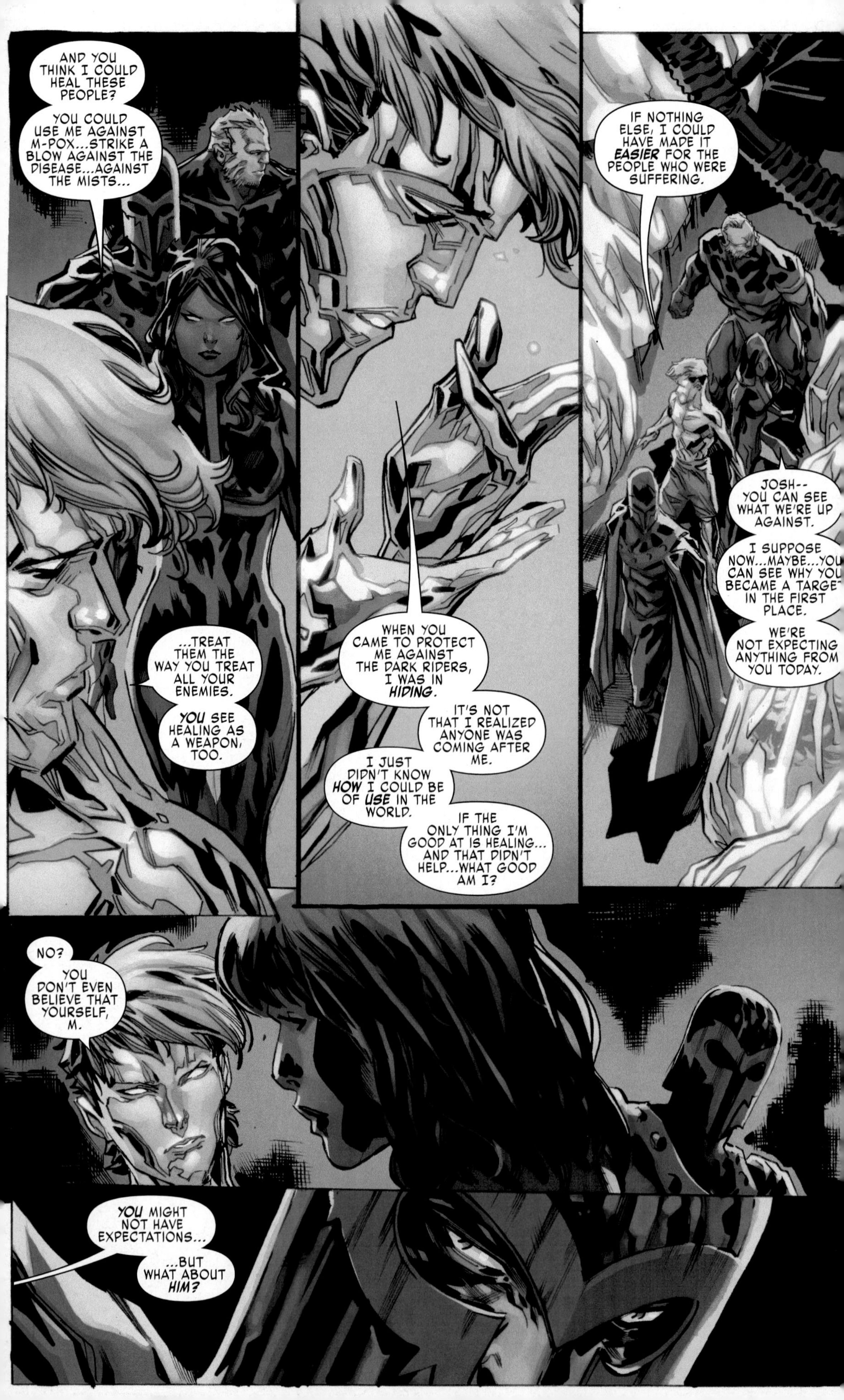
AND YOU THINK I COULD HEAL THESE PEOPLE?
YOU COULD USE ME AGAINST M-POX...STRIKE A BLOW AGAINST THE DISEASE...AGAINST THE MISTS...
...TREAT THEM THE WAY YOU TREAT ALL YOUR ENEMIES.
YOU SEE HEALING AS A WEAPON, TOO.
WHEN YOU CAME TO PROTECT ME AGAINST THE DARK RIDERS, I WAS IN HIDING.
IT'S NOT THAT I REALIZED ANYONE WAS COMING AFTER ME.
I JUST DIDN'T KNOW HOW I COULD BE OF USE IN THE WORLD.
IF THE ONLY THING I'M GOOD AT IS HEALING... AND THAT DIDN'T HELP...WHAT GOOD AM I?
IF NOTHING ELSE, I COULD HAVE MADE IT EASIER FOR THE PEOPLE WHO WERE SUFFERING.
JOSH-- YOU CAN SEE WHAT WE'RE UP AGAINST.
I SUPPOSE NOW...MAYBE...YOU CAN SEE WHY YOU BECAME A TARGET IN THE FIRST PLACE.
WE'RE NOT EXPECTING ANYTHING FROM YOU TODAY.
NO?
YOU DON'T EVEN BELIEVE THAT YOURSELF, M.
YOU MIGHT NOT HAVE EXPECTATIONS...
...BUT WHAT ABOUT HIM?

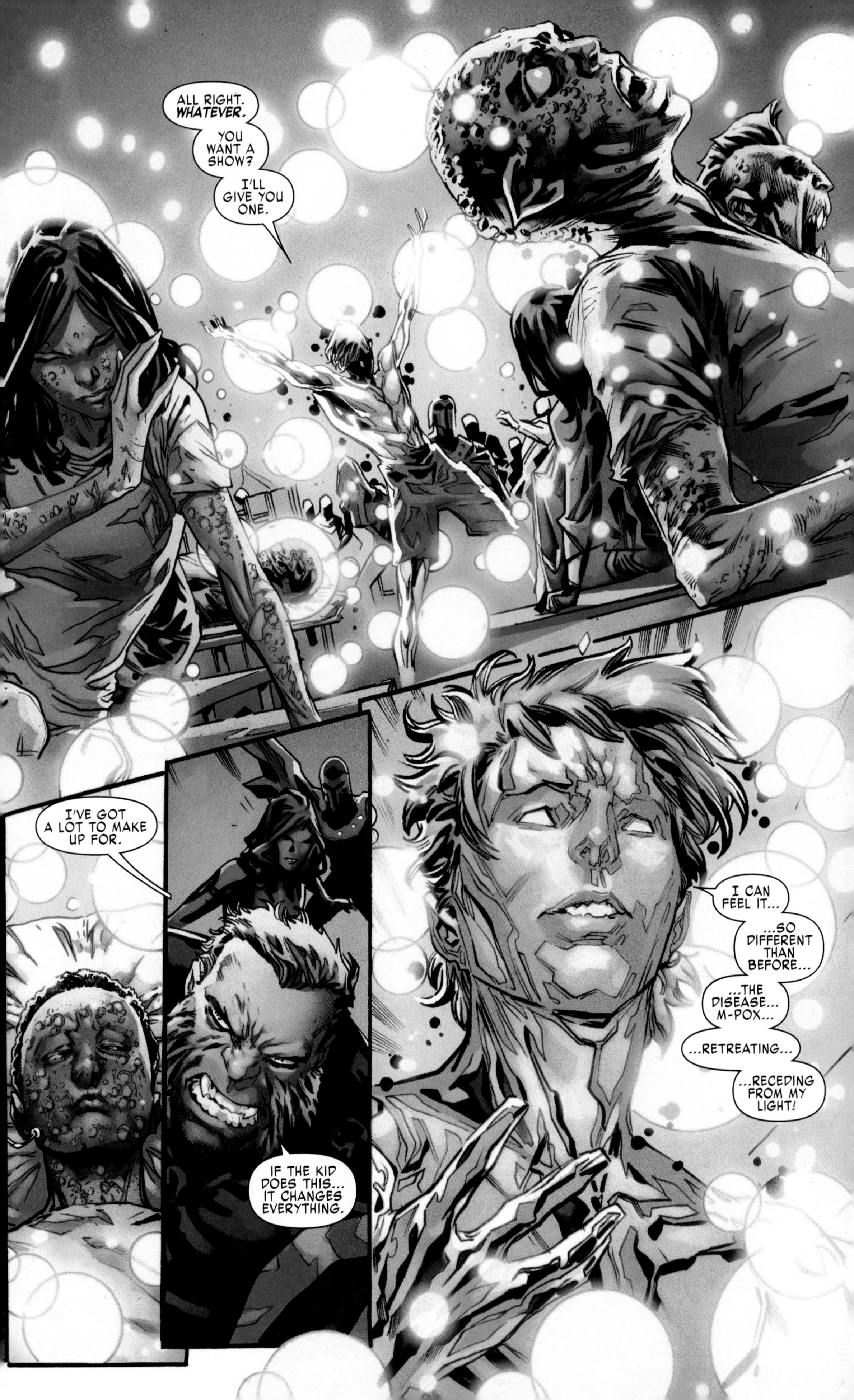
ALL RIGHT. *WHATEVER.*
YOU WANT A SHOW?
I'LL GIVE YOU ONE.
I'VE GOT A LOT TO MAKE UP FOR.
IF THE KID DOES THIS... IT CHANGES EVERYTHING.
I CAN FEEL IT...
...SO DIFFERENT THAN BEFORE...
...THE DISEASE... M-POX...
...RETREATING...
...RECEDING FROM MY LIGHT!

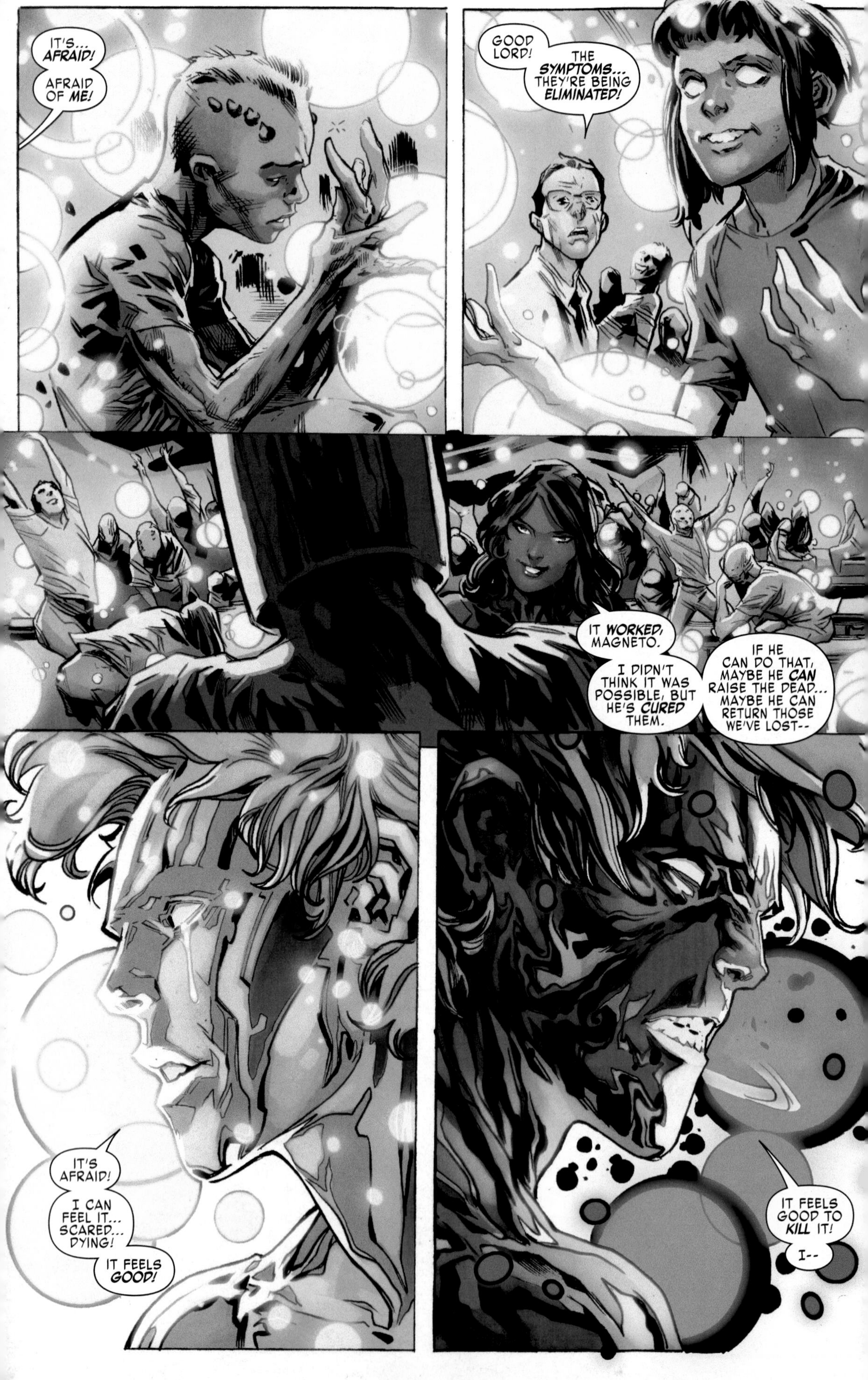
IT'S... AFRAID!
AFRAID OF ME!
GOOD LORD!
THE SYMPTOMS... THEY'RE BEING ELIMINATED!
IT WORKED, MAGNETO.
I DIDN'T THINK IT WAS POSSIBLE, BUT HE'S CURED THEM.
IF HE CAN DO THAT, MAYBE HE CAN RAISE THE DEAD... MAYBE HE CAN RETURN THOSE WE'VE LOST--
IT'S AFRAID!
I CAN FEEL IT... SCARED... DYING!
IT FEELS GOOD!
IT FEELS GOOD TO KILL IT!
I--

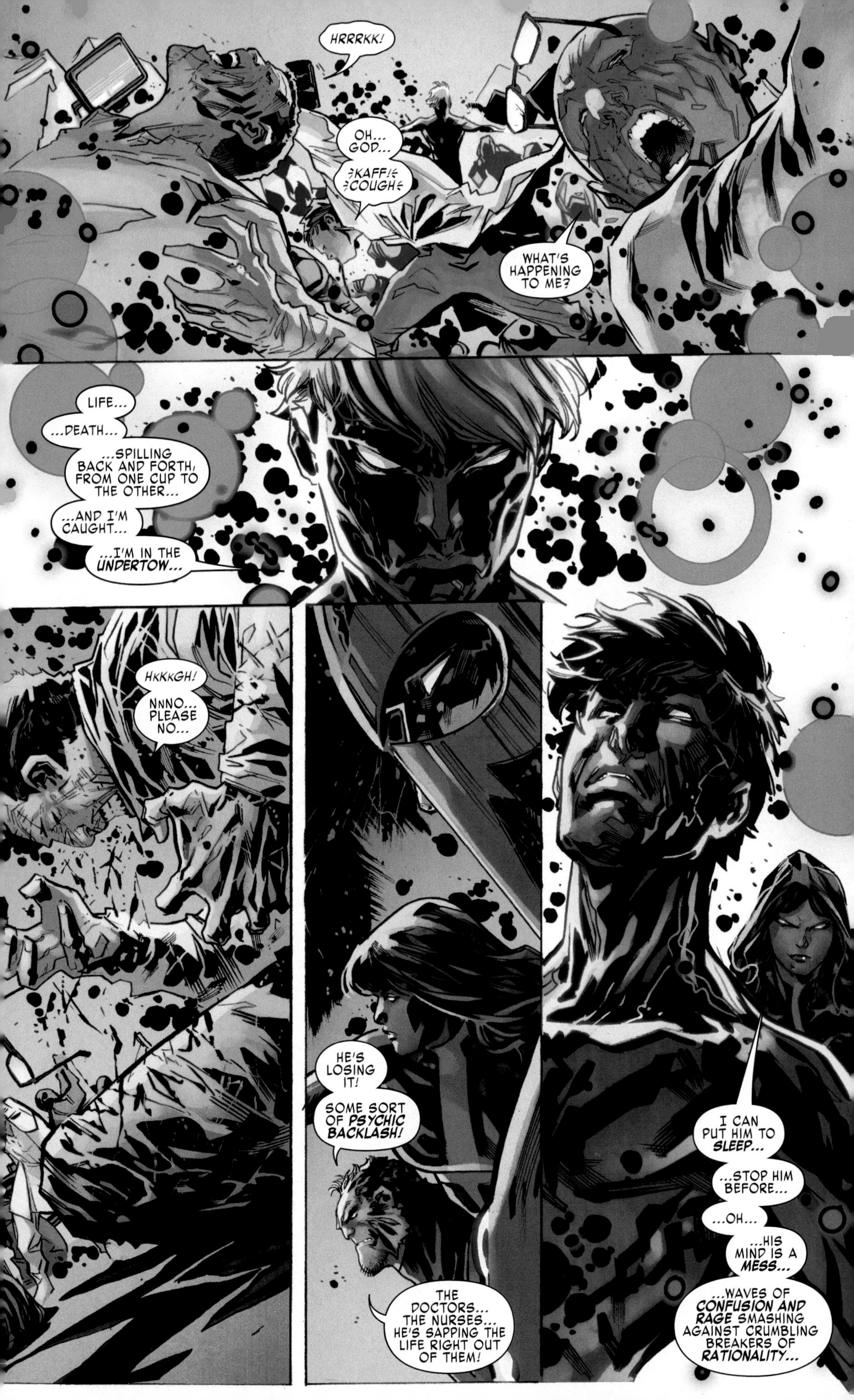
HRRRKK!
OH... GOD...
⚡KAFF⚡ ⚡COUGH⚡
WHAT'S HAPPENING TO ME?
LIFE...
...DEATH...
...SPILLING BACK AND FORTH, FROM ONE CUP TO THE OTHER...
...AND I'M CAUGHT...
...I'M IN THE *UNDERTOW*...
HKKKGH!
NNNO... PLEASE NO...
HE'S LOSING IT!
SOME SORT OF *PSYCHIC BACKLASH!*
THE DOCTORS... THE NURSES... HE'S SAPPING THE LIFE RIGHT OUT OF THEM!
I CAN PUT HIM TO *SLEEP...*
...STOP HIM BEFORE...
...OH...
...HIS MIND IS A *MESS...*
...WAVES OF *CONFUSION AND RAGE* SMASHING AGAINST CRUMBLING BREAKERS OF *RATIONALITY...*

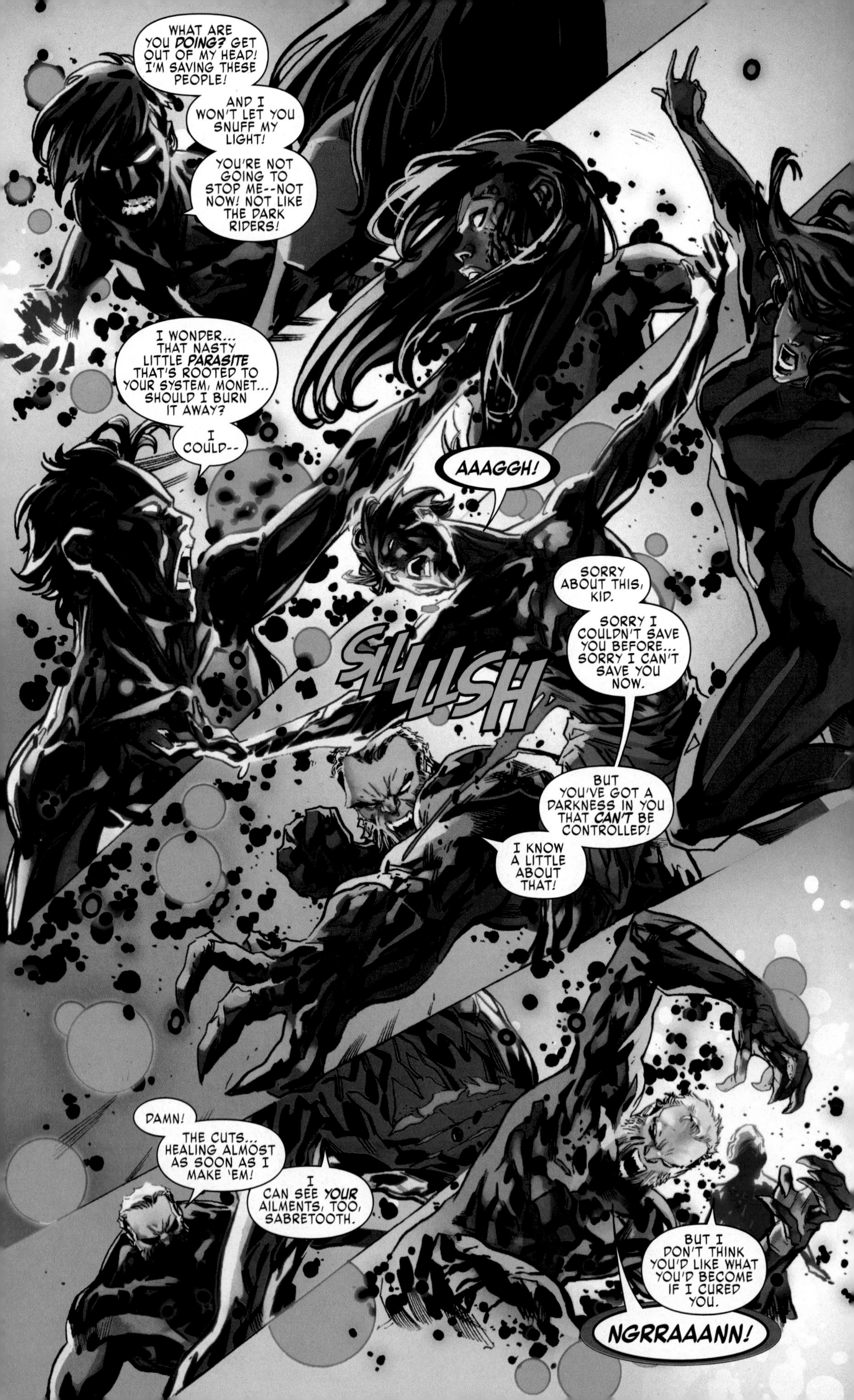

WHAT ARE YOU DOING? GET OUT OF MY HEAD! I'M SAVING THESE PEOPLE!
AND I WON'T LET YOU SNUFF MY LIGHT!
YOU'RE NOT GOING TO STOP ME--NOT NOW! NOT LIKE THE DARK RIDERS!
I WONDER... THAT NASTY LITTLE PARASITE THAT'S ROOTED TO YOUR SYSTEM, MONET... SHOULD I BURN IT AWAY?
I COULD--
AAAGGH!
SORRY ABOUT THIS, KID.
SORRY I COULDN'T SAVE YOU BEFORE... SORRY I CAN'T SAVE YOU NOW.
SLLLUSH
BUT YOU'VE GOT A DARKNESS IN YOU THAT CAN'T BE CONTROLLED!
I KNOW A LITTLE ABOUT THAT!
DAMN!
THE CUTS... HEALING ALMOST AS SOON AS I MAKE 'EM!
I CAN SEE YOUR AILMENTS, TOO, SABRETOOTH.
BUT I DON'T THINK YOU'D LIKE WHAT YOU'D BECOME IF I CURED YOU.
NGRRAAANN!

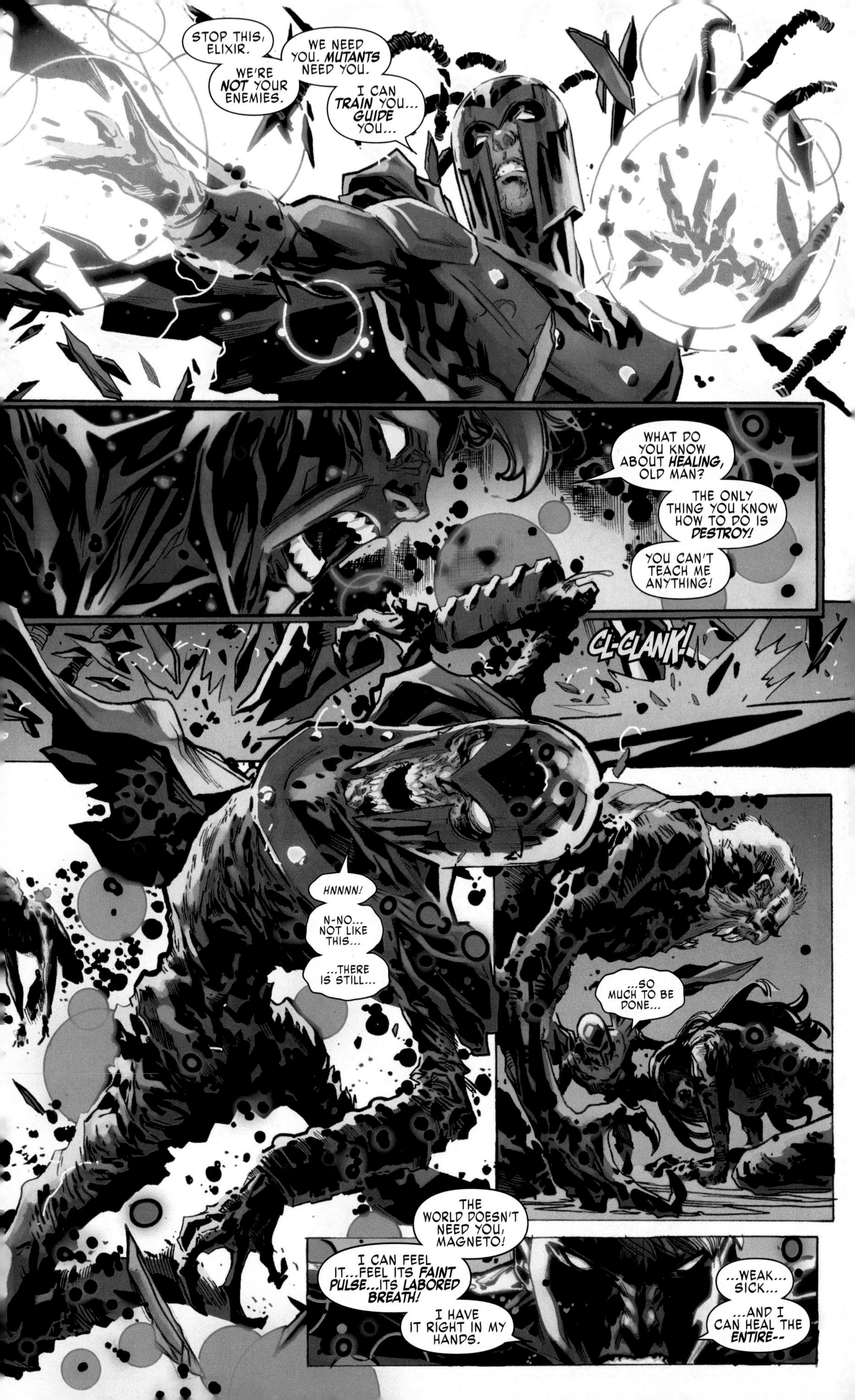
STOP THIS, ELIXIR.
WE'RE NOT YOUR ENEMIES.
WE NEED YOU. MUTANTS NEED YOU.
I CAN TRAIN YOU... GUIDE YOU...
WHAT DO YOU KNOW ABOUT HEALING, OLD MAN?
THE ONLY THING YOU KNOW HOW TO DO IS DESTROY!
YOU CAN'T TEACH ME ANYTHING!
CL-CLANK!
HNNNN!
N-NO... NOT LIKE THIS...
...THERE IS STILL...
...SO MUCH TO BE DONE...
THE WORLD DOESN'T NEED YOU, MAGNETO!
I CAN FEEL IT...FEEL ITS FAINT PULSE...ITS LABORED BREATH!
I HAVE IT RIGHT IN MY HANDS.
...WEAK... SICK...
...AND I CAN HEAL THE ENTIRE--

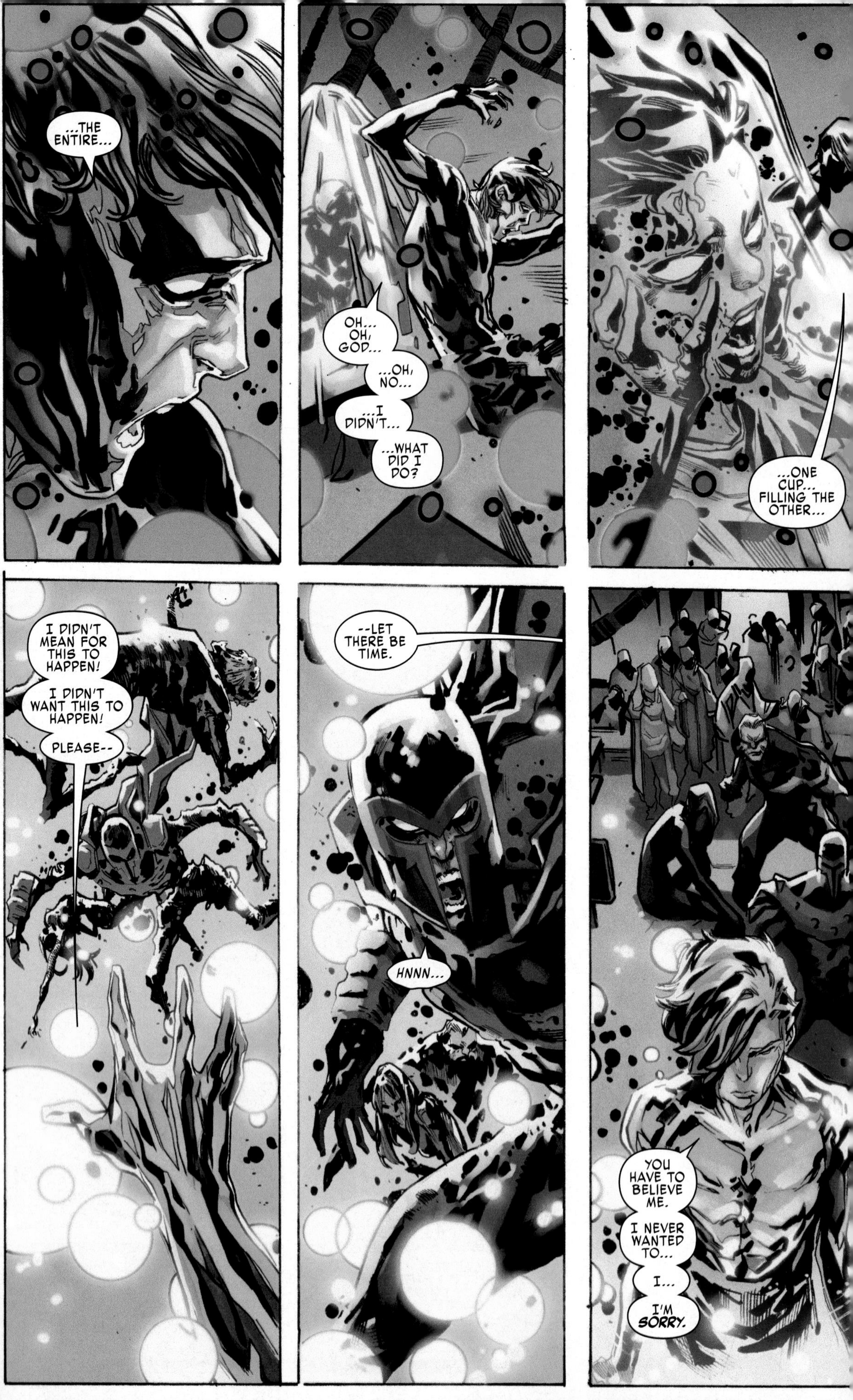
...THE ENTIRE...
OH... OH, GOD...
...OH, NO...
...I DIDN'T...
...WHAT DID I DO?
...ONE CUP... FILLING THE OTHER...
I DIDN'T MEAN FOR THIS TO HAPPEN!
I DIDN'T WANT THIS TO HAPPEN!
PLEASE--
--LET THERE BE TIME.
HNNN...
YOU HAVE TO BELIEVE ME.
I NEVER WANTED TO...
I...
I'M SORRY.

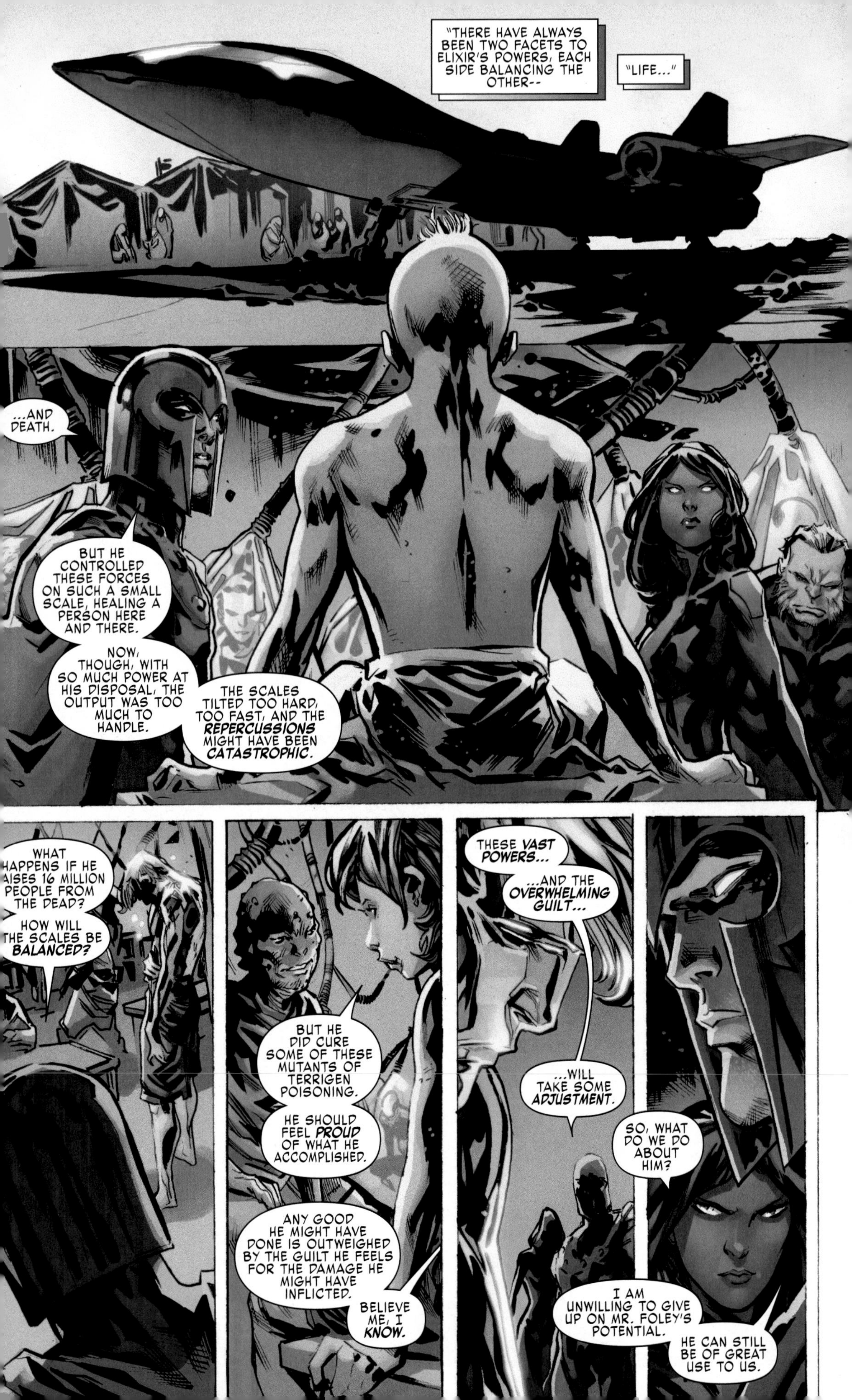
"THERE HAVE ALWAYS BEEN TWO FACETS TO ELIXIR'S POWERS, EACH SIDE BALANCING THE OTHER--
"LIFE..."
...AND DEATH.
BUT HE CONTROLLED THESE FORCES ON SUCH A SMALL SCALE, HEALING A PERSON HERE AND THERE.
NOW, THOUGH, WITH SO MUCH POWER AT HIS DISPOSAL, THE OUTPUT WAS TOO MUCH TO HANDLE.
THE SCALES TILTED TOO HARD, TOO FAST, AND THE REPERCUSSIONS MIGHT HAVE BEEN CATASTROPHIC.
WHAT HAPPENS IF HE RAISES 16 MILLION PEOPLE FROM THE DEAD?
HOW WILL THE SCALES BE BALANCED?
BUT HE DID CURE SOME OF THESE MUTANTS OF TERRIGEN POISONING.
HE SHOULD FEEL PROUD OF WHAT HE ACCOMPLISHED.
ANY GOOD HE MIGHT HAVE DONE IS OUTWEIGHED BY THE GUILT HE FEELS FOR THE DAMAGE HE MIGHT HAVE INFLICTED.
BELIEVE ME, I KNOW.
THESE VAST POWERS...
...AND THE OVERWHELMING GUILT...
...WILL TAKE SOME ADJUSTMENT.
SO, WHAT DO WE DO ABOUT HIM?
I AM UNWILLING TO GIVE UP ON MR. FOLEY'S POTENTIAL.
HE CAN STILL BE OF GREAT USE TO US.

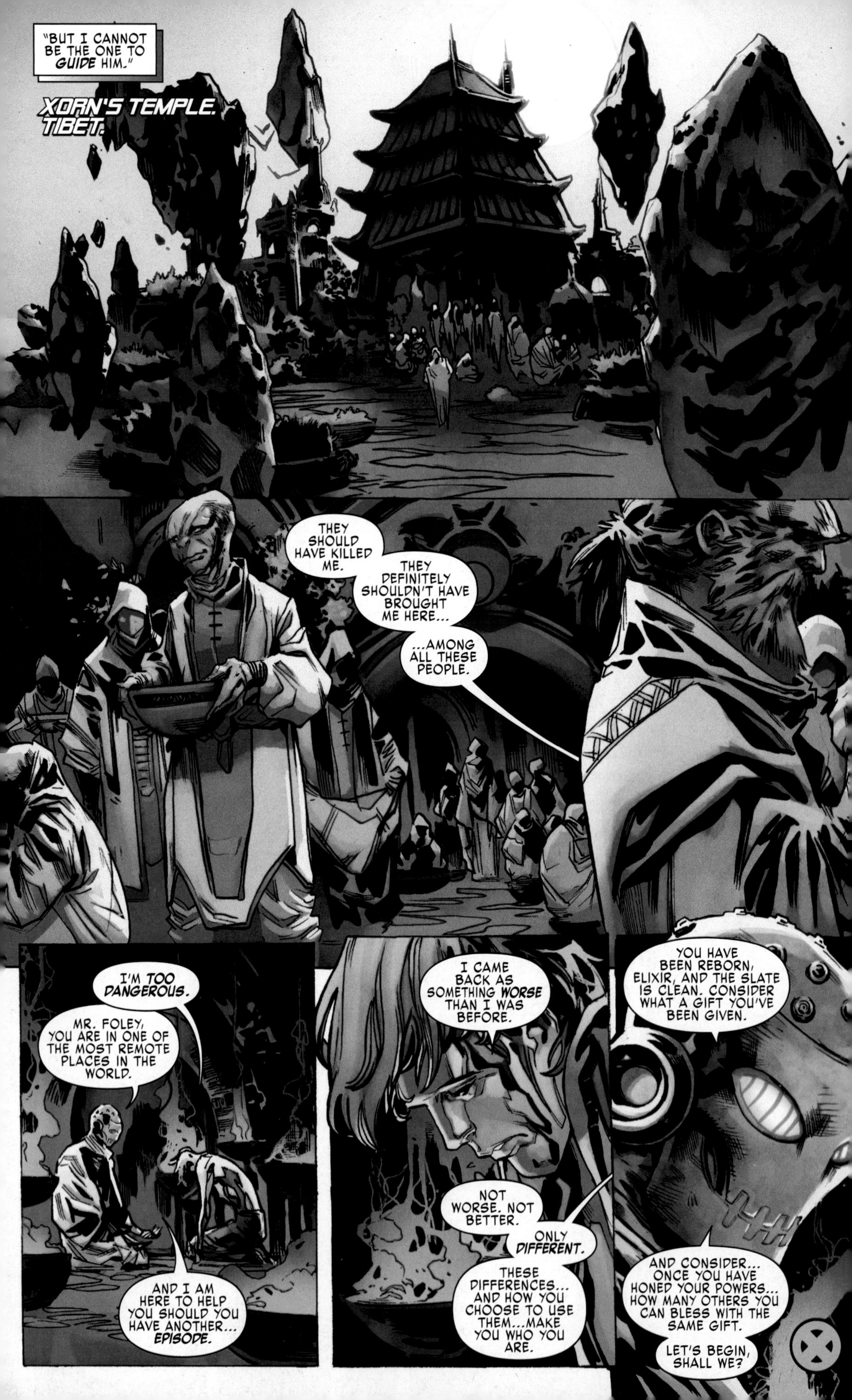
"BUT I CANNOT BE THE ONE TO GUIDE HIM."
XORN'S TEMPLE. TIBET.
THEY SHOULD HAVE KILLED ME.
THEY DEFINITELY SHOULDN'T HAVE BROUGHT ME HERE...
...AMONG ALL THESE PEOPLE.
I'M TOO DANGEROUS.
MR. FOLEY, YOU ARE IN ONE OF THE MOST REMOTE PLACES IN THE WORLD.
AND I AM HERE TO HELP YOU SHOULD YOU HAVE ANOTHER... EPISODE.
I CAME BACK AS SOMETHING WORSE THAN I WAS BEFORE.
NOT WORSE. NOT BETTER.
ONLY DIFFERENT.
THESE DIFFERENCES... AND HOW YOU CHOOSE TO USE THEM...MAKE YOU WHO YOU ARE.
YOU HAVE BEEN REBORN, ELIXIR, AND THE SLATE IS CLEAN. CONSIDER WHAT A GIFT YOU'VE BEEN GIVEN.
AND CONSIDER... ONCE YOU HAVE HONED YOUR POWERS... HOW MANY OTHERS YOU CAN BLESS WITH THE SAME GIFT.
LET'S BEGIN, SHALL WE?

ECUADOR.
350 MILES SOUTH OF THE COLOMBIAN BORDER.

PEOPLE USUALLY SUM UP MY MUTANT ABILITIES AS "LUCK."

IT'S A LI'L MORE COMPLEX THAN THAT. I'M BASICALLY TELEKINETIC...I CAN MOVE "SMALL" THINGS WITH MY MIND.

THE ONLY PROBLEM IS I CAN'T CONTROL IT. IT'S ALL SUBCONSCIOUS. I'M NOT EVEN AWARE OF WHEN I'M DOING IT. AND IT ONLY SEEMS TO WORK WHEN I'M IN NEAR-DEATH SITUATIONS.

SO I GUESS YOU'RE USING A.I.M. TO SPY ON THE GOOD GUYS NOW?

ROBERTO DA COSTA, A.K.A. SUNSPOT.
MUTANT. OWNER OF AVENGERS IDEAS MECHANICS. FORMER MEMBER OF X-FORCE.

O CALL

DURATION: 1:27

ON CALL WITH:
DA COSTA, ROBERTO

INCOMING DATA TRANSFER
767.5 of 936KB   **82%**

CANCEL TRANSFER?
YES / PAUSE

ENGTH: 74%

A.I.M.

NORMALLY NOT THE CASE, BUT I JUST RECEIVED INTEL IN REGARD TO THE LOCATION OF A CRIMINAL WE'VE BEEN TRYING TO CATCH FOR A WHILE.

I HAD A.I.M. SATELLITES SURVEYING THE AREA, AND TO MY SURPRISE... THE ONE PERSON I NEED FOR A SITUATION LIKE THIS JUST HAPPENED TO BE 80 MILES EAST OF THE THOSE EXACT COORDINATES.

I CAN'T BEGIN TO RECALL HOW MANY TIMES SOME IDIOT HAD A GUN POINTED AT MY HEAD AND IT SUDDENLY JAMMED WHEN THEY PULLED THE TRIGGER.

MY POWERS HAVE GOTTEN ME OUT OF SOME TOUGH SITUATIONS, BUT THE *GAME OF LIFE* HAS TAUGHT ME TO NEVER BET ON "LUCK" ALONE.

IN ANY GAME, IT'S ALWAYS BEST TO HAVE A GOOD STRATEGY.

NEENA THURMAN, A.K.A. DOMINO.
MUTANT. MERCENARY. FORMER MEMBER OF X-FORCE.

YAY. LUCKY ME.

HOPEFULLY VACATIONING AND NOT ROBBING ANYONE.

NO COMMENT.

ARE YOU KEEPING TABS ON ME 'CUZ OF THOSE WEAPONS YOU LENT ME? I PROMISED I'D PAY YOU BACK. DID YOU GET THOSE CHECKS I MAILED?

YEAH, BOTH OF THEM. THAT $15.75 PUT A REAL DENT IN THE $260,000 YOU STILL OWE.

HOWEVER, THAT'S NOT WHY I REQUESTED YOU. I REALLY NEED YOUR HELP ON THIS ONE.

THIS INTEL REGARDS A GUY NAMED DANILO "BONES" ROJAS. BECAUSE OF HIS MILITARY TRAINING, HE'S A VERY DIFFICULT MAN TO TRACK.

HOWEVER, AN HOUR AGO AN ENCRYPTED COMM LOG WAS ANONYMOUSLY LEAKED INTO OUR INTERNAL NETWORK.

ONCE WE WERE ABLE TO DECODE IT, WE DISCOVERED ROJAS AND HIS MEN WERE STATIONED AT AN ABANDONED MILITARY FACILITY IN ECUADOR.

SO, WHAT'S THE DEAL WITH THIS GUY?

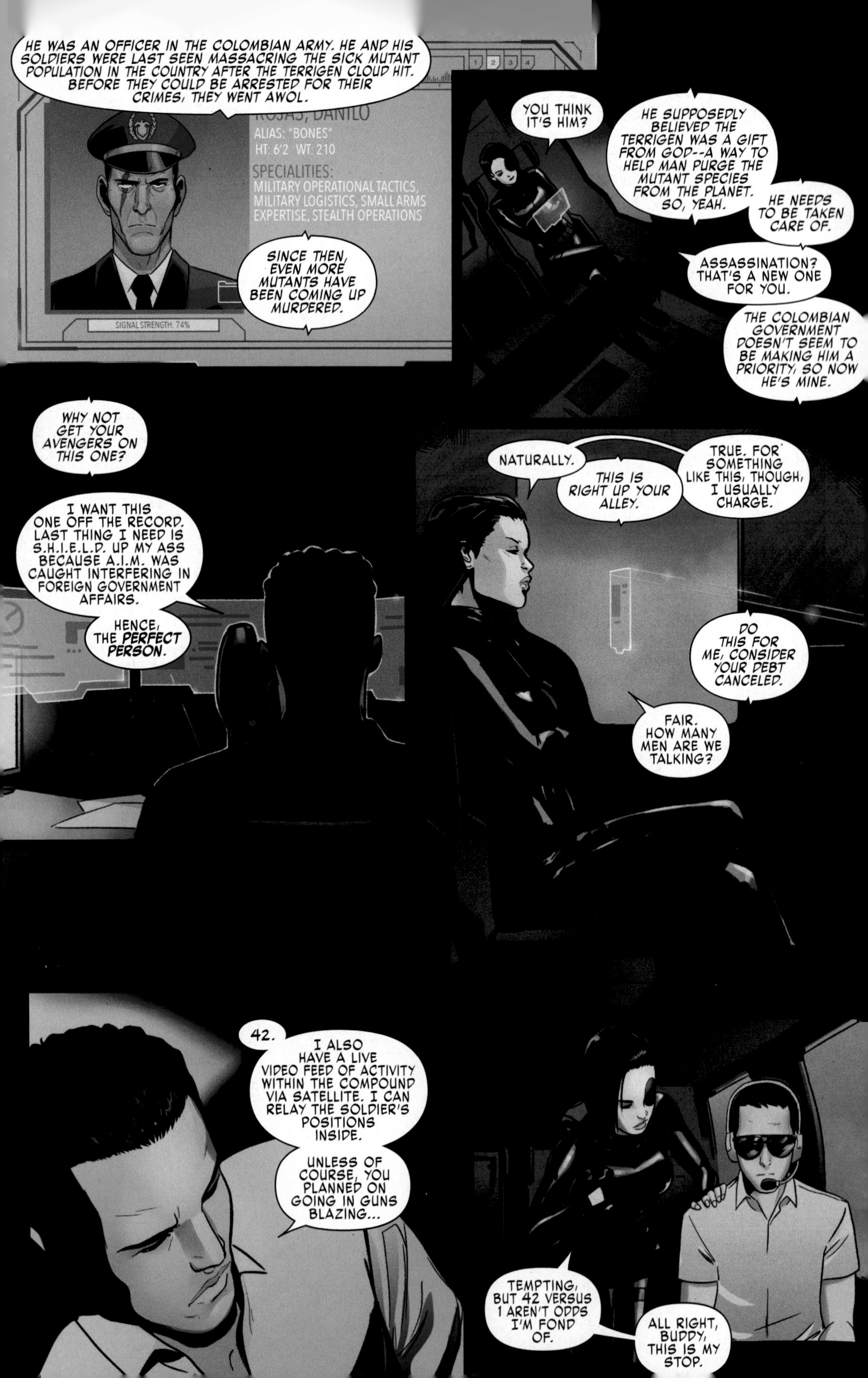

HE WAS AN OFFICER IN THE COLOMBIAN ARMY. HE AND HIS SOLDIERS WERE LAST SEEN MASSACRING THE SICK MUTANT POPULATION IN THE COUNTRY AFTER THE TERRIGEN CLOUD HIT. BEFORE THEY COULD BE ARRESTED FOR THEIR CRIMES, THEY WENT AWOL.
ROJAS, DANILO
ALIAS: "BONES"
HT: 6'2 WT: 210
SPECIALITIES:
MILITARY OPERATIONAL TACTICS, MILITARY LOGISTICS, SMALL ARMS EXPERTISE, STEALTH OPERATIONS
SIGNAL STRENGTH: 74%
SINCE THEN, EVEN MORE MUTANTS HAVE BEEN COMING UP MURDERED.
YOU THINK IT'S HIM?
HE SUPPOSEDLY BELIEVED THE TERRIGEN WAS A GIFT FROM GOD--A WAY TO HELP MAN PURGE THE MUTANT SPECIES FROM THE PLANET. SO, YEAH.
HE NEEDS TO BE TAKEN CARE OF.
ASSASSINATION? THAT'S A NEW ONE FOR YOU.
THE COLOMBIAN GOVERNMENT DOESN'T SEEM TO BE MAKING HIM A PRIORITY, SO NOW HE'S MINE.
WHY NOT GET YOUR AVENGERS ON THIS ONE?
I WANT THIS ONE OFF THE RECORD. LAST THING I NEED IS S.H.I.E.L.D. UP MY ASS BECAUSE A.I.M. WAS CAUGHT INTERFERING IN FOREIGN GOVERNMENT AFFAIRS.
HENCE, THE PERFECT PERSON.
NATURALLY.
THIS IS RIGHT UP YOUR ALLEY.
TRUE. FOR SOMETHING LIKE THIS, THOUGH, I USUALLY CHARGE.
DO THIS FOR ME, CONSIDER YOUR DEBT CANCELED.
FAIR. HOW MANY MEN ARE WE TALKING?
42.
I ALSO HAVE A LIVE VIDEO FEED OF ACTIVITY WITHIN THE COMPOUND VIA SATELLITE. I CAN RELAY THE SOLDIER'S POSITIONS INSIDE.
UNLESS OF COURSE, YOU PLANNED ON GOING IN GUNS BLAZING...
TEMPTING, BUT 42 VERSUS 1 AREN'T ODDS I'M FOND OF.
ALL RIGHT, BUDDY, THIS IS MY STOP.

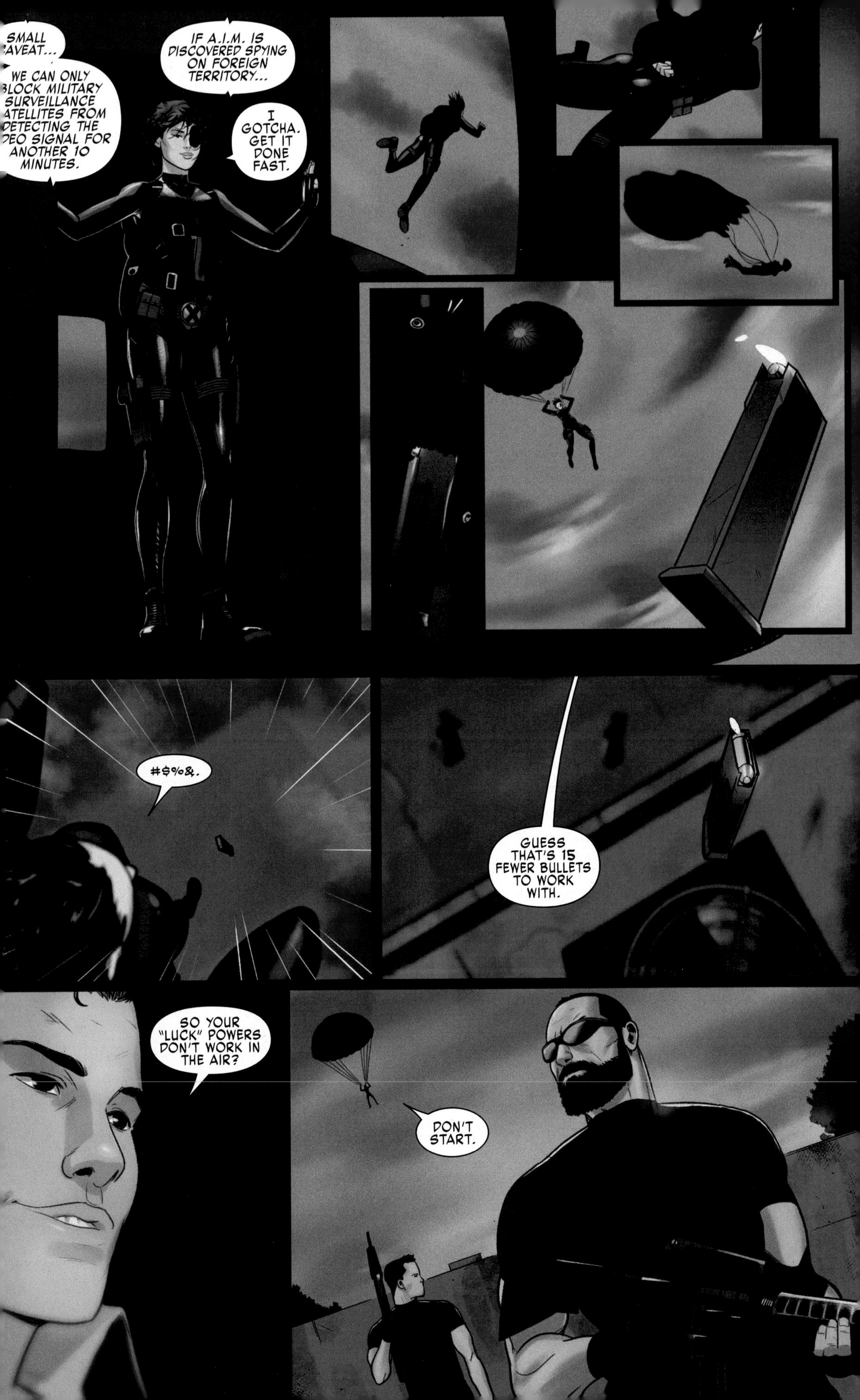

SMALL
CAVEAT...
WE CAN ONLY BLOCK MILITARY SURVEILLANCE SATELLITES FROM DETECTING THE DEO SIGNAL FOR ANOTHER 10 MINUTES.
IF A.I.M. IS DISCOVERED SPYING ON FOREIGN TERRITORY...
I GOTCHA. GET IT DONE FAST.
#$%&.
GUESS THAT'S 15 FEWER BULLETS TO WORK WITH.
SO YOUR "LUCK" POWERS DON'T WORK IN THE AIR?
DON'T START.

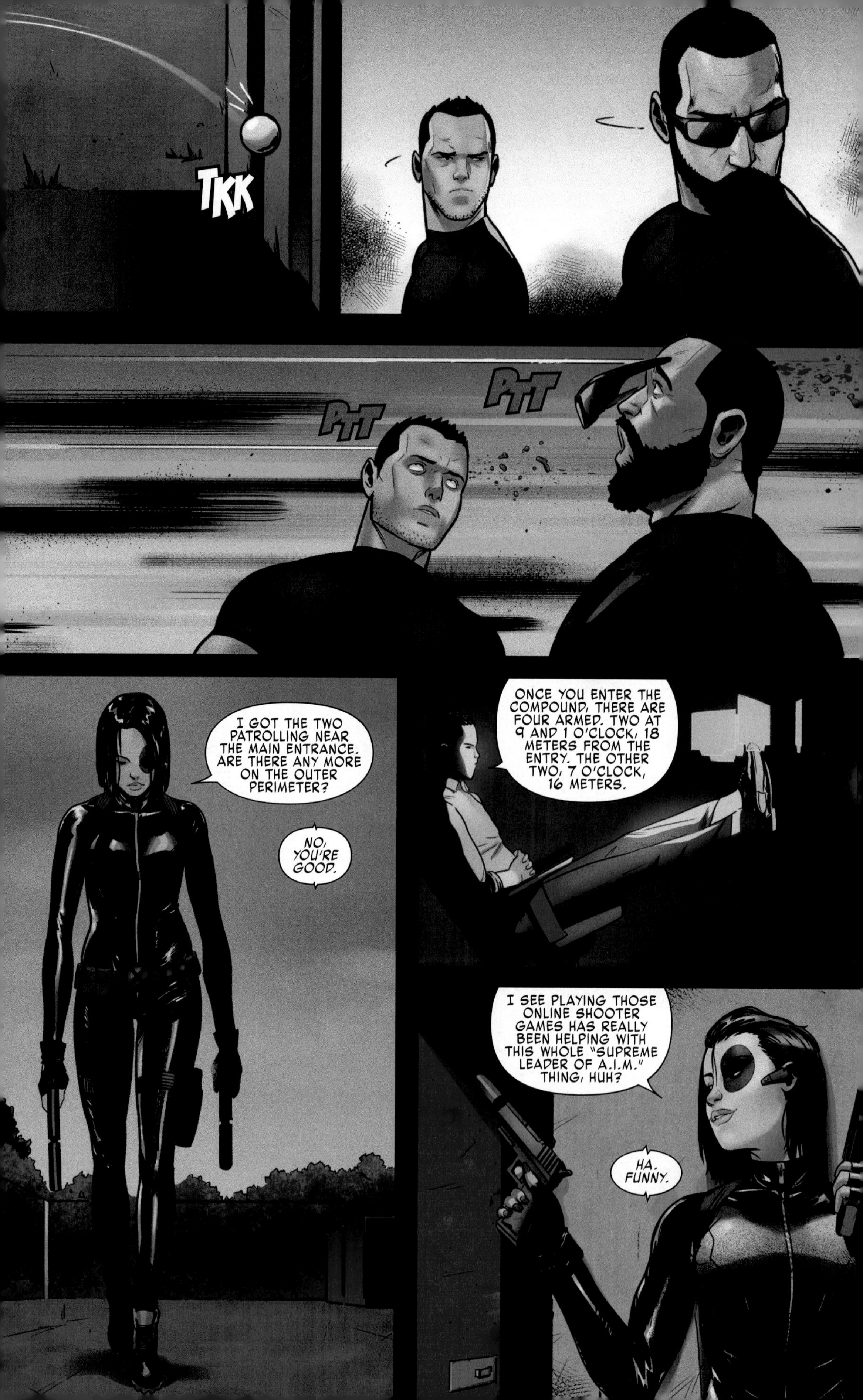
TKK
PTT
PTT
I GOT THE TWO PATROLLING NEAR THE MAIN ENTRANCE. ARE THERE ANY MORE ON THE OUTER PERIMETER?
NO, YOU'RE GOOD.
ONCE YOU ENTER THE COMPOUND, THERE ARE FOUR ARMED. TWO AT 9 AND 1 O'CLOCK, 18 METERS FROM THE ENTRY. THE OTHER TWO, 7 O'CLOCK, 16 METERS.
I SEE PLAYING THOSE ONLINE SHOOTER GAMES HAS REALLY BEEN HELPING WITH THIS WHOLE "SUPREME LEADER OF A.I.M." THING, HUH?
HA. FUNNY.

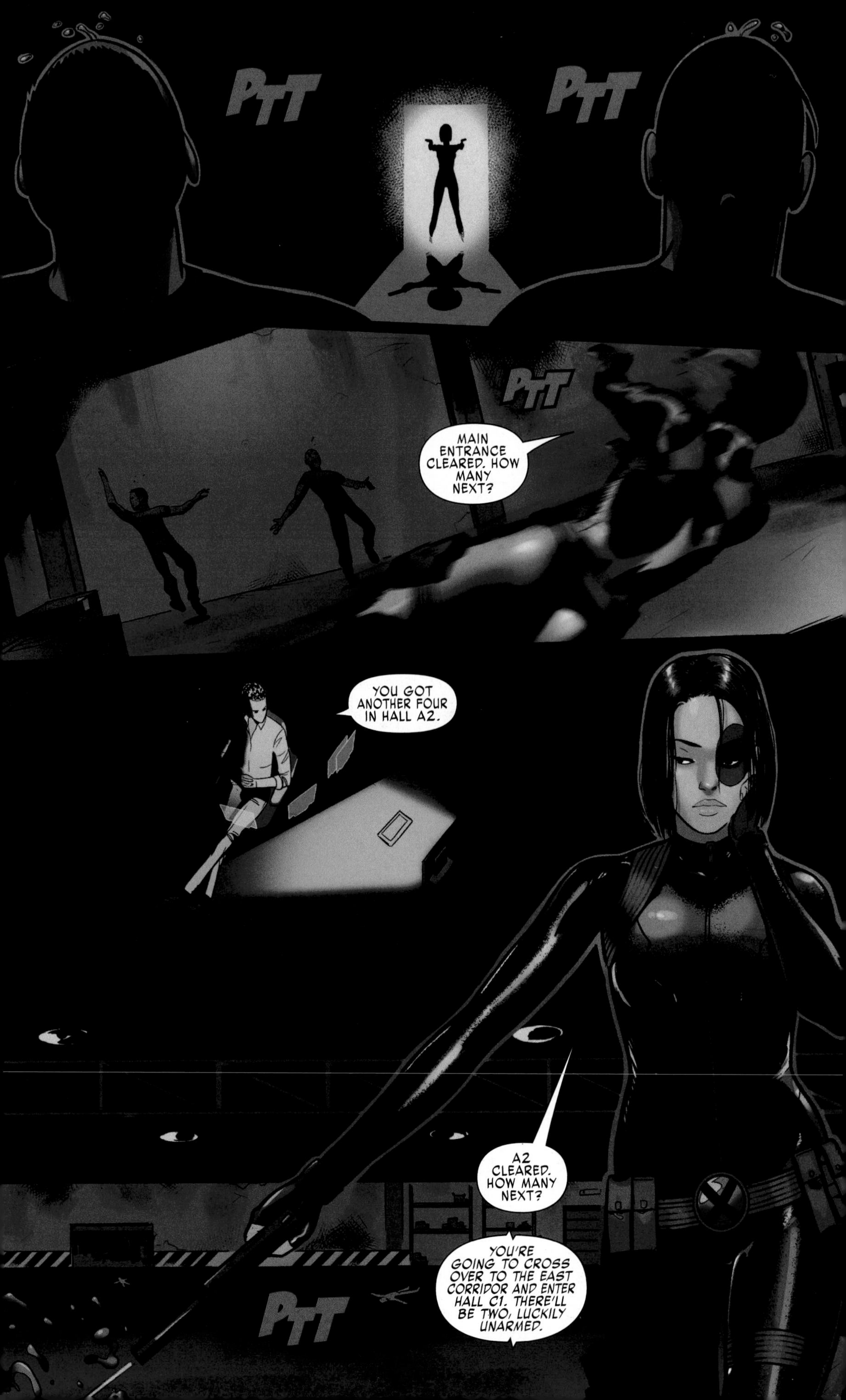
PTT
PTT
PTT
MAIN ENTRANCE CLEARED. HOW MANY NEXT?
YOU GOT ANOTHER FOUR IN HALL A2.
A2 CLEARED. HOW MANY NEXT?
YOU'RE GOING TO CROSS OVER TO THE EAST CORRIDOR AND ENTER HALL C1. THERE'LL BE TWO, LUCKILY UNARMED.
PTT

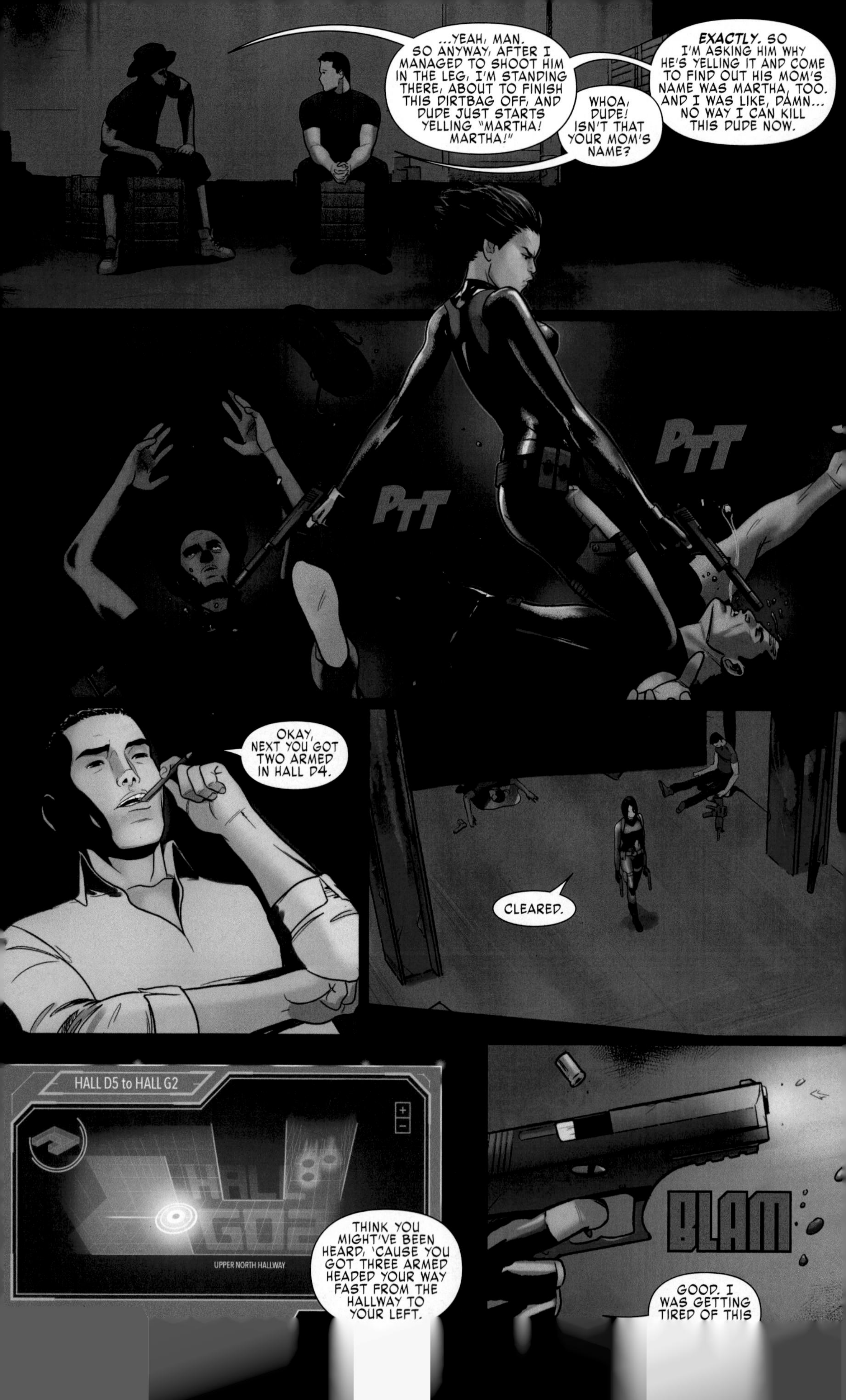
...YEAH, MAN. SO ANYWAY, AFTER I MANAGED TO SHOOT HIM IN THE LEG, I'M STANDING THERE, ABOUT TO FINISH THIS DIRTBAG OFF, AND DUDE JUST STARTS YELLING "MARTHA! MARTHA!"
WHOA, DUDE! ISN'T THAT YOUR MOM'S NAME?
EXACTLY. SO I'M ASKING HIM WHY HE'S YELLING IT AND COME TO FIND OUT HIS MOM'S NAME WAS MARTHA, TOO. AND I WAS LIKE, DAMN... NO WAY I CAN KILL THIS DUDE NOW.
PTT
PTT
OKAY, NEXT YOU GOT TWO ARMED IN HALL D4.
CLEARED.
HALL D5 to HALL G2
HALL G02
UPPER NORTH HALLWAY
THINK YOU MIGHT'VE BEEN HEARD, 'CAUSE YOU GOT THREE ARMED HEADED YOUR WAY FAST FROM THE HALLWAY TO YOUR LEFT.
BLAM
GOOD. I WAS GETTING TIRED OF THIS

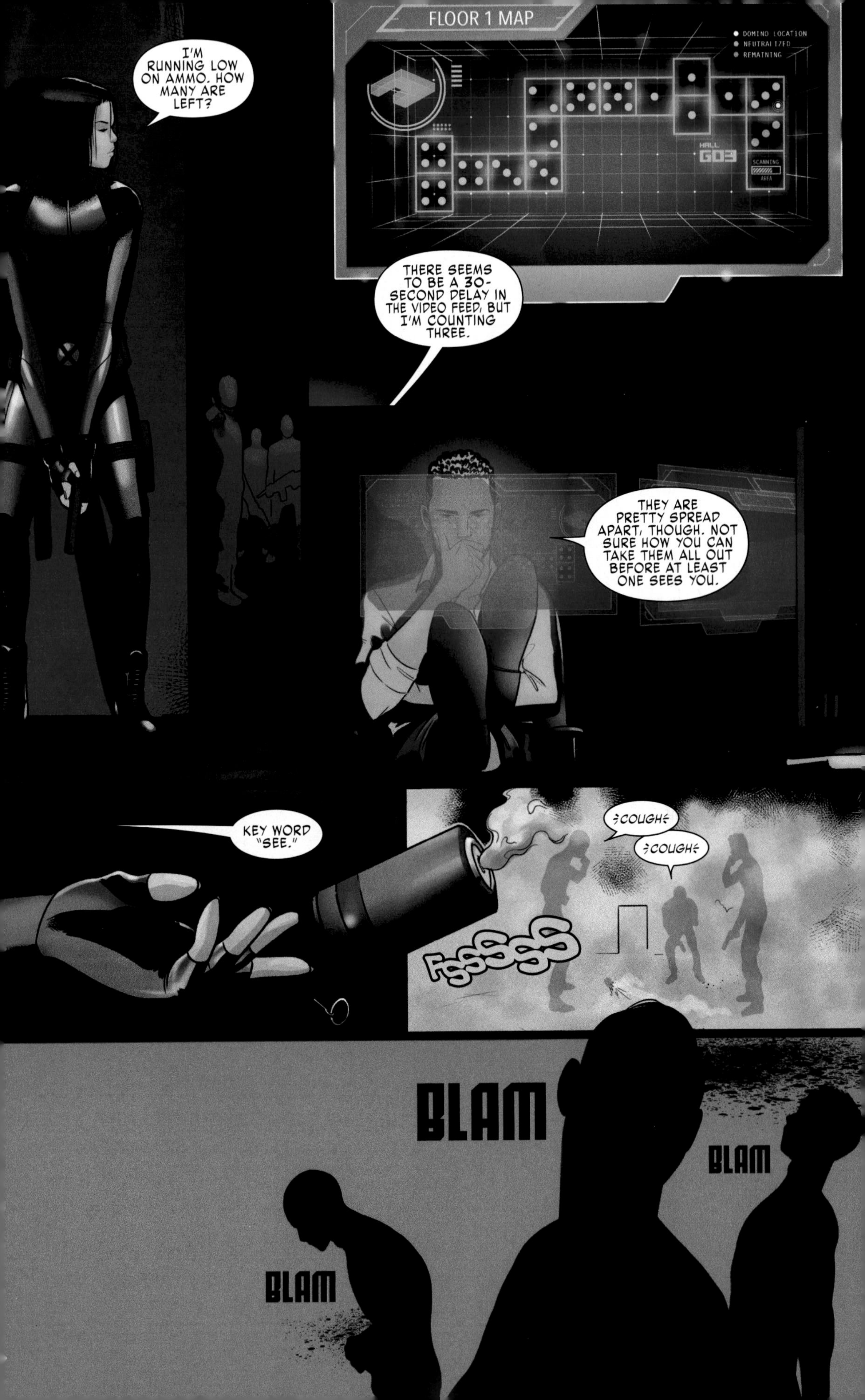

FLOOR 1 MAP
DOMINO LOCATION
NEUTRALIZED
REMAINING
HALL G03
SCANNING AREA
I'M RUNNING LOW ON AMMO. HOW MANY ARE LEFT?
THERE SEEMS TO BE A 30-SECOND DELAY IN THE VIDEO FEED, BUT I'M COUNTING THREE.
THEY ARE PRETTY SPREAD APART, THOUGH. NOT SURE HOW YOU CAN TAKE THEM ALL OUT BEFORE AT LEAST ONE SEES YOU.
KEY WORD "SEE."
FSSSSS
COUGH
COUGH
BLAM
BLAM
BLAM

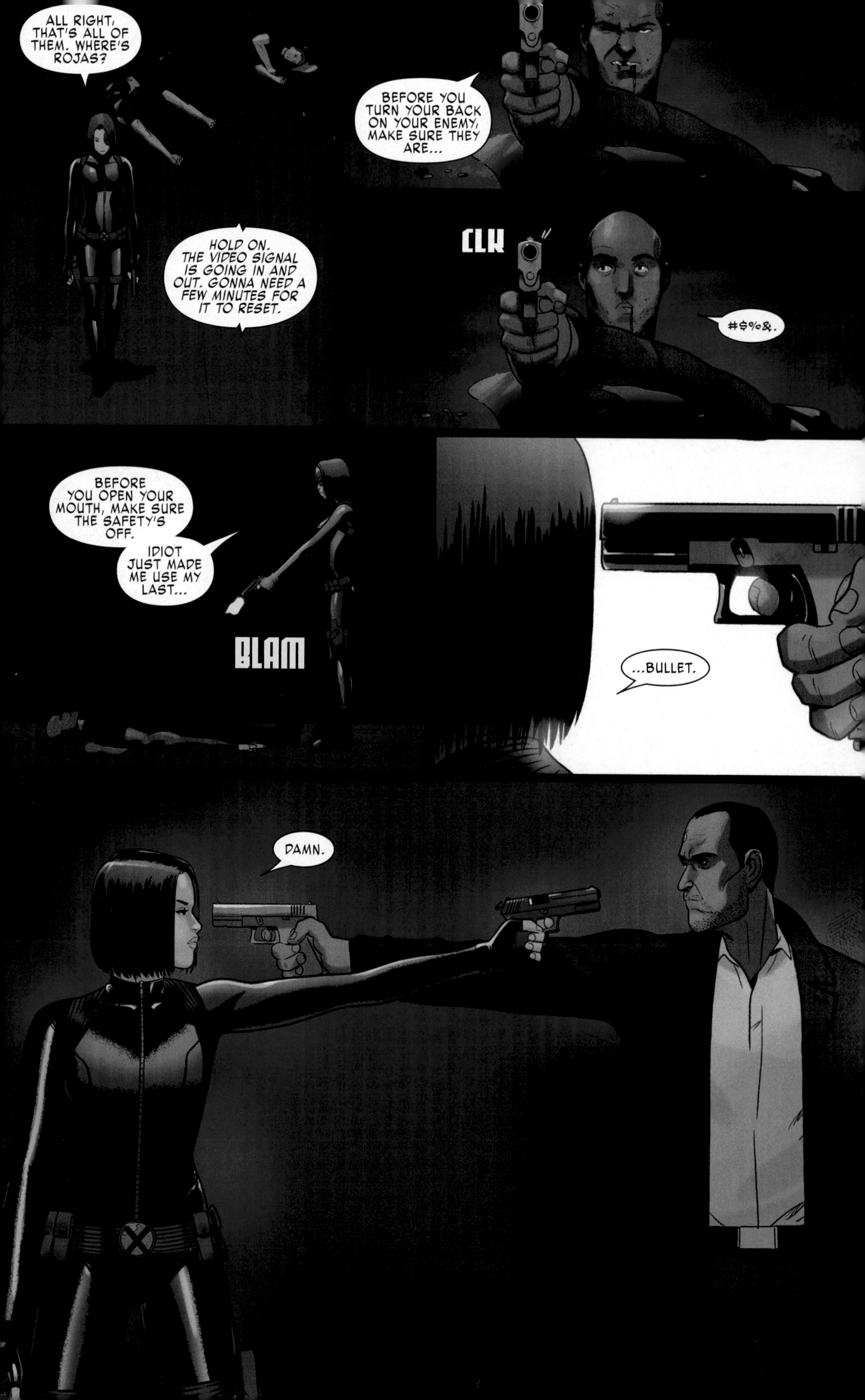
ALL RIGHT, THAT'S ALL OF THEM. WHERE'S ROJAS?
BEFORE YOU TURN YOUR BACK ON YOUR ENEMY, MAKE SURE THEY ARE...
HOLD ON. THE VIDEO SIGNAL IS GOING IN AND OUT. GONNA NEED A FEW MINUTES FOR IT TO RESET.
CLK
#$%&.
BEFORE YOU OPEN YOUR MOUTH, MAKE SURE THE SAFETY'S OFF.
IDIOT JUST MADE ME USE MY LAST...
BLAM
...BULLET.
DAMN.

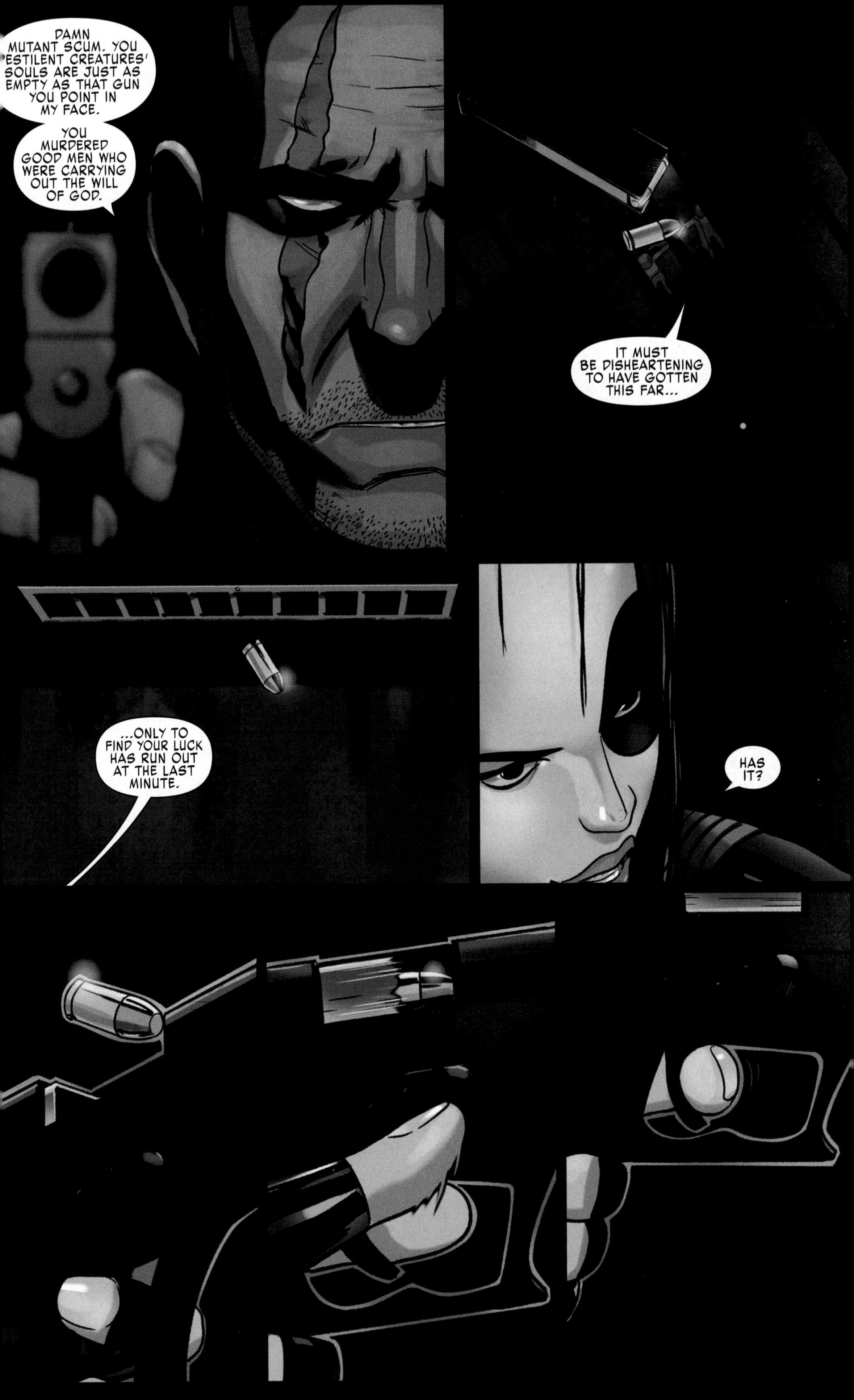
DAMN MUTANT SCUM. YOU PESTILENT CREATURES' SOULS ARE JUST AS EMPTY AS THAT GUN YOU POINT IN MY FACE.
YOU MURDERED GOOD MEN WHO WERE CARRYING OUT THE WILL OF GOD.
IT MUST BE DISHEARTENING TO HAVE GOTTEN THIS FAR...
...ONLY TO FIND YOUR LUCK HAS RUN OUT AT THE LAST MINUTE.
HAS IT?

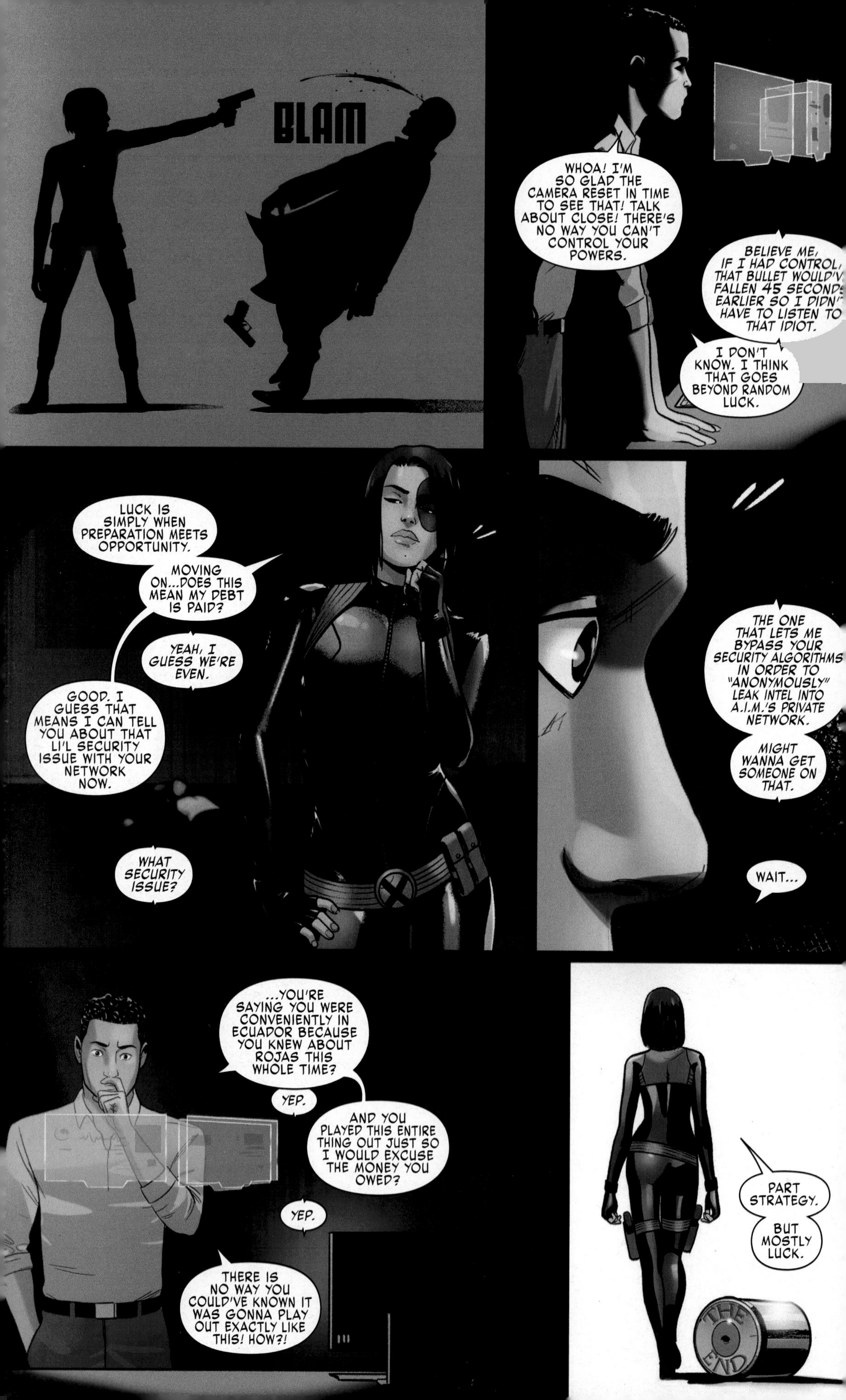
BLAM
WHOA! I'M SO GLAD THE CAMERA RESET IN TIME TO SEE THAT! TALK ABOUT CLOSE! THERE'S NO WAY YOU CAN'T CONTROL YOUR POWERS.
BELIEVE ME, IF I HAD CONTROL, THAT BULLET WOULD'VE FALLEN 45 SECONDS EARLIER SO I DIDN'T HAVE TO LISTEN TO THAT IDIOT.
I DON'T KNOW. I THINK THAT GOES BEYOND RANDOM LUCK.
LUCK IS SIMPLY WHEN PREPARATION MEETS OPPORTUNITY.
MOVING ON...DOES THIS MEAN MY DEBT IS PAID?
YEAH, I GUESS WE'RE EVEN.
GOOD. I GUESS THAT MEANS I CAN TELL YOU ABOUT THAT LI'L SECURITY ISSUE WITH YOUR NETWORK NOW.
WHAT SECURITY ISSUE?
THE ONE THAT LETS ME BYPASS YOUR SECURITY ALGORITHMS IN ORDER TO "ANONYMOUSLY" LEAK INTEL INTO A.I.M.'S PRIVATE NETWORK.
MIGHT WANNA GET SOMEONE ON THAT.
WAIT...
...YOU'RE SAYING YOU WERE CONVENIENTLY IN ECUADOR BECAUSE YOU KNEW ABOUT ROJAS THIS WHOLE TIME?
YEP.
AND YOU PLAYED THIS ENTIRE THING OUT JUST SO I WOULD EXCUSE THE MONEY YOU OWED?
YEP.
THERE IS NO WAY YOU COULD'VE KNOWN IT WAS GONNA PLAY OUT EXACTLY LIKE THIS! HOW?!
PART STRATEGY.
BUT MOSTLY LUCK.
THE END

#16 VARIANT BY ***TRADD MOORE*** & ***RICO RENZI***

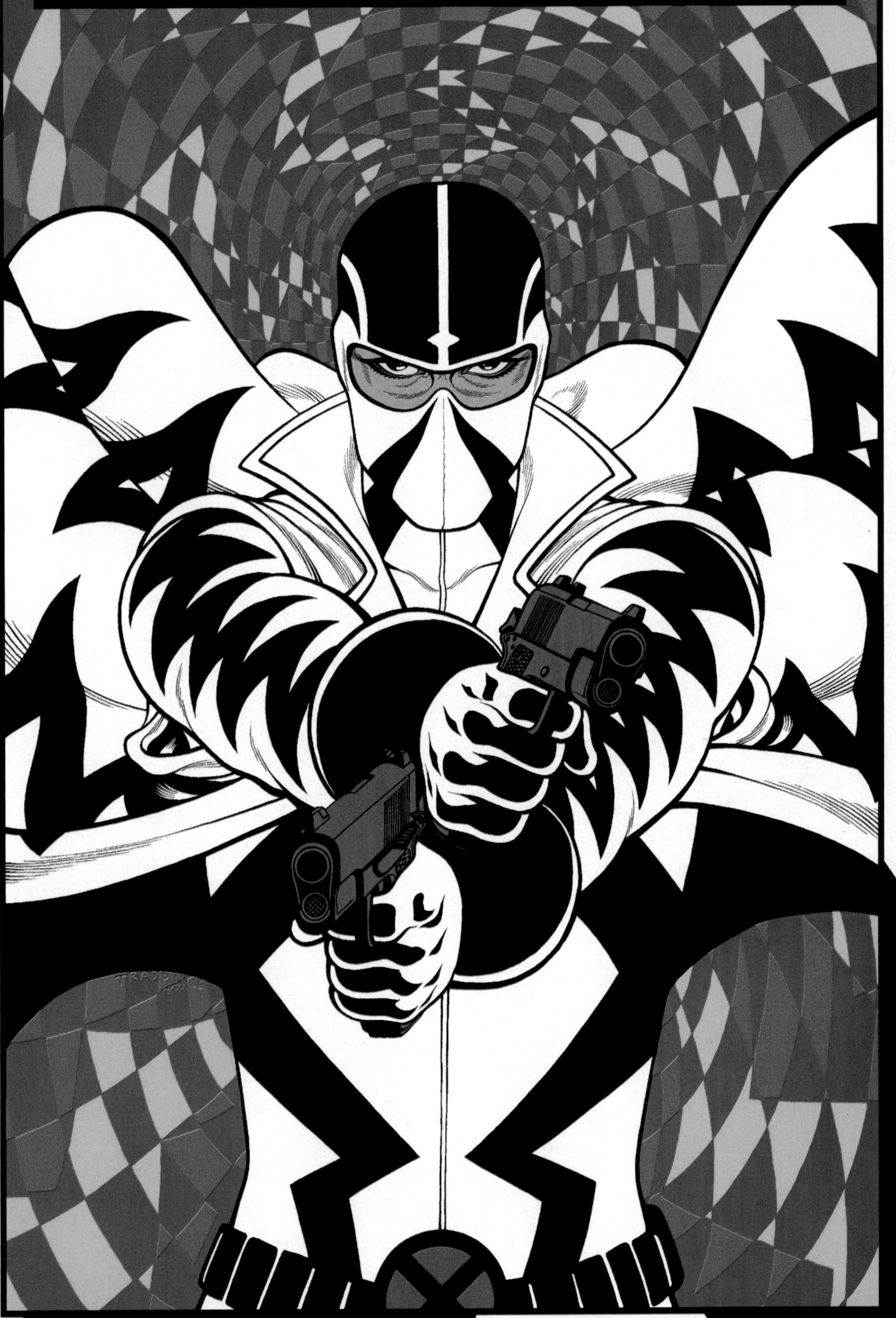

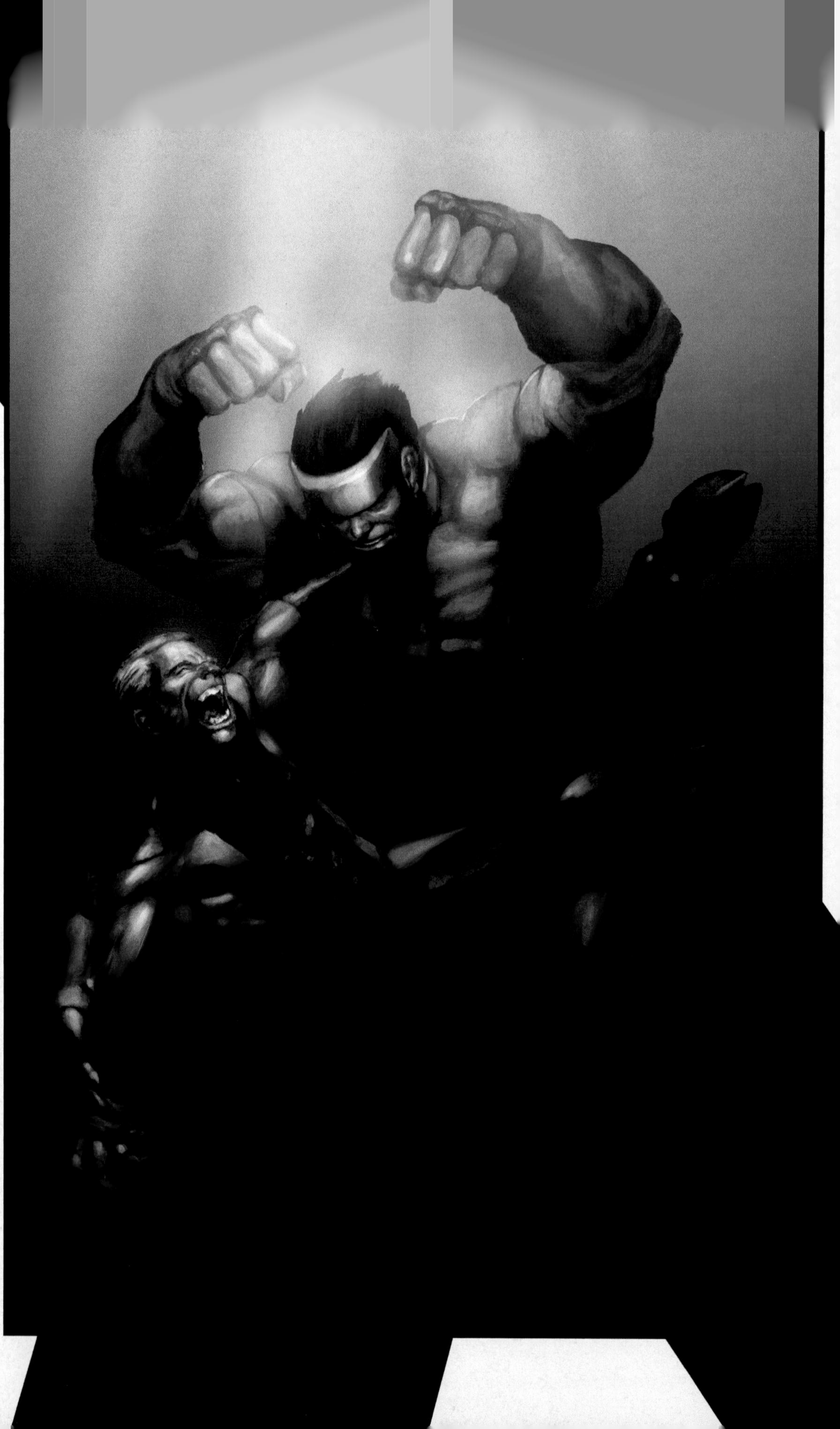

#18 VARIANT BY *JUAN DOE*

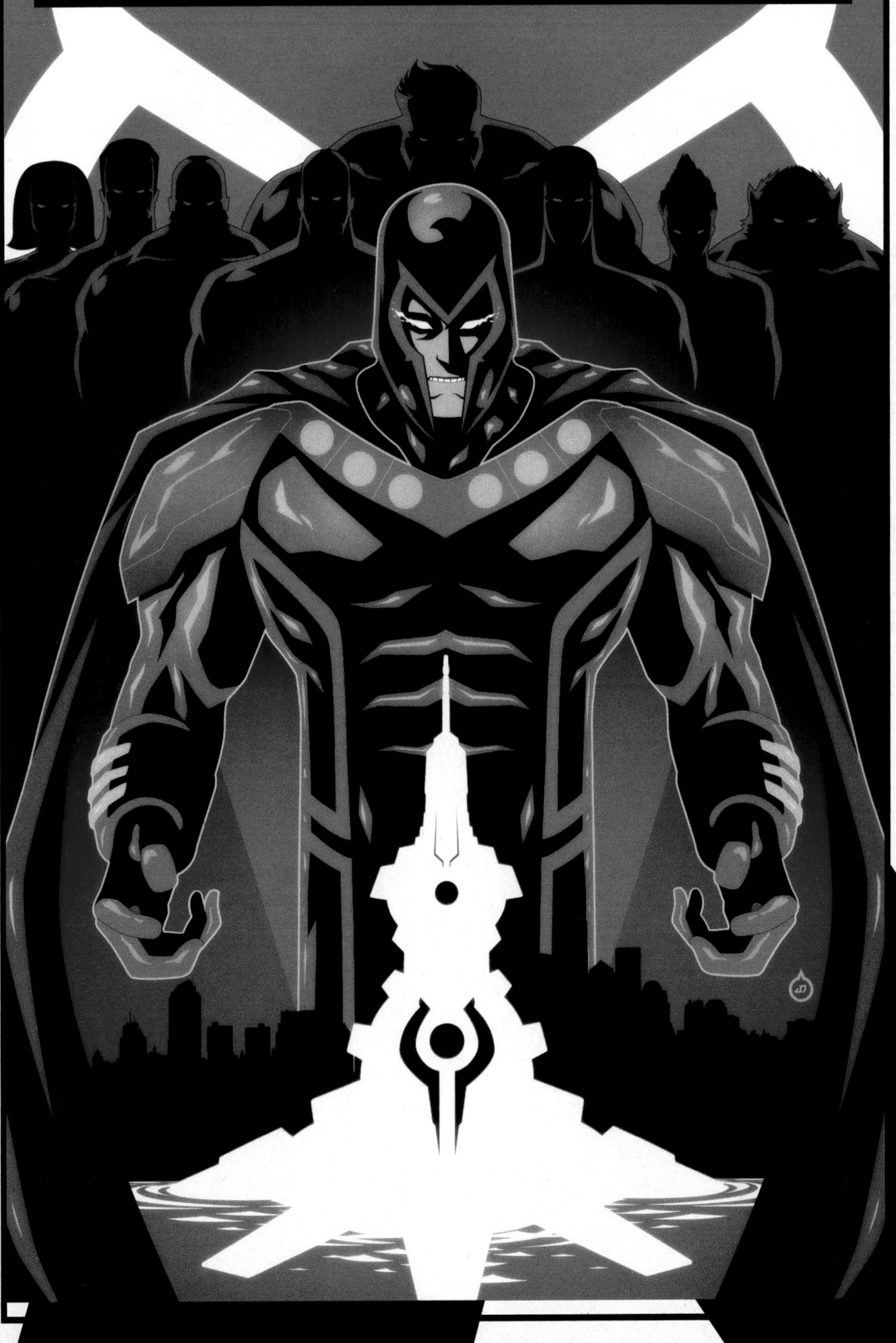

ANNUAL #1 VARIANT BY ***KEN LASHLEY*** & ***NOLAN WOODARD***

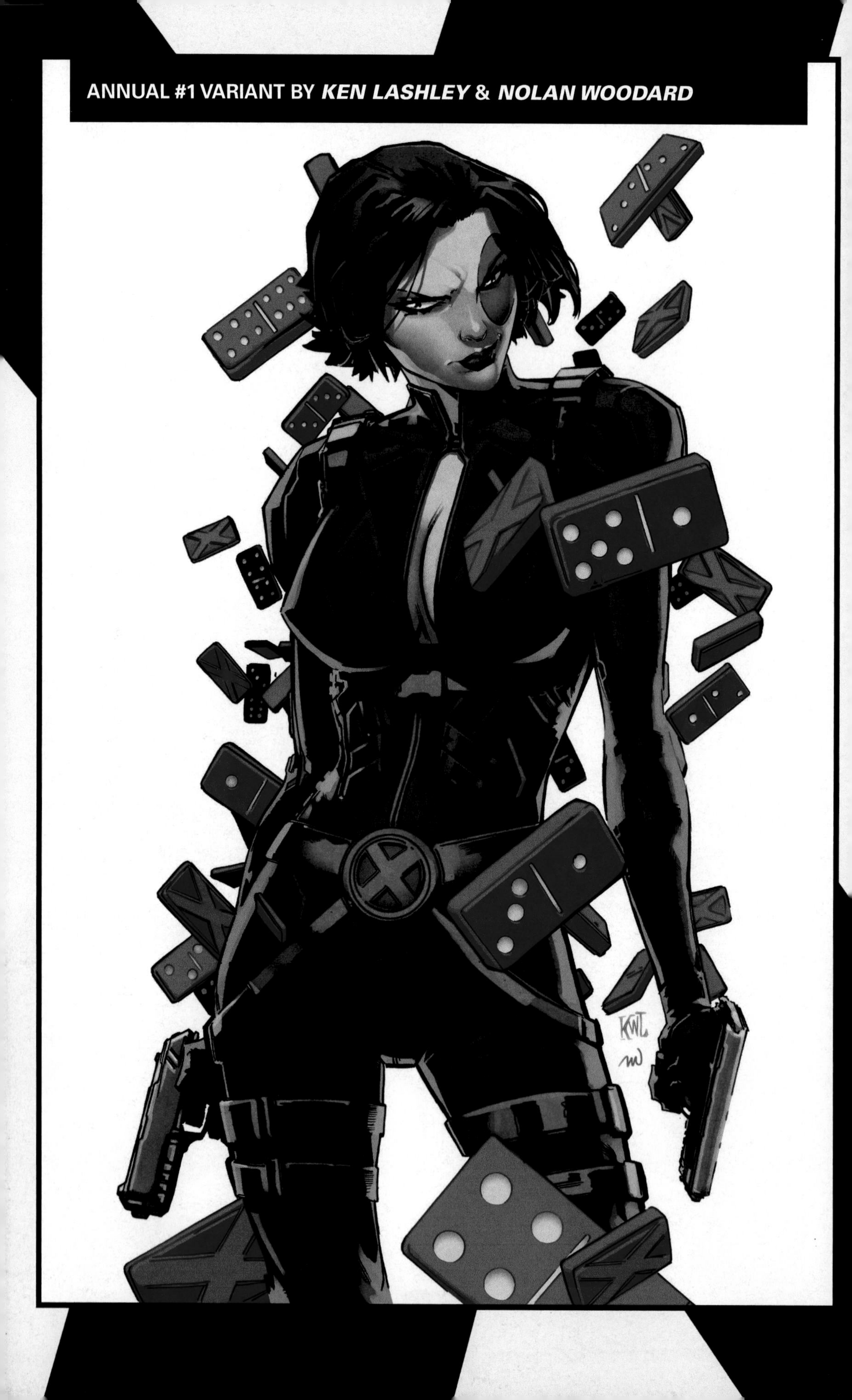

ANNUAL #1 VARIANT BY *VICTOR IBAÑEZ*

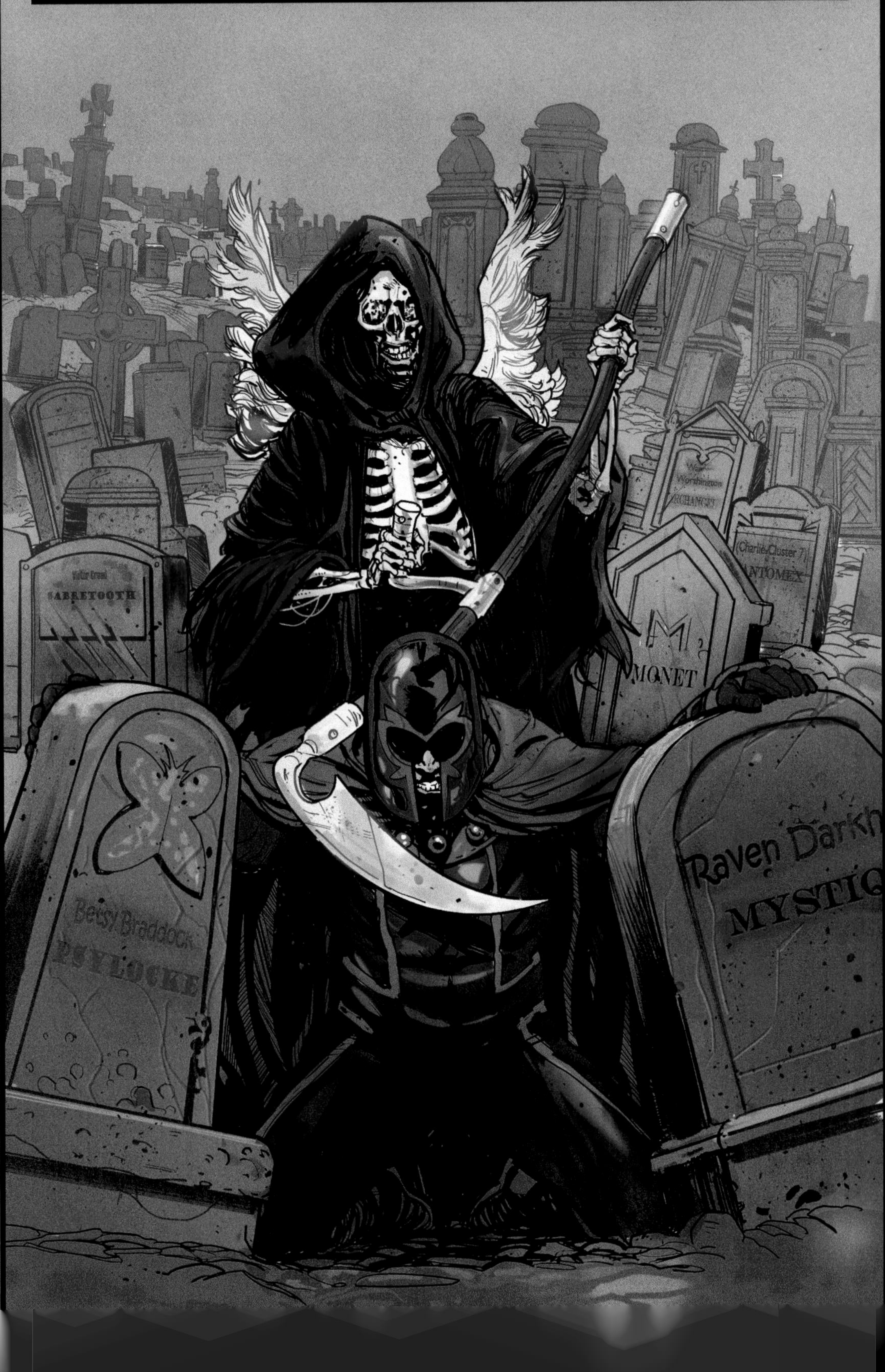
SABRETOOTH
Charlie Cluster 7
MONET
Betsy Braddock
PSYLOCKE
Raven Darkh
MYSTIQ

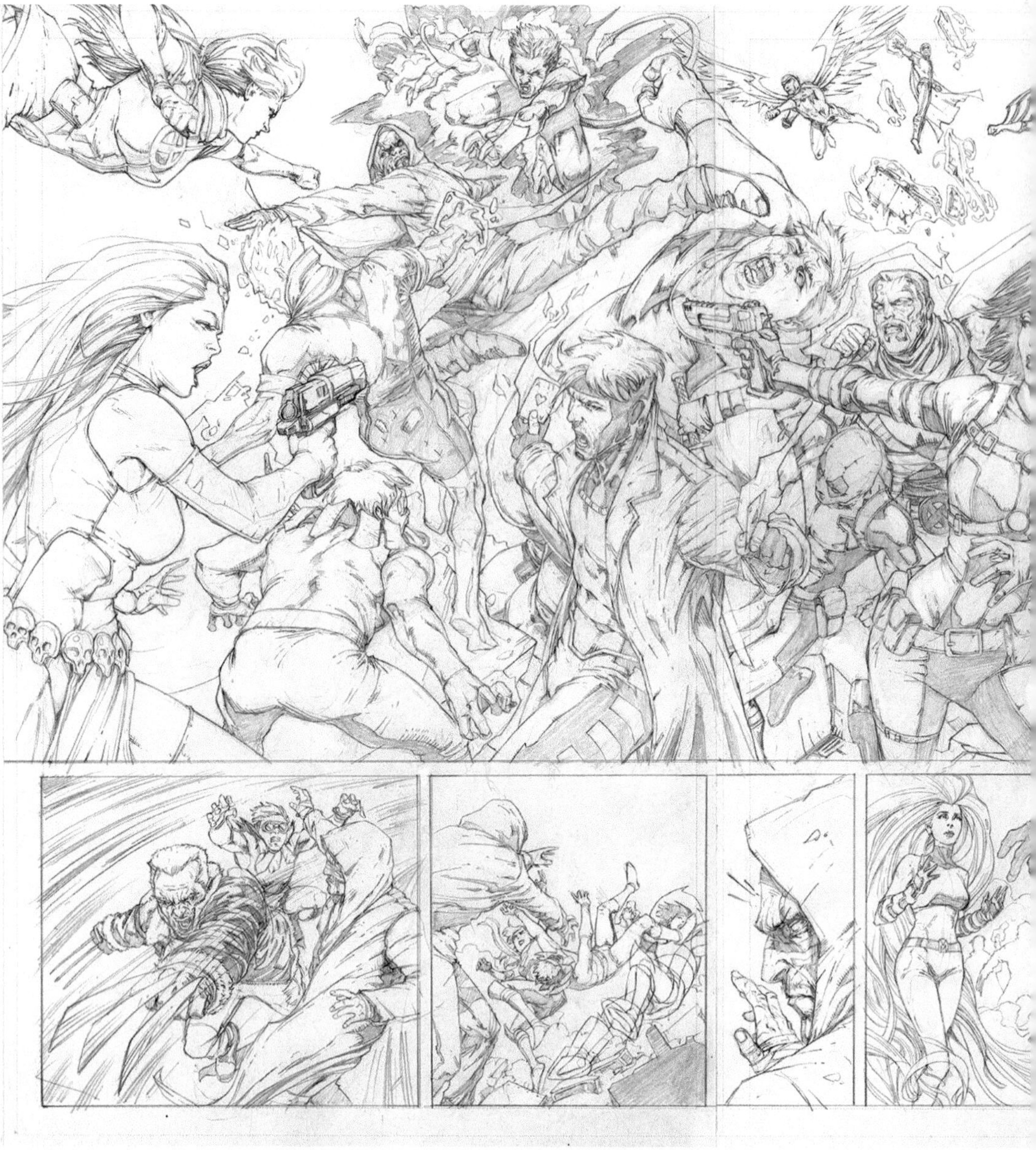

#16, PAGES 14-15
PENCILS BY **EDGAR SALAZAR**
INKS BY **ED TADEO**

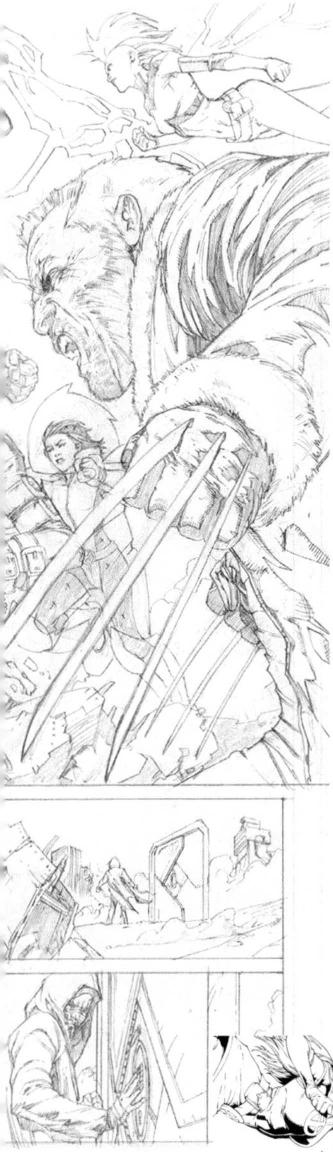

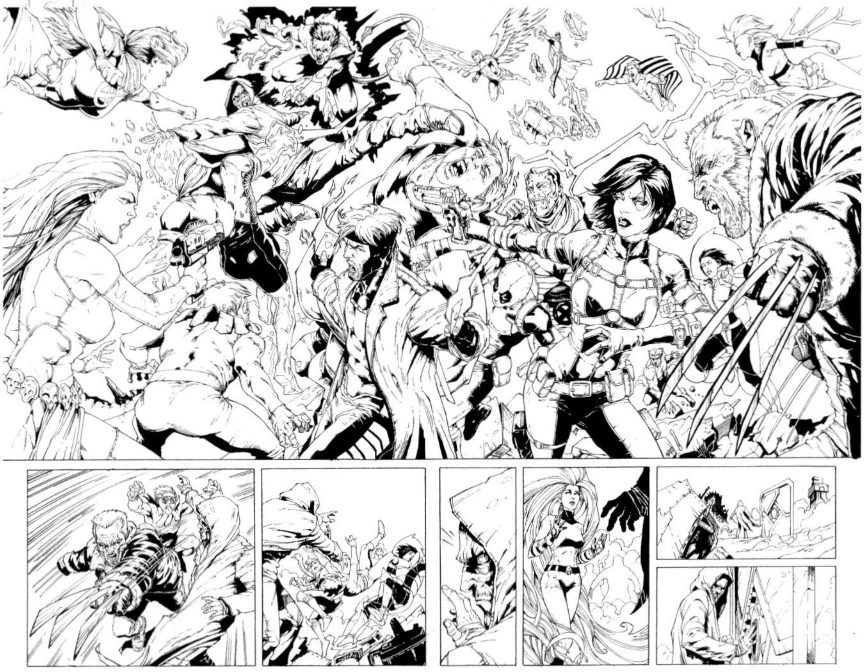

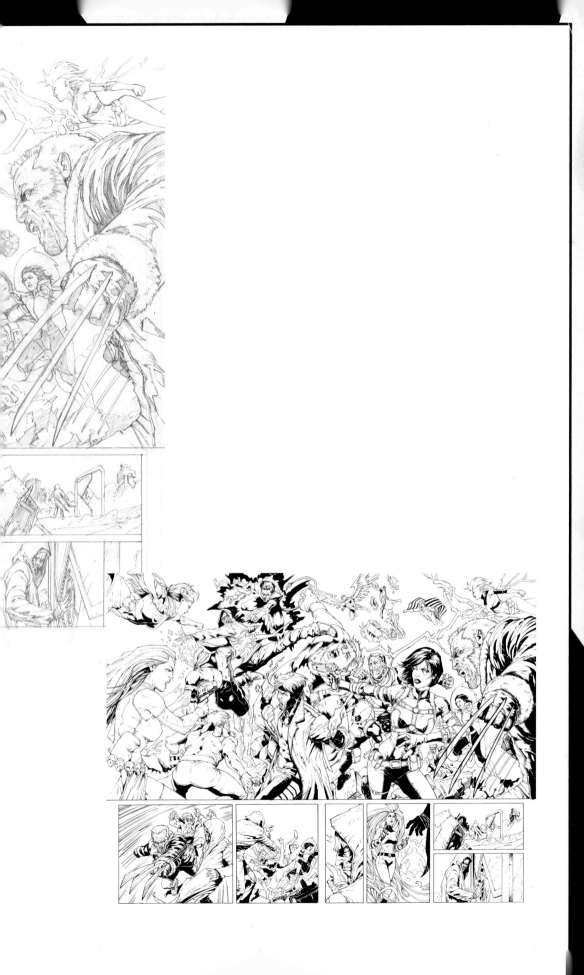

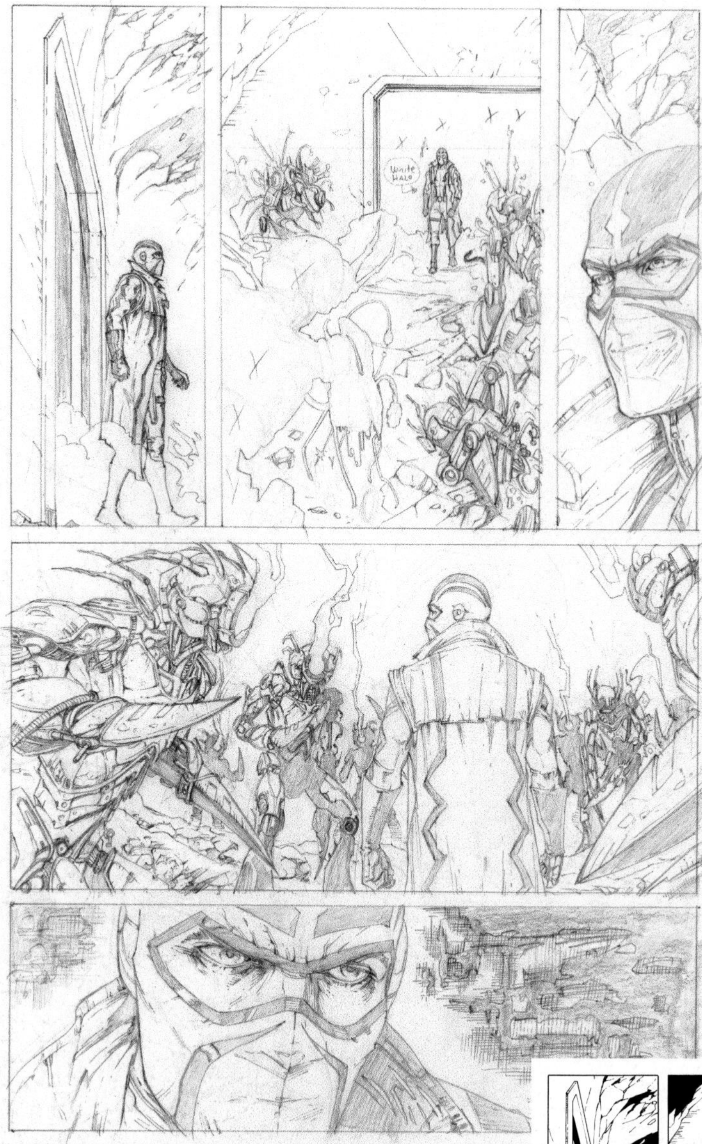
White HALO

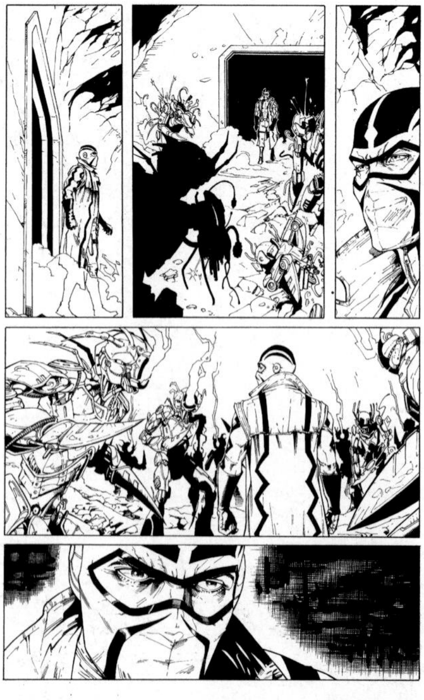

#16, PAGES 20

PENCILS BY **EDGAR SALAZAR**

INKS BY **ED TADEO**